# I Am from Iceland
## A Memoir

by
Edith Andersen

Lulu.com

ISBN: 978-0-557-51048-1

*This book is dedicated with affection
to my granddaughters,
Amanda, Elizabeth, Sophie, Sunnie,
Moira, Isobel, and little Edith.*

# Where I Am From

I am from the axe and the sword, honor and revenge
From the hidden people and mountain spirits
I'm from short growing seasons, ice, fire,
and life-sustaining warmth of the Gulf Stream current.

I am from the woman at the bus stop, facing the wind
And the sewing machine that awaits her and sleepless nights
I'm from the fish store, house-flies, and never enough money
From sheets on the clotheslines billowing in the wind.

I am from the Dane, roses, music, and books
And the Trabant that barely made it up hills
From footsteps on the stairs that move mountains and daughters
And "help your mother" and "now I've had enough."

I am from Sigga, Margrét, Inga, and Magnea
Sewing clubs and poker on Thursdays
From belonging, knowing, light, and darkness
Family tragedies and celebrations.

I am from Adda, Gunna, Villi, Ásta
Jórunn, and Stella, laughter, mischief, and quarrels
I'm from a divan under the beams papered with ballerinas
And a feather quilt, skylight, rainbows, and northern lights.

I am from the spirits that have gone before me
Friendships made, friendships ended
An Atlantic crossing and letters never written
I'm from regret and growth, humility, and gratitude.

# Contents

# Table of Photographs

# Introduction

After I retired from teaching, I told my husband, Tim, that I wanted to write my story, about my childhood. He said, "Why not?" Interesting response. There were plenty of reasons not to—starting with my family's reaction to having their lives recorded. A week later, I told him again. This time he said, "Do you want tea?" I couldn't read anything into that so I went into a mulling phase. When you retire, you have no deadlines, so my mulling period lasted approximately one year or until Tim interrupted it asking when I was going to write my story. I asked if he wanted a cup of tea.

My story sweeps over a millennium. It tells of poets, lawmen, farmers, and fair maidens. It tells of pagan ways and the Northern Star. Granted, most of it takes place in the 1950s and '60s. It's a portrait frozen in time of a girl's life from a little country on the Arctic Circle. It's a story of an average girl living, laughing, hurting and growing up. Her father called her an old soul. It's a story that's not been told before.

I was born and raised in Reykjavík to an Icelandic mother whose ancestors can be traced to the ninth century and a Danish father who immigrated to Iceland in his early twenties.

When I was growing up, Iceland's nature nourished my soul. Waves cresting on the Atlantic, snow-capped mountain ranges, temperamental winds, and frequent rains became a part of me. Memories of picking berries in green valleys, scents of nature that surpassed any manmade perfume, sipping glacier water from cupped hands—to this day calm my active mind.Then there were the hidden people, elves, or as we called them, *huldufólk*, that lived in our mountains and boulders. Did they influence me? Just in case, let me answer that in the affirmative.

Fishing, weather, and tradition were the pillars of my childhood. My family and people around me had clothes on their backs, boots on their feet, and food on their plates. Extravagance was a vocabulary word seldom used. Borrowing money for *things*—unheard of. Kids were expected to entertain themselves; friends and school problems were solved outside parents' sphere of awareness. Physical affection between family members rare, tattling rarer, talking about your problems rarest of all. We grew up with books, music on the national radio on Saturday from two to four o'clock and three o'clock Sunday matinees—Roy Rogers and Tarzan. Lunch at noon was eaten in silence so the adults could hear the news on the radio. Newspapers were read religiously. Church attendance was confirmation, marriage, and death. Dinner at six.

While writing the book, I reached out to family and friends for help. Without my sister, Adda Andersen, this book would have died in infancy. Two other sisters, Jórunn and Stella, enhanced my memory while enjoying a few more laughs of days gone by. There were others: Arnþór Ævarsson, Ágústa Andersen, Bragi Valgeirsson, Carole Puzzuoli, Guðrún Kristindsóttir, Donna Hayward, Iris Underwood, Jóhann Ævarsson, Magga Bragadóttir, Maureen Travalini, Norman Briggs, Rebecca Harris, Wendell Anderson, Guru editor, my Troy Library Writing Group and the Troy Women's Association Book Club. To you, I say, *takk takk*. To my children, Cliff, Jens, Naomi, Rakel, Gréta, and Andrea in my dreams, thank you for listening and helping whenever I asked. For finishing the book, cheering me to the end, and many cups of tea, I thank my best friend,Tim Watts.

# Chapter 1
## Ancestors

*This chapter is about Paganism, a love affair, and Denmark—832 to 1906.*

Before delving into ancestors' history and my childhood, an explanation of how Icelanders are named. This unique system of naming arrived with Iceland's first settlers from Norway in the ninth century.

Bragi, son of Valgeir, and Jóhann, son of Ævar, are examples of how the Vikings kept track of who was who. Surnames were not important. Still aren't. If you know that Bragi is the son of Valgeir, you know his last name is Valgeirsson. For a female, daughter instead of son is used. Margrét, daughter of Bragi, is Margrét Bragadóttir. For an added insight, Vikings attached nicknames, like Eric the Red, who got his name from his red hair. Considering his place in history, Red seems like an understatement. However, I suppose it's better than Eric the Nohair. There were also Þorfinn the Skull-Splitter—(many chose to be his friend), Eystein the Farter and Auðun the Uninspired—enough said. Growing up in the 1950s, this name-calling tradition continued. On my street there was Magga the Worm, who let worms crawl down her throat.

Across the street there was Nonni the Dead who whined and cried too much for Viking descendants' sensibilities. Ásdís the Cabbage-Head stayed away from neighborhood kids. Lovísa the Lumber-Leg was a widow whose knee had been damaged in a childhood accident.

On occasion I've bragged that I can trace my maternal family to the ninth century. This is interesting when you consider that in high school I detested history and anything that entailed memorization. History was a scroll of names and years. Snorri Narfason, born in 1175, was the son of Narfi Snorrason, born in 1135, who was the son of Snorri Húnbogason, born in 1100, with no end in sight. After high school, any thought of my heritage was a hope that nobody would ask questions beyond the year of Iceland's settlement and its subsequent independence from Denmark. For those who asked if Iceland belonged to the United States or if I drove home from Michigan to visit, I felt empathy. History and geography were probably not their favorite subjects either. For me swim class was the only class with a lower rating than history. Yet today, researching my gene pool and finding thirty generations of poets, priests, warriors, berserks, farmers, fishermen, housewives and lawyers thrills me.

The reader should know that Icelanders are known for their love of story telling. It is something to do while we wait for winter dark to ease. As a matter of fact, we know details and major events of the first settlers from around 900 from the *Book of Icelanders* (*Íslendingabók*) written by my grandfather's brother, Ari Þorgeilsson. So now as his brother's granddaughter (x23), I retell our family history, condensed, five-second sound bytes, the way it should be told.

The earliest people who settled in Iceland (ninth century) were aristocratic families from Norway. They yielded power and had a good life, that is, until King Harald Handsome-Hair put an end to independent sovereignty, ousting one king after another and setting himself up as the sole ruler of the country. What remained was a feudal system that reduced every freeman in the country to king's tenants.

Borrowing from Madame Magnusson in *A Sketch of Home-life in Iceland*:

> *The oldest aristocratic families in Norway could not endure this, and rather than sign their own degradation by a willing submission, or to become dependent on Harald's royal grace, they preferred to commit themselves, with their relatives and the holy things from their temples and homes, to the treacherous Atlantic.*

Irish monks were already living in Iceland. With the arrival of the Norwegian heathens, aka Vikings, they left. For me this is a tad problematic. Shouldn't the godly men have tried to convert the new immigrants? Granted, it might be intimidating to walk up to a wild warrior on horseback waving an axe suggesting baptism, but it was the right thing to do.

Most of my ancestors, with a few exceptions, were farmers whose journeys were not sufficiently extraordinary to earn their way into the *Sagas* (ancient history) or *Sturlungasaga* (medieval history). In fairness to early scribes, when your writing tools are quill pens, duck blood, and animal hide, you have every right to be selective.

Norwegian Björn Brynjólfsson (b. 890) was my grandfather (x28). The story goes that when my grandfather met the beautiful Þóra "with Bracelet" Þórisdóttir, he asked Þóra's father for her hand in marriage. *With bracelet* implied a high social standing and wealth. Her father refused. Björn, out of his mind with love or lust, kidnapped Þóra, bracelet and all. Back at his family farm, Björn's father ordered his son to return Þóra. Disobedient son fled with the love of his life and sailed to Iceland. In 910 they have a daughter, Ásgerður, who married Egil Skallagrímsson—next on our list. How Þóra felt about this, we don't know. Let's speculate. A big smelly guy shows up at a family party, ogles you all night, then at parting instead of "nice to meet you," grabs you like left-over dessert in a doggy bag. It's a safe bet that the rest of your bracelets were left behind. He takes you on a voyage with even smellier guys where you end up in a country at the Arctic Circle. Then you have six children in five years a big price to stay warm. Þóra and Björn returned to Norway to settle with her father. Björn wanted to tell him he was sorry, and she wanted the rest of her bracelets. However, Þóra died before returning to Iceland.

Egil Skallagrímsson (b. 910), my grandfather (x26), was one of those proud aristocrats. His life is chronicled in *Egil's Saga*. There were early signs that this grandfather would be a credit to his family. The first documented incident to support this view tells of Egil in his seventh winter. After losing a fight with an older boy, the boy jeers and taunts him. Egil does not go crying to his mother, instead he goes home for an axe he then uses to cut the offender's brain in half. "Now, who is the loser?" he mumbles to himself. His father made little of this, but his mother told him that he had the makings of a true Viking. *That's my boy.*

Egil was not an attractive man, a victim of Paget's disease, characterized by a large head. Yet he possessed valued traits of that era. He was a healer. His renowned poetic skills, which are as easy to understand as today's rap, served him well. In one situation, sitting in a dungeon facing death after killing one of King Erick's men, he composed a poem praising the king. In those days writing poems about the Norwegian king was really in—as in the thing to do. If you flattered the king enough, you could become his friend, and, better yet, he might give you gifts that gave you bragging rights at the next cocktail party. Pleased with Egil's eloquence in verse, the king forgave him and granted him his freedom. Eventually, though, his berserk ways and continued disputes with the Norwegian royalty put an end to his shopping trips to Norway.

In 930 a group of men came together in a place called Þingvellir and declared Iceland an independent nation. They called it Alþing (Parliament)—as in prepare my horse and pack me some grub and ale. I'm going to Alþing. It would become the main social event of the year where all free-men could attend to settle disputes, work out marriage deals, make rash remarks that would lead to more conflicts, and get drunk. Always well attended.

Iceland's entire legal code had to be memorized by the law-speaker and recited at the assembly. These lawmen couldn't remember what they had for dinner the night before, certainly not anniversaries, but this they remembered. Instead of swearing on the Bible, they swore an oath on a blood-reddened ring. A couple of centuries later, the laws were written into a book, *Gray Goose*. Seriously.

At Alþing in the year 1000, the pagans were told they were Christians. Imagine their surprise. "Really? I'm a Christian?" Anyway, some got a little hot under the lapel, but they knew that summers were short and battles were long. June nights are light enough to pick a flea from your tablet-woven tunic, but winter's dark makes finding the enemy an arduous affair. Patience prevented later trouble, but patience exercised for too long was a sign of cowardice. So they stood tall, picked their teeth, burped, farted, and waited.

The law-speaker that year was Þorgeir Þorkelsson, grandfather (x26), a pagan priest. It fell to him to decide: Christianity or Paganism. Both sides, for and against Christianity, would abide by his decision. After a night alone under his sheep-fur blanket listening to a gurgling river, he reached a decision. The next morning, or thereabout, he collected all his hand-carved pagan symbols and tossed them into a waterfall that is now called Goðafoss, the waterfall of the gods. When the pagans saw that, I bet they lost that winning feeling. Back at Alþing he announced, "Let it be the foundation of our law that everyone in this land shall be Christian as in Catholic Christian and believe in one God: Father, Son, and Holy Spirit."

To appease grumblings of a few pagan farmers and avert civil war, the assembly allowed some exceptions. Eating of horseflesh and private pagan worship were permitted. Under your sod roof you could pray to Óðinn, the god of poetry and war. Of course, if he were roaming around on Earth dressed like a human and impregnating women, he might not hear you. This is why some Icelanders contend that Óðinn is in their family linage. "Father, please believe me, my pregnancy is a miracle. Óðinn is the father." Þór (Thor) was another popular god. He drove around the heavens with his hammer, Mjöllnir, creating ruckus, killing everything that moved. So praying for blood, battle, or a black-eye, Þór was your god.

Exposure of infants would continue—but it was to be carried out in secret. Immediately after birth, before child tasted food or was seen by its father, it was left out to die, or it was drowned. It was medieval form of birth control. Surplus children were a burden and could bring disaster to families or the country that could not support them. Pope Gregory III relented and said that three concessions—exposure of infants, eating horseflesh, and private worship of pagan gods—were guaranteed by Rome in perpetuity. But like Loki, a Viking god of trickery, the pope lied. Once the church was firmly grounded, it reneged on its promise.

Snorri Húnbogason, grandfather (x21), was a man of the clergy, a powerful chieftain, and a lawyer. He was lawspeaker of the Alþing from 1156 to 1170. Unlike Egil's, his head was of normal size.

Icelanders, perhaps for lack of other entertainment during the long winters, were prolific story tellers, thus the *Sagas*. Telling of the *Sagas* continued until they were finally written down in the twelfth and thirteenth centuries. During this time, the country was controlled by a few families and aptly named after the most powerful of the chiefs, Sturlunga period. The rest of the people, mostly farmers, gave their loyalties to one of these power brokers. After four generations of bloody battles between the *goðords* (the areas the chieftains ruled) weary Icelanders signed the "Old Covenant"(1262-1264), agreeing to the authority of Norway's rule. It was the cost of peace. The *Gray Goose* was abolished. Shortly thereafter a new lawbook was written, one that better met the needs of the Icelanders.

In this legal text, *Jónsbók*, we learn what mattered to everyday people. This late thirteenth-century book is divided into chapters covering such issues as land use, farming, marriage and family law, inheritance, maritime law, personal rights and laws governing the poor. Maritime laws included how to prove ownership of a beached whale and what marks to mark (brand) cattle. Family law explained options if a woman's dowry was less than her sister's who married before her. Then there was the issue of support for the indigent. A millennium later, we find many of these human issues remain.

Ormur Snorrason (1320-1401) was my grandfather (x15). He was from Skarð Farm near Helgafell—(Holy Mountain—) on a peninsula on Iceland's west side. He served as a lawyer from 1359 to 1368 and as a county magistrate for a few years. He is given credit for donating a book, *Skarðsbók*, the story of the eleven apostles, to the church. Yes, there were 12 apostles, but my resource say that *Skarðsbók* told about eleven. This is a book within a book, in this case within *Jónsbook*. It was elaborately illustrated in the Augustinian monastery at Helgafell near Skarð Farm, giving credence to my grandfather's generosity.

With Olav IV's death, the Norwegian male royal line ends. Iceland went under Danish rule. Danes didn't need Iceland's fish and wool as the Norwegians had, creating hardship and a trade deficit for inhabitants.

From 1402 to 1404, the Black Death, bubonic plague, took more than half of the population. Soon after the White Death—patients' pallor, also known as tuberculosis—would plague the nation for millenniums and touch my immediate family. Unlike the Black Death, which moves in like a hurricane taking lives swiftly with little warning, TB is sly, slow, persistent.

Before 1542, Englishman Andrew Boorde, the earliest foreign traveler to visit Icelandic farms and write about it is quoted in a book by R. F. Thomasson, "Is no corn growing there, nor they have lytle bread or none. In stead of bread they do eat stockfish ... they be beastly creatures. ... They have no houses, yet doth lye in causes al together, lyke swine. "I bet Andrew was glad to get back to his world and you, the reader, glad to know that our history lesson is half over.

In the sixteenth century, enforced by the Danes, we became Lutheran Christians. This unleashed another period of violence, this time directed at the Catholic clergy and property. As did King Henry the VIII, the Danish king declared himself the supreme head of the church.

Minister Hallgrímur Pétursson (1614-1674), one of the most famous people in my linage, was a rebellious young man who dropped out of school, married a slave (more on that later), contracted leprosy, and wrote the *Passion Hymns* (*Passíusálmar*). Today, a church in his name towers over Reykjavik like a gigantic GPS.

In 1627 Westman Island, just south of the country, was invaded—courtesy of Muslims from the African continent. It was blamed on the Turks and is still referred to as the Turkish Raid. Four hundred abducted inhabitants were sold into slavery. Young and old, not worth the trouble of taking, were killed. Among the abducted was a woman nicknamed Gudda and her son. A decade later Gudda was rescued and taken to Denmark where Hallgrímur, a theology student, was instructed to reindoctrinate her in the Lutheran faith before she is returned to Iceland. Halldóra Guðmundsdóttir, my grandmother (x8), is Hallgrímur's aunt. (I stretch the linage thread to reach Hallgrímur even though we share a mere scant of DNA—I couldn't resist.) Gudda got pregnant, with my cousin Hallgrímur Péturs-son's help. With news of her husband's drowning, she was free to marry Hallgrímur. When they returned to Iceland, Gudda received a cold welcome from the Christian community for marrying a man sixteen years her junior. Her slavery status earned her no kudos.

In the 1970s, a law stating that any Turk found in Iceland should be killed on sight was abolished. We may be Christians, we may sing the Passion Hymns, but when someone really

10

ticks us off, we are beserks who return to our pagan ways of behaving.

Iceland's most famous murders involved my great-great-great grandparents, Steinunn Sveinsdóttir (1776-1805) and Bjarni Jónsson (1771-1805). Tim said that I should have told him before we married. I said he shouldn't make me mad.

Steinunn and Bjarni were farmers on Redsand on one of Iceland's Westfjords. Bjarni was a large, hard-working, muscular man with blue eyes, blond hair, and a beard. Steinunn was five feet tall with a fair complexion and long brown hair. They were married, but not to each other. Therein lay the problem. For those interested, a book, *Blackbird*, chronicles their affair. For those not inclined to read the book, what happened is this. My grandfather (x3) wanted to be with my grandmother (x3), but their respective spouses were uncooperative. My grandparents all-consuming love for one another refused to let others get in their way. Bjarni killed Steinunn's husband, Jón, and threw his body over a cliff. This way he made sure Jón was dead and didn't suffer unnecessarily. Bjarni's wife, Sólveig, was the gossiping type and hinted to nearby farmers that my grandparents were out to get her. Sólveig met her maker returning from the barn when my grandparents pushed her down and choked her to death. They had had enough of her gossiping. From the court records, Bjarni is quoted saying: "We wanted so much to have each other—as man and wife—Steinunn and I. To be really married to each other." They had a son together, my great-great-grandfather, Jón Bjarnason.

My grandparents confessed. Grandmother Steinunn died in jail waiting to be transported to Norway. Bjarni was found guilty of a godless act, killing his wife, and of murdering Jón. On October 4, 1805, in Kristianssand in Norway, he received his punishment—pinched with red-hot tongs, his right hand severed from his body while he was alive, and then his head chopped off with an axe. A dire day in the family.

Their granddaughter, Juliana Jónsdóttir, married Pétur Guðmundsson, my great-grandfather (1804-1884). They lived on a farm, Brekkuvöllur, in 1870 when Iceland's first census was taken. It was probably the world's first listing of an entire nation's population. The population count was 50,366.

Social conditions and every-day life in Iceland during the nineteenth and early twentieth centuries were not for the faint of heart. With few alternatives available, people expected and accepted what this arctic country offered. In the short summers with around-the-clock daylight, they worked. In winter they were marooned with their family in the *baðstofa* (a long room for sleeping and living). This acceptance, no–nonsense-take–no-prisoners attitude was in mother's blood. Depression or mental dysfunction was explained in terms of lack of work. For those whose life had taken a bad turn, she quipped, *"Neiðin kennir naktri konu að spinna"*—(Desperation teaches a naked woman to spin).

Iceland yields no timber. Driftwood from the American continents and northern Eurasia was important to Icelanders. Pieces of wood, soaked in brine, tossed on the shoreline by the waves of the Atlantic were put to good use. Purchasing lumber from Norway was expensive, and farmers had to make do with the same timber that housed their families for decades, if not centuries. Consequently, they used turf and stones to keep the family from the arctic winds. In pictures from the 19th century and earlier, buildings look like heaps of earth.

Traveling between farms, mainly in summer, was done on horseback. If necessity dictated winter travel, travelers made sure to arrive before dark when the doors were locked to keep out ghosts. Roads and bridges across glacier rivers were few. This often- hostile environment was the cause of many untimely deaths.

When spring arrived, sedentary life was replaced with agricultural activities. Icelanders had little experience in agriculture or farming as we think of it today in North America. Icelandic agriculture was and is the raising of sheep and cows. Men and women took an equal part; age and strength dictated children's contributions.

Again, borrowing from Madame Sigrid E. Magnusson's article published in 1894, she writes:

*After this [winter] sets in the long, and in many laces dreary, winter. All life in the country seems to crouch despondingly under roof and thatch. The animals are now attended to in their stalls, or huts, by the men, and the women set to work in earnest at what may be properly called the domestic industry of the country. During the day various acts of routine work disturb, to a certain degree, he industry proper of some of the women; but toward dusk everybody has settled down, and this is the appearance of an Icelandic household generally during the long winter evenings: At the upper end of a long room, the so-called badstofa, the sitting-room of the family, which in most cases also serves as a dormitory for the women, sits the mistress of the house at her spinning-wheel, surrounded by her children, the master often also by her side, carding the wool for her, or perhaps making some utensils required for the house. Next, in a row down the room on either side sit the hand-maidens, all at their spinning-wheels. Then the men are seated next, at the lower end of the room, carding the wool for the women, or some may by exercising their skill at woodcarving, making ornamental horn spoons or other things required for the house. For the most part, the whole company sits in silence, because one of the party, generally a youth, or one of the better readers among the men, is sitting in a central position in the room reading an Icelandic Saga to the company, an act that*

*no one disturbs for a moment until the end of
a chapter gives the reader an opportunity for
a pause. Then there is a lively interchange of
opinion between both sexes as to the merits
and demerits of the of the Saga, and it is striking to hear how intensely the girls realize, and
how intelligently they rush with a freshman's
boldness into a discussion of the subject. This
kind of life accounts for our language being
kept pure, and practically unaltered, for over a
thousand years-the whole of the people working together, indoors and out of doors.*

My maternal grandfather, Ingimundur Pétursson (1873–
1957), a hard-working, disciplined man, spent his early years
on a farm. His father, thirty-eight years older than his mother,
died when he was 11 years old. He was one of five children
but the only one to survive beyond the age of one. His mother,
Juliana, died in 1886, four years after his father. At the age of
15, he moved to Reykjavik where he would spend the rest of
his life.

At the turn of the twentieth century, a controversy was
brewing. Any issue that involved fish was debated with passion akin to religious fervor. The subject was the international
market. Fish caught and processed in the Westfjords brought
better price than fish from the nation's capital. Newspapers
claimed that lack of uniform standards resulted in sloppy
unsanitary processing of fish in Reykjavik. In the Westfjords,
fishermen applied consistent ratios of water and salt, used
sharp knives to cut the heads off, and processed the catch
quickly and cleanly.

Iceland was a poor country. Its growing season too short
and cold to grow grains or fruit, with the exception of black-
berries and bilberries that grew in bushes on the ground. On
farms and in garden plots behind town homes, people grew
potatoes, carrots, cabbages, turnips, rutabagas and rhubarb.

Fish, a seemingly endless natural resource, was the nation's hope for prosperity. At times, it was used as a currency. In November of 1895, a Norwegian baker placed an ad in the paper announcing that he was selling his bakery and that customers who owed him money could pay using fish or wool. This was not an extraordinary practice; it was ordinary.

So while Ingimundur pulled on his waders, wool sweater, and oil skins and trudged to the harbor, members of Parliament debated the merits for a maritime school, soon the main topic of conversation on the docks.

September 9, 1890, the newspaper Fjallkonan reported that Parliament's accomplishments were minimal but that there was a consensus that a maritime school was needed if money had been available. The momentum and the citizenry's interest reached a tipping point, and by 1891 fourteen young men had enrolled in the first class at the school. The school offered two tracks, a mini and a maxi. The mini was for those who wished to sail and fish around Iceland. The maxi, attended by far fewer students, rendered them qualified to sail and fish farther out and transporting fish to other countries. A few years later, Ingimundur, now in his twenties, was admitted to Iceland's Maritime School.

Ingimundur rented a room in Reykjavík from Sigríður Sigurðadóttir, a widow in her mid thirties. In 1895 they had a son together, Sigurður Einar Ingimundarson. For the next three years, it's likely that they remained together as a family. Then, Sigurður, a toddler, was sent to live as a foster child with a couple on the west side of town. A child born out of wedlock was not an earth-shaking event, barely interesting enough to gossip about over a cup of coffee and crepes. Sigurður would always be considered a part of our family, attending parties and celebrations.

Ingimundur met my grandmother, Jórunn Magnúsdóttir, who was deaf, while attending the maritime school. Feeling more confident about the future, he proposed, and they married on January 2, 1900.

April 27, the same year, along with thirty-four other young men, Ingimundur graduated with a degree (mini) as a helmsmen. His test score, 54 of 60, the fourth highest.

My grandparents' first of eight children together is Ásta Magnea who died in infancy. Then Pétur was born in 1902; Magnea, 1905; Mamma, my mother, 1906; Inga, 1908; Magnús, 1909; and Margrét 1912. Karl Björgvin, mother's brother—I learned about him during my research for the book—died in childhood, 1914.

In the early years of child rearing, grandfather fished off his own boat, Björgvin, while grandmother learned to accommodate for her deafness by positioning a mirror in the kitchen to monitor her babies who slept in the livingroom. In later years Ingimundur owned and operated a fish factory.

I was eight years old when my grandfather died, but I had met him only once at Aunt Magnea's home. My memory is of an old man with piercing eyes offering me a piece of hard candy from a bowl where the pieces had all stuck together. My sister Jórunn recalls meeting him at another aunt's home and his asking, "Is this one of Ágústa's brats?"

My maternal grandmother had two sisters, one that married into a "better" family (Thorberg) and one brother, Magnús. It's reasonable to speculate that Amma (Grandmother) Jórunn had fond memories of her childhood and family. She named her second son after her brother and Mamma after both her sisters. Naming a child after a relative is viewed as a sign of affection and respect.

# Iceland

My motherland may be the last inhabitable country where in less than an hour you can drive from a city to places unpolluted by trash, water pollution, gift shops and golden arches. In Iceland's countryside, sloshing oceans of commercial noise is replaced by rhythmic sound of rivers and waterfall cascading down mountain sides. Camping in my motherland we experience nature the way our ancestors did.

Nature aside, Icelanders love to swim and soak in sulphurous water. A village of 150 people will have an Olympic-sized pool. A required competency to enter high school was swimming 200 meters.

Names in phone books are listed by first name. The only two people in the country addressed by last name are the Bishop of Iceland and the president.

When women marry, me included, they retain their maiden name. Because my father was Danish, instead of following Iceland's tradition—which would have resulted in Edith Kaisdóttir—I was given his surname, Andersen.

# Pabbi (Father)

In the hundred years before Kai's (my father) birth, Denmark was involved in conflicts that tested the Danes' character. In 1807 the British bombed Copenhagen and seized the Danish fleet to keep it from joining Napoleon. Danes had sided with the French. Thirty percent of Copenhagen was destroyed and more than two thousand were killed. When Napoleon was defeated in 1814, Denmark paid for this alliance and lost Norway to the king of Sweden. Fifty years later, 1864, after a war with Prussia (a German kingdom) and Austria, Danes were ousted from the Schleswig-Holstein region, a rich province in southern Jutland. In response nationalism among Danes flourished and their hostility towards Germans continued for another hundred years.

After the loss of the Schleswig-Holstein region, what remained of Jutland were "great stretches of wind-blown heather sands, oozing bogs, and clay soil mixed with pebbles." The constant winds from the ocean and poor soil conditions made farming difficult. Jutlanders were left to rebuild and rethink. It led to a motto: What is lost externally is regained internally."

This was the environment where my paternal great-grand-parents made a life for themselves. Although knowledge of my ancestors before these grandparents is nonexistent, it's likely that they were farmers or lived in a small town. By the end of the nineteenth century, 60 percent of the Danish population lived in rural settings or villages. Under the leadership of an engineer, Enrico Dalgas, Danes turned their energy to cultivating the rest of the Jutland, making it more suitable for farming. This is the world Pabbi was born into. His life options were vagabond, farmer, tradesman or educator.

Lineage of Danish ancestors goes back to 1872, Dalby, Denmark, where my paternal grandfather, Mads Ulrik Vilhelm Andersen, was born. My grandmother was Adeline Karoline Dagmar Andersen (born Iversen). Around 1900 my grandparents moved to Egtved, Jutland, a rural community, for a teaching position.

At the beginning of the twentieth century, it was said that the Danish farmer leaned with one shoulder on the church and the other on the school for support while plowing his fields. While Taagelund's pastor ministered to his people, baptizing them, marrying, and finally burying them in the graveyard by Egtved Church, my *bedstefar* (grandfather), prepared young people for occupations. His students became blacksmiths, wheel-wrights, cobblers, and weavers for country occupations. Others—became builders for villages or towns, and a few continued on to universities to become scholarly men.

The Andersens were one of the leading families in Taage-lund. My *bedstefar*, when not teaching, spent his time in his library with shelves full of books on husbandry, philosophy, poetry, history and novels of worth. Village people and farmers alike sought his advice. He served on various local boards and committees and was in charge of bookkeeping for health premium payment. Mads provided a good home for his family and a pleasant childhood for his children.

Fearful of Germans, Danes remained neutral through both World Wars. Even so, Germans invaded Denmark in April of

1940 allowing Danes self-rule until August 23, 1943. My father's dislike for Germans ran deep.

# Denmark

July 2008, I visited Taagelund School and Egtved church, where my father was baptized, and the site of my grandparents' graves. Jutland is a Heidi–and–Peter environment with oceans instead of mountains. Meandering through apple-pie orderly villages with cobblestone streets and old churches, keepers of history, was like traveling back in time. The homes are well preserved and often handed down through generations. As my sisters Jórunn and Stella and I drove to the northernmost tip of Jutland, Skagen, I saw cow pastures where once only marshlands existed. Some of Jutland's flat land is still covered with heather, aspen, and beech trees as it was when Pabbi grew up. We were a month too early to see the blossom of the crowberry and cranberry shrub. I thought to myself, here I could live. Then a voice from the GPS brought me back to the moment at hand, "Take the second roundabout."

"Taking all things together, would you say you are very happy, rather happy, not very happy, or not at all happy?" In 2008, University of Michigan researcher posed this question to people all over the world. Danes, reported by CNN, are the happiest people in the world. After my visit to the Jutland peninsula, I was willing to accept that.

Surveys aside, reading about the country, I learned that Denmark has an egalitarian, social–welfare system that fosters the idea that all are the same. The Law of Jante states that we should not think ourselves better than others. With no masters, no servants. Dignity and self-assured humility is highly regarded. Free education and medical assistance are available to all. Danish kids are independent at an early age, and couples don't expect help from their parents. The state provides free education and health. It's also written that Danes are shockingly honest—a trait I recognized in my father.

# Chapter 2

## My Parents

*This chapter is about a stubborn boy, a hard working girl, and a marriage—1906 to 1932.*

Father seldom talked about his childhood or his life before me, and I never asked. Any life before he was cutting my nails, mending my boots, or teaching me how to tell time-I gave little thought to. He was like Esja, Reyjavik's mountain built up during the Ice Age, always there.

What little I knew about my father, Kai (Kaj on his birth certificate), was that he was a Dane who never mastered Icelandic grammar, loved nature, played poker on Thursdays, frequently visited his grown children, and said help your mother too often. He moved without haste, was slow to anger, and chose harmony over drama. Father had a mischievous twinkle in his eyes that saw mostly good in his fellow man—until life bruised it. After a time of research and reflection, like a film in the soaking tray, little by little, a picture of a man I called Pabbi emerged.

Kai spent the first two decades of his life in Taagelund, a farming community near Egtved village, west of Vejle in Jutland, Denmark. My *bedstefar* was the headmaster and one of two teachers at Taagelund School. The school consisted of two rooms at the end of the home where my grandparents lived. Pupils were divided into two classes, one for older and the other for the younger children. Owing to the necessities of agricultural work, older children attended more days in winter, whereas the younger children reversed the order. Six Egtved country schools were spread around the community to make it easier for students to attend. Even so, some children walked many kilometers through the fields creating school paths. Bicycles were a luxury afforded only to a few children.

Jens Nikolaj Kai, my father, came into the world on Saturday, February 3, 1906. He was the first of two sons. My *bedstemor* (grandmother) Adeline was devoted to her family, but Kai was said to have been her favorite. They had six children who lived to old age. Anna, mentally impaired, was their first born, three years older than Kai. So on this day, when they looked at their first-born son, a healthy bundle of life, they had faith that his life would be of an educated man spent in contemplation and in serving others.

Kai, the boy, grew up carefree, loved and doted on. His home was surrounded by gently rolling hills, scattered coniferous juniper berry bushes, grass and heather. Cats, dogs, little furry creatures, horses, and school friends filled his days. Cats were kept more because of mice than sentiment. It was a landscape and an atmosphere that nurtured the soul of a growing boy. On Sundays on a horse and in a buggy, they rode to services at Egtved Church.

Kai was enrolled in dance classes. My mother told my sister Adda that Pabbi loved to dance. As an adult he would strut his stuff, the envy of other men not blessed with his childhood experiences. However, it was in his music lessons that spawned a lifelong hobby that brought him peace and joy. Kai was able to pick up any instrument and quickly learn to play it. When he came to Iceland, he brought his mandolin. When absentmindedly he sat on the mandolin—well, mandolin player no more.

Academics came easily to Kai, but the studying part didn't come at all. He lacked interest and self-discipline for the academic path. In spite of that Adeline hoped her son's vocational aspiration would lean to the spiritual side.

Childhood days were filled with horseback riding and chasing hares, badgers, and foxes. He and his brother Svend, with elastic around the hem of their pants to keep mice from crawling up their legs, explored the meadows and hills behind Taagelund School. When the winds howled and fog blanketed the countryside, Kai stayed indoors teasing his sisters, Anna, Helga, Esther, and Ely.

School, under the tutelage of his father, became a cause of friction and disappointment to my *bedstefar.* Mads Ulrik's high hopes were continually reassessed and lowered as he watched his first-born son carve his name into his wooden school chair. Years later Uncle Svend showed Adda this unappreciated artwork. The charm of Kai's childhood was marred by his stubbornness to grow up, meaning, to take steps that would lead him to a life of comfort and contemplation.

After mandatory schooling Kai went to work at a farm in Jutland, operating agricultural machinery. This new technology made mowing heather-clad ridges, tilling the soil, and planting tasks easier than using the sweat of men's brows. Of the many jobs Pabbi tried his hand at, farming had his heart. Later in life mowing the lawn and tending to his vegetable garden in our backyard suited him. He was one with nature and the only person I knew who found his own company enough. But in the late 1920s, young in years, enjoying his new-found freedom, spending time alone or taking responsibility for himself was not on his mind.

At the cobbler's store in Vejle, Adeline learned that Kai was charging his shoe repair to his parents' account. This was understandable when he lived at home, she reasoned, but now he was living and working elsewhere, a grown man. She was truly dismayed and wondered if she'd been too easy on him—Mads had suggested that possibility as an explanation for her son's lack of self-discipline. Years later, when she retold this story to my mother, the sting of disappointment still pricked.

Bored with Danish farm life, Kai shares with his parents his plan to work in Iceland, then under the Danish crown. Arriving in Iceland in 1931, Kai went to work for Thor Jensen, a Dane who came to Iceland at the age of fifteen with lots of plans and no money. Thor, at the age of 60, after a successful life as a wholesaler and a engineer, decided to pursue a childhood dream of building a dairy farm, Korpúlfsstaðir (1922–1926). Pabbi, in his mid twenties, was eager to be a part of the adventure. It's from the children on Korpúlfsstaðir that Pabbi learned to speak Icelandic. Something, he said, he'd always be grateful for.

Thor Jensen's goal was to provide the highest quality dairy products in the land. Icelanders would no longer have to look across the Atlantic for an example of how to treat live-stock, harvest fields, or operate a sanitary dairy farm. If not for milk, the Vikings might not have survived in this tempermental land with its high population to volcanoe ratio. In the mid-1950s, milk and fish continued to be the two most consumed foods in the country. For Icelanders, milk production and fishing quotas are important—real important.

Taking advantage of new technology, Thor Jensen purchased machines to increase and improve hay production. Where before workers lined up, raking rows in tandem, now one machine operated by one worker did the work of twenty. Instead of using horses and wagons to transport the hay, farmers used trucks.

The dairy barn on Korpúlfsstaðir housed 200 to 300 heads of cattle. It was roomy, well lit, and clean, cleanliness ranking number one in importance. Milk, with the exception of infant milk, was pasteurized and processed and then shipped in metal containers to milk stores in Reykjavik. Milk intended for infants came from Korpúlfsstaðir's best cows; the fat content was higher than it was for the rest of the milk. Cows showing the slightest signs of illness were slaughtered. A veterinarian made regular visits.

May 1926, ten people in Ísafjörður, a town north west of Reykjavík, were hospitalized with typhoid fever that was traced to two farms. Dr. Björnsson, surgeon-general of Iceland, wrote in the newspaper that the cause was unsanitary conditions of the milking cows. He added that these farms were not the exception; on the contrary, they were the norm. After a visit to Korpúlfsstaðir in the same year, Dr. Björnsson, wrote to Hr. Jensen.

> *I thank you for inviting me to Korpúlfsstaðir, but it could be that you don't know the reason for my recent comments in the newspaper about typhoid fever. But it explains my eagerness to visit your miracle at Korpúlfsstaðir. The reason is this: Typhoid fever has become an embarrassment to the nation. I wish for our nation's longevity to be the world's longest ... If two could be reduced, typhoid fever and accidents, we could achieve this. ... you are one man that the Icelandic farmer can least be without.*

Korpúlfsstaðir hired foreign and Icelandic farm laborers, but paid foreign laborers lower wages than Icelanders doing the same work. Unhappy with unequal pay, foreign laborers made a formal complaint. The results were that the number of immigrant workers was reduced and, of greater consequence to Pabbi, was the additional ruling "one farm, one foreign farm laborer." Kai had to look for work elsewhere.

In the next few decades, Thor Jensen's immigrant status faded. Instead of being the outsider who made it big, he was one of us. His children, who took his first name as their last with s added, Thors, rose to become one of Iceland's most influential families. One of his sons, Ólafur Thors, was elected prime minister five times. Growing up, I heard his name so often that I thought he was the entire government.

Sleeping at the Salvation Army, gambling, partying—1932 was a good year. That year, Kai befriended Arni Strandberg, a relationship built on their shared interest in bootlegging. Kai appreciated the young women he met at the dance halls. They were easy on the eyes, but in Ágústa, my mother, he discovered traits he admired. She was ambitious, competent, responsible, and a tireless worker who put her family first. When he and Arni were arrested and incarcerated for 15 days and fined 800 *krónur* for bootlegging, he'd come to a fork in the road: Arni or Ágústa?

If I knew little about my father's childhood. I knew even less about my mother's. To learn about my mother, I spent time perusing newspaper articles, interviewing family members, and reading bits and pieces from books of that era. After a while she, like my father, came into focus.

Mother came into the world at a time of social change centered around the right to self-government without interference from outside, in this case Denmark. Our national sentiment was depicted in the so-called turn of the century poems. They stroked the flame of Iceland's independent spirit.

Along with national sentiment, the winds of socialism gained strength. Authors and poets wrote about the little people in society, and most of us were. They wrote about poverty, misery, inequality, and death. In the early part of the twentieth century, poverty was the norm. The *better citizens*, Danes—my father excluded—politicians, and a few Icelandic entrepreneurs were a small group. But, no doubt, large enough for others to see the disparity in lifestyles creating a desire to share in the prosperity.

After mandatory education mother attended an all–girls junior college (Kvennaskóli, RVK). She was the only one of her family to seek advanced education. Cutting mother no slack, her father expected her to continue working in the fish factory and helping with the younger children.

Working outdoors processing fish, Mamma and my aunts created newspaper hats to shield their faces from the summer sun. Outdoor appearance suggested that they were fish workers, a revelation best kept from others.

Eventually, school demands and working proved too much. Something had to go. Her education went. It's hard to walk in another's waders, but self-sacrifice started early. Ágústa inherited her father's work ethic and sense of responsibility. Life was work. You didn't complain about your lot in life. As long as there was breath in your body, you got out of bed and took care of your responsibilities. Signs of weakness were considered a personal flaw to be corrected—quickly.

Mother left school, but the desire to make something of herself didn't leave her. When her sister, Inga, decided to follow her boyfriend, Siggi, to Denmark—he was there to study mechanical engineering—Mamma, with her mother's blessings and her brother Pétur's financial support, enrolled in an early childhood education program in Copenhagen. The sisters resided with Lára and her husband, Viggo Nielsen. Mamma and Lára's friendship lasted a lifetime. In 1994 my niece Kata named her daughter Lára Kristín in honor of this friendship.

Ágústa's training took place at an orphanage. The woman in charge was a miser. She cut corners every way she could. The children were bathed without soap. Just rub hard enough and the dirt will come off, workers were told. By the end of the bath, their little ear lobes, faces, hands, and feet looked like ripe apples about to fall off. Food rations were minimal. On the other hand, the miser, a gargantuan woman with a titanic appetite, carried enough blubber to sustain life for years. Mamma used her spare time off to patch dresses and pants and used her money to buy soap and candy for the ragamuffins. Their needs tugged at her soul. She loved the work and learning.

Back in Iceland, Amma (grandmother) had a stroke precipitating a summon from her father for her to return to Iceland. Her mother asked for Ágústa, not her two daughters who still lived at home. Mamma's loyalty and sense of responsibility left her no choice but to pack up and return—again, her aspiration shelved. Inga, 22, remained and gave birth to a son, Karl Björgvin Sigurðsson.

After Mamma returned from Denmark, her relationship with her father was strained. Ingimundur was impatient with his wife's condition. Like many of his generation, surviving required most of their lives' energy. But his lack of compassion for his wife created a chasm between him and my mother, one too deep for either to cross. Her mother died in 1938.

June 24, 1933, in their mid-twenties, Kai and pregnant Ágústa married. Their marriage certificate lists mother in her childhood home, Sólvallagata 45, and Kai in Bárugata 32, Reykjavík.

# Chapter 3
## Leifsgata 7, Reykjavik

*This chapter is about a gray cloud, a soldier,*
*and rats—April 1944.*

Remember when Adda promised Villi a caramel for running in his underwear down four flights of stairs and around Ceasar Mar's truck?" "Remember what happened when Stella and Jórunn lit a bonfire under our parents' bed?" When you are the youngest, much had happened before you came along. Your family had this whole big life without you. So it was in my family. The year was 1944. The month was April. Outside—cloudy but dry.

Pushing open the front door of Leifsgata 7, Adda, then ten, looked around the first floor of the apartment building. She was looking for her seven-year-old brother, Villi. It was a four-story building that smelled of dirt, gravel, and damp rubber boots. Adda's family lived on the top floor, high enough where street noises were muted. An unwritten house rule gave their floor claim to the roof and clothes lines. Adda, an imaginative bookworm, enjoyed accompanying Mamma to the roof. Clothes fluttering in the wind straining against the wooden pins, she imagined them as people escaping they tyranny of

a Russian tsar. At other times the colored towels flapping like sails on sea were flags of nations.

The clotheslines stood against a cement chimney next to a box Pabbi built to keep food cold. From there you could see the neighborhood school, Austurbæjarskóli, (East Side School). To the north across an inlet of the Atlantic Ocean, was a chain of mountains, Esja. Many poems have been written about Esja that glowed under the summer sun and looked like a gigantic lace on the barren winter landscape. East and south you could see people. Adda pretended they were Lilliputians from *Gulliver's Travels*. It was from this vantage point that Adda first spied the American soldier coming to visit Elma who lived on the third floor.

Most days Mamma stayed home with the three kids. That day she'd left Adda in charge while she took care of something. Adda didn't know what, and the sound of Mamma's voice told her it would remain so.

On weekends Adda and Villi helped Pabbi at his fish-and-chips hut at Melavelli. Their job was to sort and bundle money according to its issuing country, British pounds, American dollars, or Danish *krónur*. It could have been the warmth of the hut and unlimited supply of chips that created harmony between the siblings, but more likely it was just being with father. Pabbi, an entrepreneur at heart, found ways to support his family through days of scarcity, often working two jobs. But, after the British soldiers left Iceland in 1941, he had to close the hut. The palate of American soldiers, who occupied Iceland in 1943, leaned towards hoofed, not finned, animals.

Walking out the apartment door earlier that day, Mamma reminded Adda to keep a close eye on Villi. Pabbi had fixed many broken window-panes in the building caused by rocks his son was accused of throwing. Adda could get mad just thinking about it. The older boys in the building, especially Bjarni, used Villi. One foolish sheep will lead the flock; "That's fitting," she thought to herself. "He could be such a wimp and never stick up for himself." She could shake him silly. But, right now, she just wanted to find him before Mamma got home. She wanted Mamma to know that she was responsible, especially now that Mamma had a dark cloud inside her. She'd asked Pabbi if Mamma was sick. She told him how Mamma sat without talking to them. Mamma sitting down instead of doing ten different things around the apartment, Adda couldn't remember that ever happening. She told Pabbi that Mamma had stopped reading *Morgunblaðið* (the *Morning News*) with her cup of coffee. He said Mamma would be OK. His tone said something different. Lately, on Sundays, he'd taken the three kids for a ride on the city buses for no reason. They'd spend hours riding around in the heated bus. Adda suspected it had something to do with Mamma's darkness.

Leifsgata 7 was like an ant colony with people coming and going all hours of the day. Adda and Villi knew every family, two on each floor. Lára, the fortune-teller, lived on the first floor with her unmarried sons. She had gray hair she pulled back into a bun seated at the nape of her neck. Most of the time she wore a hairnet to constrain the gray wiry strands attempting to escape like prey from a spider's web.

People came to Lára for a reading. That's what they called it, a reading. Lára and a guest would sit, visit, and drink coffee together. Then Lára placed the cup upside down on a saucer to dry. For an express reading, when a person was in a hurry, Lára rested the cup on the radiator. Looking at the patterns inside the cup Lára would say things like, "In midst of great darkness, a light will shine." Or "A journey is in your future." Adda had seen glimpses of the process. It was mystical, exciting, and scary all wrapped together. However, she knew that going to a fortune-teller was a right of passage. She'd have to wait.

The previous summer, on an errand for Mamma, Adda had stopped at Lára's apartment offering to shop for her. She was on her way to the fish shop for salt fish and the grocer's for margarine and sugar. Shopping was her chore. Thought of compensation, a few *aura* (pennies) for her efforts, didn't occur to Adda, but shopping for the resident fortune-teller could be lucrative. That thought did occur to her.

"I don't have extra money, so I can't pay you anything." Adda told Lára that it didn't matter. She knew she'd give her a few auras. She always did. This time, before she could press the bell, the door opened and Lára was almost pushing a young man across the threshold. "No, no, no, I didn't see anything. Try another reader." Later that summer, Adda learned that the young man had drowned.

Jón and Þórunn lived in the other first-floor apartment. They were old. Adda had heard Mamma say that they'd celebrated their golden anniversary, and she wondered if that meant they'd been married for a hundred years. Well, not a hundred, that can't be right. A hundred years? Nobody lives that long.

Villi—under Bjarni and Eggert's tutelage, Elma's boys from the third floor—much to his sister's dismay, found entertainment in pestering the old people playing ding-dong ditch.

After ringing the bell, they ran off like Grýla (an evil she ogre) was on their heels. It took Jón and Jórunn several minutes to answer. One time Adda was coming up from the coal cellar just as Jón opened the door. "What do you want?" he barked. She explained that she didn't ring the bell. Jón, who had grown into a grumpy old person with poor hearing, snapped, "Then stop ringing my doorbell." Hearing the conversation, the real culprits, hanging over the rail of the second floor, laughed like hyenas.

Adda was tall for her age, thin, with blue eyes and thick wavy brown hair swept up to the side and tied with a ribbon that matched her outfits. She had a quicker temper and less patience than her brother. Her favorite chore was ironing her and Ásta's hair ribbons. She loved to read; hang out with her best friend, Erna; spend time with Pabbi, and go with Mamma to clean at Feldurinn (a fabric store). While Mamma cleaned, Adda walked up and down the aisles touching bolts of velvet, brocades, and damask, imagining what her confirmation gown would look like. That date was still four years away, but it didn't hurt anything to think about it.

Unnur, the tailor at Feldurinn, left remnants of fabric for Mamma to keep. Mamma had taken sewing classes and made all the children's clothing. Thanks to Unnur in a small way and Mamma in a big way, Adda and Ásta were better dressed, better behaved, and cleaner than the rest of the kids in the apartment building. Mamma's children would do better in the world than she had done. For Mamma Leifsgata was a stopping point for the family, not a final destination. Villi didn't share his mother's ambition or opinion about their dwelling. It was clear to Adda that to keep him clean and behaving would take religious effort, and, frankly, religion was an afterthought for the Andersens. She thought Mamma should be tougher on him. No point wishing Pabbi would be. He seemed to think Villi was fine the way he was. He was way wrong about that.

By the time they reached the second floor, Ásta was spent. She wanted to stop and see her friend on this floor. "We have

35

to find Villi before Mamma comes home." Adda reasoned with her. Ásta was headstrong and stubborn and could be difficult to reason with. There were days when the only person who could bring her around was Pabbi. Right now, Adda did not want a confrontation with a five-year-old.

Ásta had the darkest complexion of the three children. She was an exceptionally beautiful child. Using Adda's Shirley Temple paper–doll books, Mamma created new dresses, smocks, shirts, pants, and blouses for Ásta. When Ásta was a baby, Mamma had made her a snowsuit with little cub ears and tail, with pink roses embroidered down the front and around the hood. Seeing Ásta, women cooed and complimented. They'd stroke her cheek, "You are a beautiful little girl." It gave Adda a warm feeling, and she thanked them for her sister, who seemed indifferent. Now urging Ásta to continue the climb, Adda didn't know that a few years hence, she'd wonder why the family allotment of bad luck always seemed to land on this little sister's shoulders.

Downstairs she heard the front door open and close. Looking over the banister, no, not Villi. She needed to teach him a lesson. His disappearing acts were not endearing. She could lock him in the closet, but it was also their bathroom, making it an unlikely success. A seven-year–old boy should know better. If she yelled at him, she was reprimanded. In her home you didn't yell or use bad words.

Reaching the third floor landing outside Elma's apartment, the sisters faced an obstacle course of children's shoes and boots flung every which way. Adda kicked boots toward the wall. Elma had five kids. People said that her husband had one. That made no sense to her.

"Adda, maybe Villi went with the soldier that visits Elma when her Pabbi is not home. Maybe he took him on a big ship. Maybe…"

"Maybe, if you walk a little faster we'll get upstairs before Mamma comes home. Besides, Elma doesn't have a Pabbi." Well she did, but she wasn't going to try to explain that. "That is her husband, and his name is Óskar." Because Ásta was not a talkative child it was hard to be snappy when she did talk. She was serious for a five-year-old. Heck, she was serious for a kid of any age. In a softer tone Adda added, "Maybe the soldier is looking for a cab driver. That's what her husband does, drives a taxi to make money."

"Does the soldier have a lot of money?" Ásta knew that money was important. Her parents talked about money. They talked about how to make more money. They never talked about having too much. In those days the only things equally as scarce as money were housing and jobs. New homes and well-paid jobs were almost as rare as a polar bear floating ashore. Almost. Sometimes polar bears carried by icebergs drifted from Greenland and came ashore in the north. It happened—but rarely. Her parents talking about having too much money never happened on or off an iceberg.

After our parents married in 1933, they rented an apartment with Mother's sister, Margrét, and her family on Vesturgata. Each family had two rooms, a bedroom and a living room; they shared a bathroom and a kitchen. Margrét was a late riser, so Mamma took care of the cousins. What Margrét lacked in industriousness, Mamma made up for it.

After that they moved to Bergstaðagata to an attic apartment. Steep narrow stairs led to a 400-sq-foot space with one bedroom and an area that had a coal stove for heating and cooking.

In the Depression era, Father's inventive ways to sell himself to employers landed him jobs that eluded other unemployed men. For a while he was a coal-delivery man. Then he worked in the northern part of the country, Akureyri, butchering pigs. The owners must have been elated to hire him, Pabbi being a pig farmer from Denmark and all. Pabbi considered retelling of the truth to find a suitable frame for the occasion acceptable. He had fed pigs and witnessed their slaughter—close enough. Besides, he was a quick learner.

After inheriting money from his parents, he used it to import Christmas trees. Pabbi and his two oldest kids set up a tree sale downtown outside Eymundsbókaverslun, a book-store. Spruce trees were corded to hold back the branches and to make transporting easier. Christmas time was always bitter cold, with bakery and pine smells filling the air. Pabbi walked back and forth blowing on his stiff cold fingers, rubbing them together.

Adda and Villi's jobs were to take branches that had come detached and collect pinecones from the trees. Using wax, they made berry-sized balls, threaded a wire through them, and dipped them in red varnish. After dying the pinecones bronze, they decorated the branches that were sold for grave sites. On the last day, Pabbi gave them money to go Christmas shopping for coloring books and other trinkets. This continued for several years until the inheritance was exhausted.

Ascending the stairs at Ásta's pace, Adda also wondered why the American visited Elma. She'd overheard Pabbi say, "The American is back. Elma must be home alone." He laughed. Mamma didn't. She told him to keep his voice down. It was the way Pabbi made jokes about it. He had that same smile that Villi did when he was up to something no good. It made no sense that Óskar, Elma's husband, was always gone when the soldier came. In the marrow of her bones, Adda knew that the American visited for a different reason, but she didn't know what.

"Villi, are you in here?" she hollered into their apartment. She saw the clock on the wall—the next bus was twenty minutes away and Mamma would be on it.

Jóhanna, Ágústa's best friend, and Caesar Mar lived across the hall. She was a large woman, big boned with generous thighs. She exuded warmth, laughed easily, and sang to the delight of some and not others. Caesar worked on the sea, a fisherman. Later in his life he became an author and wrote about his war adventures in his book *From the Depth of Time*. Ceasar liked to invent things—an Icelandic version of Thomas Edison, but not famous for it. Their three children, like my siblings, went to East Side Elementary School.

Adda hung up their jackets on the coat rack on the left wall. Most days the threshold of the flat was a boundary between stagnant air and the aroma of baked goods, between grubby and clean, and between bedlam and equanimity. Adda loved everything about her home, from the green curtains with white sheers in her parents' bedroom to their ironed ribbons in the kitchen window.

"Villi, are you back!" she yelled for the second time. Looking at her big sister, Ásta's big blue eyes were a question mark. Even she could tell that Villi was not home. "He's impossible," Adda snapped to herself. Sometimes he was so exasperating that she hit him. Last Bolludagur (Punski Tuesday) Mamma said they could eat the last two *punskis* before they went to bed. Mamma made them light and fluffy with whipped cream and homemade jam. To say that they were good would distort their taste. Adda could think of no adjective to describe them adequately. In the kitchen they discovered that one was almost twice the size of the other. Adda insisted that Villi pick first. He did. He picked the big one. She couldn't believe it. He should have better manners than that. He knew that when two pieces remained, you never, ever, ever took the bigger one. She smacked him hard to help him remember next time.

Another time, before Christmas, Adda knew that Mamma had bought her Christmas gift with Villi in tow. She tried to get it out of him. He wouldn't budge. Hinting that she knew what he was getting, she suggested that they draw the gift on paper so it wouldn't be like telling. Telling, she explained, is only if you use words. Sitting down, they each drew the gift. Villi had done quite a handsome job for a five-year-old. She was getting a shoulder purse, exactly what she wanted. She could barely contain herself from jumping up and down. On her paper she scribbled a bunch of lines. When he saw it, he started crying. Then he ran out and hid. "He's just too sensitive," Adda thought to herself.

Inside the apartment there were windows on the right, and on the left was a broom closet with a toilet. It was large enough to store a coal bucket, mop, broom, and dustpan but not a sink. Toilet paper, shredded newspaper, was piled up next to the toilet bowl high enough to reach it without getting off the toilet. Adda took Villi and Ásta to the Sundhöll (the Swim Palace) on Fridays for showers. At the end of the hall of the 560 sq foot apartment was a kitchen. It wasn't a kitchen in the strictest sense of the word but a space at the end of the hall with a coal stove and an airshaft window. A one-plate-burner sat in middle of the kitchen table big enough for two people to sit at. On the street side of the apartment were two air-shaft windows, too small for a body to squeeze through, one for our parents' bedroom and the other for the living room where my siblings slept on bedrolls.

Leaving Ásta with a chunk of cheese and a slice of French bread, Adda crossed the hall to see if Jóhanna had seen Villi. When Villi hid this well, it usually meant trouble. Villi's friends Bjanri and Eggert were bad news on the move. They were older than Villi and had taught him skills—not in great demand. Mamma's warning to keep a close eye on him had his friends' names all over it. She didn't tell Villi he couldn't play with Elma's boys; this would've fallen on deaf ears. With Mother it was never what she said, it was the unsaid that hung in the air. That's what mattered. To Mother how her children were seen by others—mattered. That their clothes were clean and they were well dressed—mattered. Her children's conduct—mattered. That they were safe from harm—mattered. On this day Adda was the guardian of what mattered to her mother. She was ten years old, plenty old enough to be responsible, but she had failed. Playing with Erna, jumping off the swings, measuring each others' distance, she'd forgotten her promise. Leaning over the banister, she thought hard of places Villi liked to frequent. That's when she heard the thump of the front door and boots hitting the stairs.

Sound of heavy breathing came nearer and got louder, and she knew who they belonged to. Walking backwards towards the apartment, she reached behind her for the doorknob and, without a sound, slid inside. Chewing, kicking her feet back and forth, Ásta was back in her own world.

"Your brother is on the roof." Mamma, heaving, her lungs marred by prolonged smoking, tossed her purse and grocery bag inside the apartment and continued up the stairs that led to the roof.

Legs dangling over the ledge, smoking and yelling at people below, sat Villi, Bjarni, and Eggert. Mamma had seen them, but they had missed her. Now holding back panic, in slow motion, Mamma eased towards the edge. "Stay where you are." She met Villi's eyes full of flight. Wind pushed at her back. Her legs shook from combined effort and gut fear. Her eyes willed him not to move. Close enough she bent and grabbed his arm down to the bone and dragged him away. "You boys away from there, right now." Bjarni and Eggert skedaddled back to their lair with the quickness of convicted felons outside prison walls.

On the steps she let go of his arm. "We were not doing anything." Villi rubbed his arm, embarrassed that his friends were privy to Mamma's hysteria. "We were only there for a little bit," he reasoned.

She pushed him inside the apartment. "Sit on the sofa," was all she said. After hanging up her coat, she went to the kitchen sink to wash her hands. Although relieved to see her brother again, Adda felt the heaviness, the gray cloud, emanate from mother. It was stronger than were the worries for the consequences of her negligence.

"Did you get candy from the soldier?" Ásta was glad to have her brother back. Villi sat on the couch like a rag doll with droopy shoulders not answering. She tried again. "Is Mamma mad at you? Did you do something bad?" Giving up on her brother, Ásta looked out the window for Pabbi. He would fix her broken home.

Mamma didn't admonish Adda. She dropped potatoes into a pan with cold water, sprinkled salt into the pan and turned the burner on high. She didn't even look at her. Adda looked. She looked at her brother, the cause of all this. She glared, daring him to look back. It was all his fault. Minutes later he asked Mamma for milk and a piece of marble cake. "He is just too much," Adda thought to herself. Mamma ignored him.

Finally, after what seemed like a silence long enough for monks to want to leave the monastery, Mamma reminded Adda that the coal bucket was empty. This was her most-hated chore. Ten swimming pool trips with her siblings was better than one to the cellar. Don't complain was an established rule in the Andersen household. Adda sulked in silence, kicking Villi's leg as she passed by whispering, "I ate the rest of the marble cake."

When she picked up the handle, the bucket clanged against the side of the toilet. A proverb, although not one she was particularly found of, *bestu illu aflokið* (what you dread, do first) was fitting for this moment. She knew lots of proverbs and used them. Besides being an avid reader, she was a poet. The only person who got to read her poems was Pabbi. It meant a lot to her that Pabbi liked her ballads; that's what he said they were. She could tell from how he nodded his head that he liked them.

Outside the cellar door, below Jón and Jórunn's apartment, Adda repeated to herself, "*bestu illu aflokið.*" She repeated it like a chant on her way to the coal cellar where a truck came once-a-week and dumped coal down the shoot. The cellar had a dirty smell, not like dirty ground, but like dirty air that came in through your nostrils. Opening the cellar door she told herself, "Go down quickly, grab the shovel, fill the bucket, and run."

She had read in *Morgunblaðið (The Morning News)* that the culprit for the rats' proliferation was to be found at the feet of the fishermen. The harbor, twenty minutes walk from their apartment, housed not only ships, but also debris, over-flowing garbage cans, rusty pipes, and fish guts covered with houseflies. The seagulls were well fed but so were the rats. It was an Eden for pests to feast and procreate. She agreed with the health department when it called for fishermen and families with trashy yards to take responsibility for their environment.

Rung by rung Adda descended into the blackness of the coal cellar. Walls down the stairwell were smeared with sooty handprints. A small light came from the edges of the trap door where the coal was dropped. A chill that felt like rodents' feet scurried down her spine. From the bottom step she reached out for the shovel, almost falling into the coal pile. She yelled as she caught the shovel and steadied herself. She knew the rats had poor eye-sight and used their whiskers to navigate. More than once they'd navigated across her boots. The rats stayed close to the walls, thinking they'd be harder to see. That made them stupid *and* blind. Pabbi told her that rats and mice had a good memory and were smarter than people thought. This information did not make her chore any easier. At least he didn't say they were smart enough to invent glasses for themselves. Blind rats were preferable to sharp-eyed rats. At times one would freeze in fear right in front of her, but she couldn't make herself smack or drive the edge of the shovel into it. The thought of pushing the blade of the shovel into their bodies, blood and organs squirting out, made her want to puke.

Without taking that last step into the cellar, balancing the bucket with one leg, she got a shovelful. She pushed the shovel under a pile of coal and jiggled it to give the rats a chance to scat. Five shovelfuls filled the bucket. Climbing back up the stairs, she felt light as a feather.

Back in the apartment, Villi still sat on the couch. Looking at him forlorn, miserable, his head like a flower with frost, she felt the anger drain out of her. She loved her brother and allowed no one to say one bad thing about him. He was happy and funny and never hurt a soul—if you discount ding-dong ditch. When Elma's boys turned up like bad pennies, another proverb Adda knew, Villi followed like a puppy eager to play. Life was like that; as soon as one problem was solved, another took its place. Perhaps it's a mistake to solve a problem—make it a gatekeeper to thwart others' entrance.

Mamma, ever silent, stayed home the rest of the week. Waiting for a moment alone with Pabbi, Adda asked again, "Pabbi, what is wrong with Mamma? Why does she visit Inga so much?" Pabbi was a little under six feet with a thick strong body accustomed to physical labor. He was even tempered, an approachable man, the kind people and animals gravitate to. "She doesn't even read the newspaper." She'd already told him that, but it was really queer that Mamma didn't keep up with the news. As long as Adda could remember, Mamma read *Morgunblaðið*.

Pabbi looked at his first-born, debating, then said in a low quiet voice, "You are going to have a new sibling soon. I think your Mamma didn't want no more children." So the gray cloud was just a baby? That didn't seem so bad. She felt giddy with relief. It wasn't contagious. No, she concluded, it could have been much worse. Saturday night Pabbi installed a lock on the door to the roof.

# Chapter 4
## Three More Daughters

*This chapter is about a machete, burns, and a building permit—1944 to 1951.*

Early in 1944, Adda had learned that Mamma was with child. At first she was happy that Mamma's dark mood was temporary. Now, a few months later, she wished it wasn't so. Having too many children is not like having too many flowers. Their one bedroom apartment was shrinking. Reykjavik's list for housing was growing.

June 17, 1944, Iceland declared its independence from Denmark. Mamma cooked pork chops, mashed potatoes with red cabbagec and cocoa soup for dessert.

September 1944, Jórunn Andersen was born. Mamma took care of her as she did all her babies. But the joy was gone. She was exhausted from within, and the heaviness and a sense of hopelessness continued. At times, without an explanation, she'd put on her coat and tell Pabbi she'd be back later. Those trips were always to her sister Inga's. One afternoon she told Pabbi, "I'd be better off dead."

Adda wasn't supposed to hear those words. Her almost-eleven-year-old brain tried to understand how her mother planned to end her life. Maybe then she could prevent it. As she scanned the apartment, the kitchen table with two chairs, roll-up beds shoved into corners, sewing machine, and a coal bucket in the bathroom-closet seemed harmless. It was unlikely that Mamma would use pots and pans—besides, how do you end your life with pots and pans? But there were knives. There was one really sharp knife with a brown handle used to fillet fish. Hadn't she heard her mother say, "Kai, be careful with that knife." Now she knew.

Good luck was with her. Adda's bedroll on the living room floor was between the kitchen and our parents' bedroom. At night she removed the knife, which now looked more like a machete, and hid it under her pillow. In the morning, tip-toeing over her brother, machete in hand, she returned it. It was a good plan. It worked. Mamma lived. In time, as morning follows night, darkness lifted, little Jórunn slept through the night and the family adjusted to the new addition.

By 1945 World War II came to an end, and economic conditions began to improve. For a summer Pabbi landed a job as a chef on a trawler. He borrowed a cookbook from Mamma's sister Magnea. How hard could it be? He could read. With cookbook under one arm and a canvas bag over his shoulder, he was prepared to fine-tune his culinary skills while bouncing on the Atlantic.

Pabbi was well liked and comfortable in his own skin when dealing with others. This trait supported the family. For a few summers, working with a farmers' co-op, he bought vegetables at a lower cost and resold them from wagons on the west side of town and one on Óðinstorg. The profit was marginal, but it bought fish for the table and tickets for the bus. Adda, moody and bored, spent the summers selling tomatoes, cucumbers, cabbages, and cauliflower. It was uncanny how many tomatoes she could eat in a day.

Of the four sisters, Mamma was the most self-reliant. She was disciplined, independent in thought, religious about cleanliness, and fastidious about schedules and order. She breastfed her babies at the same time every day. She bathed them in a metal pan on the kitchen table at four in the afternoon. Her babies slept through the night at an early age. She claimed that her daughters were potty trained at nine months. She said nothing about her son's training. The first three months babies were left alone in peace and quiet. They were not cuddled and seldom kissed. Diapers were boiled in a heavy, red cast iron pot—bubbling water on the stove-burner for twenty minutes. Bacteria caused illness. Penicillin would be invented some years later. Her babies were taken outside for their naps in the fresh air. A cloth covered the buggy's opening to protect them from the wind and a rope tied to a fence was to keep the winds from blowing the buggy down the street. For the rest of her life she remained firm in her view that good babies were the result of a consistent schedule. If they were fed, burped, and had on a dry diaper, you didn't give in to their between-meals whines or complaints.

As we got older, if our egos sought affirmation of worth, recognition for some accomplishment, Mamma was not the person to go to. You did what you were told—because. Nothing came after the *because*. So most of the time, my siblings did what they were supposed to do—because.

On Fridays Adda continued to take Villi and Ásta for a shower at the swimming pool a few blocks away. School-aged children got in free. It was a new building, close to East Side School. It had taken fourteen years to complete amid the haggling of politicians and newspaper editors. It served as our bathhouse.

One Friday at Swim Hall, bouncing around on the slippery shower floor, Ásta slipped, splitting her forehead open. Quick to assist, the shower attendant helped get her dressed while pressing a towel against her forehead. Walking home, Ásta alternated between shrieking and wiping blood off her cheek. Heilsuveitastöðin (the Health Station) was close enough for Mamma to walk her there. After tears shed, back home, Ásta fell asleep in Mamma and Pabbi's bed, a rare treat.

By 1946 there were five children. Stella Andersen, an exceptionally mellow infant, had arrived. The apartment was shrinking; expenses were growing. This pregnancy arrived without the darkness. Stella's temperament was appreciated. She slept well, ate well, and smiled often. Adda's friend, Erna, an only child, always chose to babysit her at the park leaving Adda to take care of Jórunn, who was plagued with frequent ear-aches and fussed wanting attention.

Around this time Pabbi was thinking about buying land between Hafnarfjörður and Keflavík to start a pig farm on. Instead of struggling with city living, he would be the master of his land, Vatnsleysuströnd. A few years earlier, when jobs were hard to get, he had landed one at KEA in Akureyri slaughtering pigs. His experience with pigs, the one he wished he'd had but didn't, was explained in such great detail that the KEA bosses thought themselves lucky to get him onboard. Now with experience in his pocket, he was so serious about buying the land that he turned off the radio to make sure that Mamma heard the benefits of being a pig-farm family. "There is enough grassland to feed the hogs and a building that can be converted to a barn. Villi and I can ..."

Mamma didn't let him finish, so Adda never found out what my father and brother could do. "I have no interest in being a pig farmer's wife and living at Vatnsleysuströnd. We don't even have to talk about it. That's how sure I am." She said that this idea was no better than some of his other schemes. Adda was curious about the others. This was not such a bad idea. If asked, which she wouldn't be, she'd say it was a good idea. Mamma should give it a chance. Eating sugar-sprinkled yogurt with cream poured around it, she thought about sheep. Pigs were dirty, but she could take care of little lambs. Then my parents stopped talking. Mamma rinsed out the coffee thermos and wiped the counter.

Pabbi tapped four fingers one after the other in a quick succession again and again. It was something he did when he was thinking hard. The sounds of the newspaper pages turning and coffee pouring were loud. The noon weather report came on the radio—he turned up the volume.

Villi, now eleven years old, had inherited his mother's energy and his father's disposition. As far as his education, he was bright but lacked self-discipline, like father, like son. In the ten-year- old class (classes were named by age group), his report card ranked him last—as in all his class-mates had done better. Mamma asked her only son to expound. How could he possibly have the worst performance in ten-year-old class? Villi had a good explanation: "Someone had to be last. It was my turn."

In our lives, of all lives' passages—birth, confirmation, marriage, and death—confirmation was the pinnacle. It was the opening of the door to the future. It was the rite of passage. It was a celebration like no other. In my family, Mother would make sure that her children would pass through that doorframe in grand style.

Adeline Dagmar Andersen, Adda, was confirmed at Dómskirkja (National Church) on April 20, 1947. She was in her fifteenth year, now a tall, slender girl with a handsome face. She had Mother's streak of independence and Father's outspokenness at times laced with scornful dubiety. When she laughed, lightheartedness from within shone through. Like Mother, she kept doubt, pain, and worry from public view.

Mamma turned to her sister Inga to sew her daughter's confirmation dress. Inga was an accomplished seamstress who had studied in Denmark. For Adda all this attention, going over to her aunt's house, the money spent on material was surreal. Visiting Aunt Inga, the most generous and compassionate of Mother's sisters, raised her "feel-good" meter. Weeks leading to the big day, Adda's Cinderella gown took shape. It was a long white dress with a silk under-satin skirt that cascaded to the floor like a waterfall spilling down a side of a mountain. The silk bodice had long, slightly puffed sleeves, ten diminutive buttons, and satin wrapped around Adda's small waist. Adda was as close to princess-hood as she had ever been.

This first of six Andersen confirmations took place at Hotel Tjarnarlundur, and the effort and expense surpassed those of most families. It was a day of doting—something Ágústa's children knew little about. Every *krónur* Mamma could bleed out of the budget, spilled out. For a few hours the family got away from the daily toil and celebrated life.

Invited guests included Mother's three sisters, three brothers, their children, and friends. Wearing Sunday's best, nylon stockings and high heels, women were transformed. Above the polished shoes, suit and tie, men's clean-shaved faces smelled of cologne. Young boys pulled at their suits in a vain attempt to escape, and girls in chiffon dresses and patent leather shoes behaved as expected. Hired caterers served lamb with gravy, potatoes, cabbage, and dessert afterwards. Surrounded by the smell of cigars, the band played, and goodwill prevailed. It was Christmas in April. To sit and have others serve us indeed was a rare moment of luxury.

Later that year Karl Björgvin Sigurðsson, seventeen, Inga's son, died of pneumonia. It was Mamma's turn to be there for her sister.

That summer, Adda and Villi crossed the Atlantic to visit our paternal grandparents in Denmark. Unna, a cousin four years older than Adda, traveled with them. My siblings brought their new bikes, which were stored in the hull along with other luggage. Although the bikes had been gifted to them, they'd been instructed *not* to bring them back. Uncle Svend would sell them and send the money to my parents.

When the ship docked in Copenhagen, Villi was nowhere to be found. The cousins on deck, suitcases packed, took turns running around looking for him. They had been derelict in their duties trusting that his escape route was confined within the perimeter of the ship, *Hekla*—named after one of Iceland's volcanoes. Merriment around the cousins, the final rocking of the ship as the ramp was lowered, brought palpitations instead of joy. People walking off the ship, waving to loved ones on land, increased the sense of urgency to find Villi. Reluctantly, Adda waved to *Tante* (Aunt) Helga, Pabbi's sister, there to meet them. Finally, Adda explained to a ship hand that her brother had fallen overboard. A search ensued ending below deck where Villi sat watching over his bike. Knowing that his first new bike came with an expiration date, by god, he'd stick by it as long as he could and that included watching it unloaded off the ship. Adda didn't like that explanation any more than Unna did. "Villi, we thought you'd drowned!"

While pregnant with Stella, Mamma had enrolled in classes for advanced sewing techniques. She was an apt student and soon a talented seamstress in her own right using wax-paper to make patterns. Clothes from taller family members, worn-out and threadbare, reincarnated as brand new skirts, pants, and shirts for shorter bodies. When she was bent over the kitchen table, adjusting pattern pieces on the fabric, time ceased to matter to Mamma. Here she could keep wrong thoughts at bay, worries about children and money. About this time concerns about one child invaded this sanctuary. Ásta struggled with most school subjects except for math in which she excelled. She had fewer friends than her older siblings and was increasingly more difficult to deal with. Her last accident, falling off the top bunk and hitting her head on a marble table, replayed in Mamma's nightmares. It was a bad fall that resulted in a concussion and a broken jaw. The worst was yet to come.

Pabbi showed great tenderness toward Ásta. Perhaps he also sensed that she had more than her share of bad luck. Perhaps he wanted to make up for all her physical pain. Perhaps he wished he could provide her with the childhood he'd been blessed with.

March 11, 1949, the weather was still a few degrees below zero with a film of snow covering the ground. An early evening sunset, around 6:30, displayed a touch of pink, a promise of a good tomorrow. During that night, Mamma awakened Pabbi, "It's time." Quietly he slipped on his robe and hastened across the hall to use Jóhanna's telephone to call for a taxi. Back in our apartment, heaving the coat over her shoulders, Mamma picked up the bag she'd packed days earlier. Wishing her well, Pabbi remained on the landing until he heard the thump of the

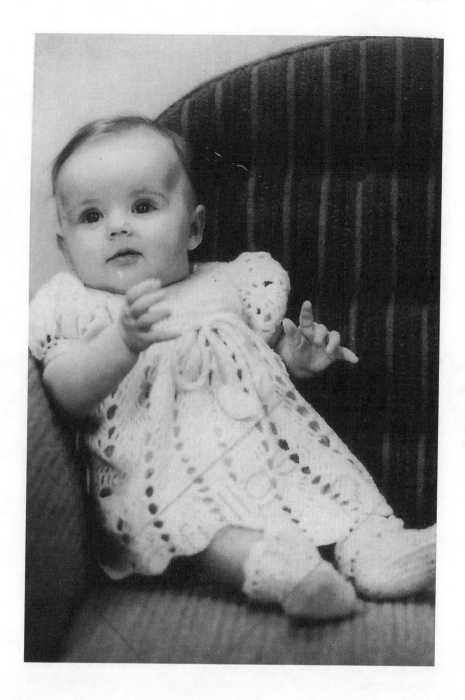

front door. North of Reykjavik, Mount Esja watched as Mamma got in the cab that took her to the hospital. Pabbi returned to bed, glad that the children remained asleep.

I was born early in the morning of Saturday, March 12. Caesar Mar got the call and trotted across the hall to our unlocked apartment with the good tidings. Wearing a *lopi peysa* (wool sweater), he made no effort to smooth his hair which stretched up like a baby waking up from sleep. Some days the luxury of a phone felt more like an unwanted responsibility.

"Kai," he spoke in whisper for respect of the early hour, "Gústa and baby are well." She was Gústa to friends, Dadda to nieces and nephews.

Sufficiently awake to remember the uneven ratio of daughters to son Pabbi asked, "What is it?"

"It's a girl." Wrong answer.

Aroma of freshly made coffee woke my siblings to the news of a new sister. Jórunn was out of sorts and wanted to know when Mamma was coming home. She was easily out of sorts. This morning she was worse than usual. Perhaps she sensed more competition coming her way. "Adda, you stay here today. I see your Mamma." Like Mamma, Adda always noticed Pabbi's incorrect grammar. Unlike Mamma, it didn't annoy her.

Earlier in the month Pabbi had bought a bathrobe for Mamma, and this morning he sent Adda to get flowers. He hummed while he waited for the water to fill the metal washbowl to shave. His kids liked his humming more than the tapping his fingers on the table. The first was a peaceful happy sound; the other meant worries on his mind. His pants and shirt, pressed and ironed, hung in his bedroom. He was sure of that. Villi and Ásta watched him walk away from the house. In his mid-forties he was still a handsome man,—although that's not what was on Villi's mind as he called to Adda, feeding Stella, "Look, look, come and look at Pabbi!" Jórunn climbed onto the sofa to take part in the fun. For the Andersen kids, this was something new, Pabbi carrying flowers. There was a first time for everything.

July 12, 1949, an announcement in *Morgunblaðið*, like a sip of strong coffee on an empty stomach, jolted my parents to high alert. The city of Reykjavík proposed a new housing development aimed at the working poor. These would be 24 two-story concrete apartment buildings between Grensás and Réttarholts roads. Each building would house four families. Apartments would be delivered roughed-in.

At a City Council meeting, a representative, Þórður Björnsson, of the Progressive Party, appealed to the council to consider this matter in earnest. On July 22 my mother turned forty-three and the City Council of Reykjavik approved a building permit to commence with the project.

By the end of 1949, Pabbi had added his names to the applicants' list for a 1,041 sq. ft. two bedroom apartment. This new community, east of downtown, was intended for families with many children and needs and few resources. Already names on the list were far greater than the number of apartments that would be available. The waiting—to hear from the city—began and another day came, a day with memories that fester like a wound that refuses to heal.

THE DAY. There was no premonition, no reading in a coffee cup, no dreams with warnings. Stella and Jórunn sat on the couch looking at a book. Instead of East Side School, which was bursting at the seams, Mamma had enrolled Stella along with Jórunn at Laugarnes School in the fall for the five-year-old class even though Stella was only four years old. The two of them fit together like a hand in a glove, a girl and her shadow. Stella knew her letters, the principal was agreeable, so why not?

Our calendar hung above and behind the kitchen table. Ásta stepped on an empty coal bin stored against the wall, next to the table. She counted the days until her birthday. Potatoes simmered in a cast iron pot on the hot plate. She would soon turn eleven. She knew Mamma wouldn't approve of her climbing adventure, but Mamma admonished her for too many things. Anyway, Mamma was feeding me in her bedroom and wouldn't see her. Reaching over the cast iron pot, she stretched her fingers as far as they would go. With her left hand on the stove for support and her index finger touching each square on the calendar—one, two, three, four—two things happened simultaneously. First, the bin slid from underneath her feet. Then the automatic reflex of her nervous system reacted, and her arm slammed down on the handle of the pot. Five-year-old Jórunn saw her sister fall. She saw the look of terror in her eyes as gravity pulled her towards the floor. She saw the pot turning in the air spewing boiling water and red hot potatoes over her sister's back and arm.

Screams, an explosion burst out of the apartment pummeling down the fourth floor, the third floor—all the way to the basement filled with coal. Still it didn't leave. It grew. Agony engulfed the apartment, crawled inside our bones. It was the scream of a young girl boiled in hot water yet denied death. Jórunn didn't move. Stella cried into the palm of her hands. Our wall clock ticked seconds. Mamma aged ten years.

Jóhanna appeared yelling for Caesar to call for help. The apartment filled with people. Strangers ceased to exist. Leifsgata 7 came together rescuing one of their own. Cold water poured over my sister brought no relief. She screamed for water to drink and flailed her arms for people not to touch her. But they did and they wrapped her in a sheet—a wounded butterfly in a cocoon.

At the hospital they moved quickly to hydrate her,— preventing her blood pressure from dropping rendering the body unable to keep blood flowing to vital organs. Burnt skin was removed to eliminate infection, and a thin layer of skin from her thighs was used to replace it. Mamma squeezed her arms around herself listening to her daughter's screams. She pushed people away. Like Ásta, her pain could not be eased.

Ásta remained at the hospital for several weeks. Her third-degree burns healed leaving the skin on her back and one arm swelled up like thick, rubbery pink leather. The physical changes were significant, but her face had been spared, handsome as ever. She'd always been reticent, but now she turned inward and closed the door. From that day on, when angst within couldn't be contained, she lashed out at Mother.

After the war Denmark experienced a severe shortage of goods. Pabbi saw it as an opportunity to make money and give his wounded daughter time to heal her soul. He convinced my Uncle Magnús that if they took his car, a big American sedan, they could store goodies to sell in it. They packed the trunk with chests full of coffee, rice, and bolts of fabric, gifts for Kai's family, they told customs. Cigarettes alone would pay for the trip. Tires were stuffed with packages of unfiltered Camels and Chesterfields. The car looked like a stuffed pig in design, and now by plan. Aunt Magnea came along with her daughter Dísa, who was Ásta's age.

Nevertheless, even the best plans go astray. Off the boat, sweet smell of money in their nostrils, Pabbi and Magnús went to liberate their future wealth from the confines of the four tires. Alas! Soaking wet—every last pack of cigarettes. Not defeated, Pabbi informed his cohort that Danes usually rolled their own cigarettes. This could be all for the best. Ásta's mental state improved. My parents watched her every smile with gratitude.

April 23, 1950, Villi was confirmed in Hallgrímskirkja (Hallgrim's Church). Again, all anchors pulled. Struggles, poverty, difficult moments were set aside. Instead of weekly trips to Inga's, his attire was store purchased, and he complained that the shirt collar was killing him. Family and friends gathered to make note of this day, a full membership to the Lutheran Church and stepping out of childhood. The reception at Breiðfirðingabúð was combined with a reception for our cousin Halldóra Magnúsdóttir. My fourteen-year-old brother was short, and our cousin, wearing high heels, towered over him. Villi's usual sunny disposition clouded. If their parents insisted on a picture of the two of them, Halldóra would have to remove her shoes. He was adamant. She relented.

The Andersens found it uncomfortable to express physical affection. Hugging, kissing, expressing love was just too hard, so we didn't. Yet on this day, Adda demonstrated her affection for her spirited brother in lyrics to the tune of a popular Icelandic song, *Á Hóli var Bóndi*. Guests sang it to Villi, whose body shrunk and face turned red. Adda received a standing ovation.

July 11, 1950, that the letter from the City Council arrived, tossed through the mail slot on the ground floor, strewn across the floor with the rest of the house mail. Some of the mail slid into wet muddy areas, the rest of it rode across the floor unmarked by wetness, grime, or gunk.

At lunch-time in the Andersen household. "Hand me a spoon." Ásta reached over to the drawer and gave Pabbi a

soup spoon. News on the radio signaled us to be quiet. After the news, the newscaster gave the names of fishing boats and number of tons of fish they'd caught. We ate *skyr* (yogurt) and open-face sandwiches with liverwurst and cheese. The city letter remained on the table unopened.

Holding me in her arms, feeding me pieces of cheese, aloud to nobody in particular Mamma said, "Well, not reading it is not going to change the content."

Mother was not a religious woman. She found no comfort in the idea of a next life. This was all we had. People spending this life looking forward to a better one in the next were ungrateful. People were always thinking that they deserved something better. Then what? Your life and comfort was what you could make it. That's all. So instead of making the sign of the cross and a short prayer, she took a deep breath and opened the letter from the city. She knew what an approval meant. It meant her kids would have beds instead of bedrolls. It meant a regular kitchen with a stove. It meant a bathroom with a sink and a bathtub.

July 7, 1950, the letter, from the office of the mayor in Reykjavik said:

> *The City Council has decided which applicants will be given an opportunity to purchase apartments from those now ready to be awarded at this time. An agreement has been reached to give you an opportunity to buy a four- room apartment* (two bedrooms, living room, and dining room) *at Hólmgarður 26 upon receipt of required deposit.*

The energy in the 560-square-foot apartment rose like a helium balloon. Mamma read it to herself. Then she read it to her family. It was the best single family news the Andersens had received in what seemed forever and then some. I remained indifferent except to the possibility that Mamma dipped my pacifier in sugar before handing it to me. I was sixteen months old, and already the sugar drawer was my favorite spot in the apartment. For my parents much work lay ahead, but work was something Mother understood, and Pabbi was grateful for the opportunity.

The letter stated that the apartment would be sold to Pabbi roughed-in and that the exact cost would be known after the first phase of the construction was completed. The approximate cost was 88,000 *krónur*. The city of Reykjavík would provide a fifty-year mortgage for the apartment at 3 percent interest. One caveat—the city had first right to purchase it back if no family member wished to continue the mortgage. The apartment could never be rented.

Roughed-in means that what's behind the walls, like plumbing and electrical works, is completed. Also, windows and exterior doors are installed. New owners were responsible for walls, painting, floor coverings, plumbing and electrical fixtures, appliances and cabinetry. To make it a home for a family of eight was up to Pabbi. All work had to be completed within two years from the date the contract was signed.

New Year's morning of 1951, Margrét's five-year-old daughter, Helga was up before her parents anxious to play with her doll, a Christmas gift. It was a lovely doll with yellow hair and brown eyes and black eyelashes that opened and shut. She and the doll had nightgowns on but only Helga had slippers. She named her Sara. Helga and Sara explored the living area scattered with ashtrays and boxes of matches. Striking a match was hard. It made her more determined. She slit the stick against different parts of the matchbox. Finally, she found the gray sides that felt like fine sandpaper and the flame found her doll's hair resting on the coffee table. Helga grabbed Sara and hugged her tight, tight enough to put out the fire. But the fire found Helga's nightgown. There would be no heroic attempt or a miracle to save her life. It was simply too late. Margrét and Leifur had now lost the oldest and youngest of their seven children.

That same year Pabbi became one of five owners of Gúmmibarðinn, a tire shop in Reykjavik. Villi was finishing his mandatory education. For months Pabbi took the bus to Hólmgarður and worked in our apartment until the last bus came. Villi helped enough to keep our parents off his back and soothe his conscience. Adda brought Pabbi his meals.

Going to Swim Hall for a shower, Jórunn now seven, found a lady's gold watch. From appearance it was an expensive one. It sat on the kitchen counter. Before my parents could place an ad, the owner beat them to it. Arriving in our apartment, wearing a mink coat, the owner asked Jórunn, "Are you the little girl who found my watch?"

Jórunn, blushing, shook her head up and down. The woman handed Jórunn 100 *krónur*. Jórunn never owned a doll. Now she would. Maybe she'd buy the one with hair and clothes. After the mink lady left, Jórunn made more plans for the money that included candy. However, Mamma flushed out all her plans when she told her that the money would be used to buy a toilet seat for our real bathroom on Hólmgarður. So, little by little, with money older siblings earned, Mamma's part-time job cleaning, and what was left over from Pabbi's paycheck, Hólmgarður 26 was taking shape.

In the meantime, other families moved in before their apartments were complete. Lilly, a friend of Adda, whose father was a postman and mother a cleaning woman, moved in when only one door, the bathroom door, had been installed.

Ágústa was adamant that the Andersens move in only when everything was done. Not one day before. Perhaps she was concerned that her husband's motivation would dwindle if they moved in early. Perhaps this was her one chance in life to move into a home—the kind she had dreams about. Whatever the case was, they would wait.

With the inside work done, a Danish paint technician was hired. The bathroom and kitchen were painted in white high gloss. The rest of the house was white flat texture. Our hall stairs to the front door, walking down, had a railing on the left.

They made a half a spiral with a few steps wide on one side and narrowing on the other like a fan. These stairs, coupled with Ágústa's passion for cleanliness, would for years to come, play havoc with children in a hurry.

"It's just damn nonsense to wax stairs making them more dangerous than climbing Mount Everest." Pabbi seldom cursed or lost his temper. His children, sliding down faster than the apple that fell on Sir Isaac Newton's head, bruised and screaming at the bottom of the steps, put him in one of those moods.

When it came it was an extraordinary moment—the night before the Andersens moved into their new home. Into the wee morning hours, Pabbi and Adda scrubbed and wiped. They cleaned left-over paint splotches, saw dust, and errant gobs of glue around the baseboard. The kitchen cupboards were washed down, and a vinegar mixture rubbed off water spots in the sink. Adda, a teenager, hung up curtains in each of the four rooms, the kitchen, and bathroom. It had taken months, and now that it was coming to an end. Pabbi and Adda worked in silence, each deep in private thoughts. She walked around the 1,000-square foot place. They were moving into a place twice the size of their apartment. The living room had new furniture; the bedrooms, beds for each person; the bathroom, a tub and a sink. Instead of torn newspaper, a roll of toilet paper hung on the wall. She rubbed her arms to calm the goose bumps and turned away so Pabbi couldn't see the tears. Every life has moments; this one belonged to Pabbi and Adda.

# Chapter 5

## Transitions

*This chapter is about bread with jelly, black
people, and a stinky baby—1951 to 1954.*

I was two years old when the family moves to Hólmgarður.
In the fall of 1951, Adda had left home to attend a nursing school, a residential program at Landspítalinn (National
Hospital). Villi finished his mandatory education and worked
full time at Gúmmibarðinn. Mamma contemplated ways to
get him back to school for his high school diploma. Ásta took
the bus to Austurbæjar School (East Side School) whose students ranged from age five to sixteen years old. Attendance
requirements were from five to fourteen. Jórunn continued
at Laugarnes School which took students from the overpopu-
lated Austurbæjar School. Laugarnes School principal encouraged Mamma to enroll Stella with her age group in the new
neighborhood instead of continuing in Jórunn's class. "Academics are not an issue," he explained. "She is just too young
in years." For the first time, Stella and Jórunn, two halves of an
apple, were separated.

Moving to the new apartment in 1951, the family living
space had doubled. When our attic was finished, a few years

later, it would add three small bedrooms, storage, and a living area in the center. Each bedroom eventually had had a skylight that could be opened. And by the time I was in high school, we had heat registers in our rooms. Ásta was the first beneficiary—her own room.

Mamma continued to work part time, cleaning. Earning money was important to her. She was tired of asking Pabbi, who seldom left money unasked, "I need money for dinner." He would put money on the counter, and Mamma would quip that this would get her through the lunch, not dinner.

"How much you want?"

"It's how much do you need," the exasperation in her voice spoke volumes, and his grammar added salt to sore.

Now that we were out of the city center, young kids played in their backyards. Instead of paved streets filled with people, buses, and cars, Bústaðahverfi (our neighborhood) had gravel roads and construction in various stages of completion. It might as well have been a different planet. A street over there were small homes, summer cottages that would not be for long. Out the living room window, we could see an expanse of grass and with a small house way in the distance. That's where the Christmas lads lived, or so I believed.

First time Stella meandered to the back of the house she couldn't find her way home. Exploring her options— one to cry, two to cry-cry, and three to cry-cry-cry—she chose option two. A rescue party of one, Ásta, found her, returned her, and fed her. Family harmony restored.

April 26, 1953, Ásta was confirmed. It was a big party and well attended. Mamma made three light yellow frocks for her younger daughters, purchased new socks and shoes, and reminded Villi to get a haircut.

Memories before 1954 are hazy, but childhood sounds and smells are vivid. There is the purring of a sewing machine; a kerplunk—mail hitting the tiles of the hall floor; thump of doors closing; coughing; tic-tock of grandfather's clock; radio reports—the tons of fish caught; zzzz from my parents' bedroom; wind and rain on the roof; Pabbi playing the piano; laughter and strained silence. Smells of the cold earthy scent in the hall pantry; aroma of glazed potatoes on the stove bub- bling in sugar and butter; pungent smell of bay leaves in a pork roast; musty stale air from cigarettes that burned your eyes and nostrils; laundry and Ivory soap; Old Spice, and on special occasions—whiff of Chanel No. 5.

From here family tales are my own memories. They begin with me five years old.

Villi is sleeping on a divan in a small room next to the dining room. I'm about the height of the dining room table, watching. It's early afternoon, and Pabbi has made a couple of unsuccessful attempts to arouse my brother. Then he pulls off his duvet. Villi lets out a deep grunt of indignation, yelling for the cover to be replaced. When it isn't, he jumps off the divan

and faces his attacker. His thick brown hair, like quills on a porcupine, makes him look taller. Grogginess has left—in its place a face full of fury. He and Pabbi chase each other around and around the dining room table. Villi has gotten a hold of a broom. Pabbi runs dragging the duvet. Villi holds up the broom, a sickle without a blade. Neither man smiling. The phase slows. It's over. This violent episode upsets me so I sweep the floor until my heart is beating a calmer rhythm. Mamma and Pabbi talk behind the glass kitchen doors.

It had been nearly twenty years since Pabbi immigrated, and he understood Icelandic perfectly. He spoke it imperfectly. It hurt my feelings when Mamma pointed this out. I wished she wouldn't correct him. She sounded so mean. "Are you talking about Helga or Helgi?" she'd snap. But when she let him finish talking, you could always figure it out. Mamma didn't want to figure it out. She wanted him to speak correctly right now.

My first year in school, a morning class, is at the teacher's house. Her name is Jóna. Fifteen kids sit on her living room floor and listen to her talk. She talks, we squirm. We are not allowed to sit on her couch and two chairs. She is tall skinny and always moving around. When we ask permission to use her bathroom, she asks if we were sure we have to go. That baffles me. How can you not know? She tells me that I use the bathroom too often. So I pay attention to the bathroom feeling inside my tummy. When the pushing feeling comes, inside my head I'd think, "Is this real, or is my body just tricking me?" Björn never uses the bathroom. Sólveig uses it every day and sometimes two times. Jóna likes Björn, Sólveig not so much. After a few weeks, I agree with my teacher. I don't have to go every morning. But my tummy hurts a little bit. Katrín, my best friend, says she doesn't want to run home from school every day so she walks back with other friends.

"Mamma, how many times do you go to the bathroom—in the morning I mean?"

"What?"

"In the morning, how many times do you go to the bathroom?"

She goes "what?"

She sure doesn't hear so good. When I tell her that my teacher says I go to the bathroom too much, she looks mad. I wished I hadn't told her.

"If you have to go the bathroom, you go to the bathroom." She is still angry with me.

School is a little bit fun and little bit not fun. It is taking a long time to learn the letters, especially when you already know them. I ask questions, but the only thing Jóna likes less than my questions are my answers. You see, if she likes your answers, she'd let you go into her kitchen for a piece of white bread with butter and jam.

One day she is teaching us how fast the world turns. Standing on a chair, she twirls her hand around as fast as she can. "Can you see it? Can you see it?" she yells. "That's how fast the world turns. Look again," she says. She looks happy. It must be her favorite lesson. But I worry that with all this commotion, she'll fall off the chair. The only time I'm allowed to stand on a chair is when Mamma is trying on clothes that she had been sewing for me or she is dressing me for a holiday or family party.

Reaching my hand high moaning "Ooohhh ooohhh," Jóna picks me to answer.

"Edith, tell the children. Did you see my hand? Did you see my hand that goes as fast as the world turns." She is smiling at me and doesn't look dizzy at all. This is good.

Triumphantly, "I can see it. It's blurry, but I can see it." The look on her face tells me that white bread, butter, and jam are not in my near future. The other kids say they can't couldn't see her hand that went as fast as the world.

I tell Mamma that my whole class needs glasses. She says, "What?"

Jóna stands in front of us and we stretch and bend. It's good for us and it feels good, stretchy kind of good. But she gets confused. "Raise your right arm," then she raises her left. All the kids raise their right except me. She explains to me that she is doing a "mirror image" and that I should do what the other kids do. But they are wrong, and I don't want to put up my left arm when she says right arm. Another thing, the "mirror image"; there are no mirrors in her living room. For a teacher she makes a lot of mistakes.

If it's nice outside, we play trolls in the mountains. Four kids are picked to be the trolls, one for each corner. That's their home. The rest of us are the sheep grazing in the mountains. The trolls chase the sheep, and the one with the most wins. Because I run home every day, I am a fast troll and lamb.

Before the year ended, I did really good on road safety. Jóna said, "Look at the light. When it's green, you can cross." She got that mixed up, so I explained that the cars can go when there is a green light. Not the walking people. She said I could go into her kitchen and have a slice of white bread with butter and jam. She said I could even have two and take my time.

Katrín Kjartansdóttir lives downstairs, and we are best friends. Her Pabbi drives an oil truck, and her mother, Gógó owns a big knitting machine. You go down the stairs where one door leads outside, the other through a small concrete hall. Opposite your hall door is the one that goes into the down-stairs apartment. We share the laundry room that's five steps down from the hall. Her mother is always happy to see me. "Edith, come in, come in. Katrín was hoping you'd visit."

We are not allowed to play in the laundry room, so we play at each other's apartments or outdoors. Outside, we climb and walk on the cement fence in front of our house. The playground area close to our house is just a field of mud. They should call it mudground.

I'm sitting on the fence waving to Adda in the kitchen win-dow. Her eyes get big, her mouth opens like she is making the "O" sound. Behind me, Katrín's pabbi's truck is inching towards my legs dangling over the fence. But I don't know that. Faster than a diving seagull, Adda is outside yelling and hollering. My leg is squished against the fence, and I figure out that she was not doing the "O" sound; she was saying oh, oh. Katrín's pabbi comes running. Adda heaves me into her arms and says, "It's not so bad." She is an almost nurse so it is true.

Sitting on the kitchen counter while she washes my knee, Adda tells me that bad things happen, but it's best not to think about the bad things, just the good ones. I can't think of anything bad that has happened to Adda so I ask her. My leg hurts and I wince when she puts alcohol on it. That's when she tells me about the scar on her arm.

"I used to tease Villi," she started. I decided not to remind her that she still teased him. "Villi liked this girl who lived on Bústaðaveg," she pointed south, "and would visit her. I called her the widow, but that's not important." I kind of thought it was important but was polite and didn't interrupt her. "Anyway," Villi said he didn't like her. But he did. So, and here comes the bad part, I was tired of him lying to me, and he was already dating Gunna, so I teased him even more. Adda said Gunna was really nice. Villi got mad and grabbed a towel off the table and threw it at me. He didn't know that there were scissors inside the towel that landed in my arm. Mamma found out a day later because my arm kept bleeding and took me to have it stitched."

She picks me up and puts me down on the floor. I've forgotten all about my leg. This is a terrible story. My family is not very nice to each other. It makes me sad, so I ask Adda if I can sweep the kitchen floor.

Wearing dresses meant wearing a middy with stiff elastic, with buttons, that were pulled down to hold up brown poopy-colored stockings. It was kept taut so your stocking wouldn't sag. By the time my middy and stockings were connected, I felt shorter. "You are not shorter," Mamma chuckled. Sometimes while fastening the stockings, the elastic snapped back hitting my stomach or hip. "Stand still," Mamma directed so I waited to rub the injured body part until I got off the chair.

Jórunn and Stella liked wearing identical clothes. That I was the third identically dressed sister, they liked less. Wearing our blue coats downtown, they made me walk on the other side. They kept an eye on me and laughed and laughed. I smiled and waved back, and that made them laugh more. My sisters sure could laugh.

Adda brought home a man, her boyfriend. Valgeir wore store-bought clothes, was a little bit tall, and had brown hair and soft hands. The night she met him, instead of their regular dance club, Gúttó, (Góðtemplarar), she and her friend Dadda went to a dance club (Mjólkurstöðinni) that served alcohol. Mamma told her sister-in-law Sigga who was drinking coffee in our kitchen, that he was an only child and well-educated.

When I was four months old, Sigga and Mamma's brother Pétur took care of me while my parents visited Denmark. When they returned, Sigga and Pétur wanted to adopt me. Their two kids, Ingimundur and Ása, were grown up, and Mamma had too many children. My parents said that six were not too many.

Nineteen fifty-four, I get to go with Mamma and Sigga to Denmark to shop for Christmas. Stella and Jórunn don't. I remind them that they can't come with us. In a nasty voice, they yell, "We know."

In Copenhagen, walking from the train station to my Aunt Helga's apartment, I point to something I have never seen before, a person painted black. "Mamma, did he paint himself," I ask. Mamma tells me to stop pointing. She says that I must never say that. Denmark is full of painted people. Wait until I tell my sisters.

Sigga, Mamma, and I sleep in the same room at Aunt Helga's. Sigga stores a giant-sized MacIntosh tin under her bed. Knowing this, makes it hard to sleep. Candy is my favorite food. Yummy, Yummy! Lying on Aunt Helga's bed unable to sleep, I see in my mind the mouth-sized treats wrapped in different colors: caramel swirls yellow, milk chocolate purple, toffee gold, vanilla fudge pink, and my favorite, noisette pate, green chocolate triangles. When both start snoring, I slink out of bed and crawl to Sigga's side and liberate a few pieces. Night after night, slinking, crawling, eating, I am tired. Empty wrappers are becoming problematic. God comes up with the answer: Hide them underneath the rest of the candy.

Sweden was next on our itinerary. A short trip on a ferry from Copenhagen to Malmo and a walk through customs. Mamma and Sigga spent hours in a big department store. Each item Sigga picked up she'd show it to my Mother and lament over the cost of this item at home. They debated which items would cost the most in Iceland—those were the ones that made sense to buy. Mamma bought glass kitchen bowls, cotton towels with orange stripes and then, and then, and then she bought a little doll with a bed! This was not only unexpected, it was unbelievable. Just like that, I had a new doll, and it wasn't even Christmas. The carrier was pink, plastic with diamond patterns. My doll was a lot smaller than the carrier was. That was good. She could grow into it. I stroked her bald head.

Returning to Copenhagen meant another dreaded walk through customs. "Don't talk," Mamma's voice is serious. "We want people to think we are Danish." She and Sigga look scared and don't talk to each other at all. A uniformed custom's guy is flailing his hands, directing traffic. Danes go in the fast lane, the rest in the slow lane. We join the fast lane. My pink baby carrier is getting heavier and heavier. She weighs a lot for such a tiny baby. Perhaps I should hold my doll in one hand and her bed in the other. I whisper, "Here little doll." But before I can lift her out, Mother shoves my baby's head back down hisses for me to be quiet. We continue in the fast no-talking lane.

On the ferry retuning to Copenhagen, Mamma orders me a Coke, smiles and says I've done a good job. Then she reaches under my baby and pulls out a bottle of wine.

Home from Denmark, Mamma continued cleaning for Dr. Ólaf Þorsteinsson. Pabbi heard all about the beautiful wall painted in an array of colors. Mamma liked it so much they hired a Danish painter who painted abstracts and liked crepes. He'd paint the wall down the stairs.

After chocolate noisette pates, crepes are my favorite food. It takes a long time to make crepes. When you are a guest, you should always remember that. It's proper manners. First, you make the batter, not too thick. When the butter in the cast iron crepe pan sizzles, you pour in the first one. The smell from the steam goes right to your stomach and all you can think about is how much you want one. You don't eat the first crepe. You throw it out because it has too much butter on it. Then you watch the crepe pile growing taller.

"Isn't it time for a cup of coffee?" Mamma calls down to the Dane who gets all happy. He's served crepes, rhubarb preserve, and sugar. I can't eat any until the guest has eaten. Well, you have never seen a crepe eater like this painter. Yes, he is Danish, but that doesn't really matter. Now he is a crepe ogre. I stand behind his chair, a hungry shadow. After peeling crepe after crepe off the pile, sprinkling sugar or spreading jam down the middle, he wraps it up and gobbles it down. The pile keeps shrinking and so does my heart. I am counting with my fingers, and when I ran out of fingers I say, "He ... he ... he ... he's eaten ten." Mamma says counting is not good manners.

When the painter finished, the wall down the stairwell was black, red, orange, green, and blue with a black border. With art on his mind, Pabbi visited a friend at an art gallery for plasterboard to finish our bedrooms upstairs. He came home with lots of boards covered with pictures, advertising, writing, even scribbles the artist had done. Ásta and Jórunn scraped off the flyers, wiped the boards down, and scrubbed spots until they were clean enough to paint over.

Pabbi knew how to do a lot of stuff. What he liked most was cutting the grass and working in our vegetable plot at the back of our lot. He whistled and the birds chirped. He liked working with the men at Gúmmibarðinn, but not enough to whistle. He got money for working in Gúmmibarðinn. Mamma reminded him she needed money for groceries. "Food costs money," she reminded him. I don't think he forgot.

Our family didn't spend much money on breakfast food. It was coffee and bread with butter. Lunch, more expensive, was *skyr* and bread with liverwurst with pickled beets, headcheese with mustard, or hard-boiled eggs. Sometimes we had sliced cucumber that we dipped in sugar. For dinner, the most expensive meal, we ate boiled fish, fried fish, fish balls, fish soup, fish plokk (stew-like fish with onion), or salt-fish. My favorite food after candy and crepes was buff (hamburgers). Mamma shaped the ground beef into patties, coated them with flour, added a salt and pepper mixture, and fried them in butter with onion and served them with mashed potatoes. The onions smelled good but tasted slimy. I pushed them off to the side of my plate. We had potatoes with the fried fish, boiled fish, fish ball, salt fish and any meat she cooked. Sundays we got meat and potatoes browned in butter and sugar. I don't think potatoes cost much money. I bet Pabbi was glad about that.

"Edith is a finicky eater," Mamma told her sisters. I thought about that. Jóna was right about my using the bathroom too much. Was Mamma right about this? But I ate everything that tasted good. Pabbi told me that children in China would appreciate the food that I didn't eat. There was a deep space next to the register where I sat and ate. I dropped food down there and asked God to let it fall to China.

December 5, 1953, my sister Adda got engaged to Valli, the one with the clean nails. Ásta showed me their engagement announcement in the newspaper.

In 1954, Mamma's pabbi turned eighty, and all his kids visited him bringing flowers and presents. He was so happy that he told them thank you in the newspaper. "I think he'd have been even happier if all his grandkids had come," I shared. Mamma said she didn't think so.

The year I turned five, two good things and one bad thing happened. Ásta finished high school was a good thing because she began to earn money to help Mamma pay for the food. Villi decided that fixing tires was not that much fun. And my brother liked to have fun!

One night when Mamma thought he was having too much fun, she said a few words about that. But he talked back to

her. My sisters and I were in bed when we heard Pabbi say in a loud deep voice, "You will never speak to your mother that way again. If you are not happy here, move." Soon after he started Samvinnuskóli, Reykjavik's business school. That was the second good thing.

The bad thing? Adda was going to have a baby and couldn't finish nursing school. Mamma told her that she can do her internship, that's what they call it when you work in a hospital, after the baby was born. I hoped Adda didn't think about this bad thing. She would have to sweep a lot of floors.

April, the bad thing was born. It was a little girl that looked like a china doll. I didn't like her. Adda didn't know how to be a mother. I told Mamma. Mamma said, "She'll learn." Adda kept touching and kissing the baby, and you were not supposed to do that. When the baby cried, Adda picked her up.

"Just let her cry," I tell her. "If you pick her up all time, she won't learn to behave." Adda should know this, but since she doesn't I'm telling her.

"We don't want her to cry, do we?" she ooohhhs. Actually, I'm fine with it. "What's the matter, little one? Talk to Mamma. Tired of laying in bed with nothing to do?" My sister's parenting incompetence is so great that I shake my head as Pabbi does when he's had enough and get my coloring book. I'm going to color the princess page where she sits by the lake with two swans floating towards her. She's a lot prettier than Adda's baby is.

It's baptized and given the name Katrín, after her pabbi's mother. Mamma is kind of old, but the kid's other *amma* is really old and has a big nose. Now there is old Katrín and young Katrín. It's easy to tell them apart. Old Katrín wears Iceland's national costume. It's the one that Fjallkonan (Lady of the Mountain) wears. Young Katrín goes "Bawwww, bawwww."

Valgeir, Adda calls him Valli, misses Adda. He doesn't miss the stinky baby. Even on a workday, he wears nice clothes. Pabbi says that people who work in nice clothes are pencil pushers. But he doesn't say that about Valli. That's how I know that Valli must change clothes before he comes for a visit.

Ásta lets only me—not Jórunn and Stella—come into her bedroom upstairs. It's the only room that's finished. She tickles me and laughs when we are together. That's the only time she laughs. Most of the time Ásta has a lot of sadness inside her, and she gets angry with Mamma. I don't think Mamma and Pabbi like her boyfriend, Agnar. As Ásta is running up to her room, Mamma tells her to come back. Ásta says, "Shut up." Mamma watches her disappear into her attic room, tears running down her face. She walks slowly to her bedroom and closes the door. Now there are tears on my face. I ask God to make Ásta behave better.

When Pabbi comes home, Mamma is still in the bedroom and dinner will be late. It doesn't take long to fix buff, and I suggest it to Pabbi. I could run to the store and get some, but

Jórunn tells me to find something to do and not bother our parents. Going to the store is helping, not bothering. Pabbi calls Ásta for a kitchen talk. Through the glass panes on the kitchen door, Pabbi looks serious, Ásta stares down at the kitchen table. When he's done talking with her, she runs down the hall like a chicken chased by kids and slams the hall door behind her. She forgot it closes really easy.

On a different day, Ásta moves even faster. Gummi the Idiot lives on Bústaðaveg, the street south of ours. He is a retarded teenager who talks to himself. He likes to touch kids. Sometimes he hugs us so hard that we cry out for him to let go. Sometimes he hits us. Now our playground, called Little Róló, has swings and see-saws, and is surrounded by a high spiky wooden fence. At the playground Gummi pushes you on the swing higher than you want to go. Then he laughs. But he's the only one having fun. If you runaway from him, he'll chase you all happy like.

One day, when Ásta ran the fastest of all, I was wading in puddles outside the front of our house. They were deep enough to cover the foot part of my boots. Pabbi had just patched them, and I was checking to see if they leaked. Gummi grabbed me and pushed my head into the puddle. Now I wished it wasn't so deep. I heard him laugh as I tried my best to pull his hand off my head. Then Ásta came running, "Gummi, that's bad!" She yelled and yelled and said that he should go home and that he was a very bad boy. She's not even a little bit afraid of him. It was good to breathe again. That night I told Pabbi what happened, but I forgot to tell him that the boots didn't leak.

Our laundry room, five concrete steps down from the ground floor, had a cement floor and walls. When Mamma did laundry, I sat on the floor with legs dangling over the landing. She wore black rubber boots and an apron over her dress. It was hard to make out Mamma's waist, but she said, "We have good legs and a good neck." That's good. Our furnace was in the back a little ways from the washing machine and the two large wooden barrels for soaking and rinsing clothes. A red hose hooked to our faucet filled the tubs and washing machine with cold water.

The washing machine was a white enamel tub on legs. A big agitator twisted back and forth, making the machine dance on the cement floor. Mamma let the clothes twist back and forth until the water was dirty. She pulled the clothes out and put them through a wringer, two rubber rolling pins turned by a motor attached to the top of the machine. Then she tossed the clothes into the rinse barrel and stirred them with a wooden paddle and put them through the wringer again. Her hands turned pink from the icy water. She piled the clean clothes in a basket and took them outside to hang on our clotheslines in the back of the house. In winter she hung them in the laundry room basement. She showed me how to hang up the clothes so I'd know when I was tall enough to do it. Sheets and towels with no stains were hung on the outside. Pants and shirts came next, and underwear was hung where nobody could see it. The hanging clothes looked nice.

One house from ours a big building was going up that was to house a milk shop, drugstore, bookstore, fabric shop, grocery shop, and fish shop all on the ground floor. In the middle on the second floor, was a library. It was open two hours, three days a week. My neighborhood was a good place to live.

December 23, 1954, Saint Þorlákur Day, Pabbi asks, "Do you want to come with me to buy Mamma a present?" He was talking to me because there was nobody else in the kitchen. Adda, who had been baking and selling cookies, had left the kitchen to check on stinky baby. She had put an ad in the paper, and people came to the house to buy the cookies. She gave me the ones that didn't turn out so good. I got a lot of cookies. Pabbi waited for my answer and I shook my head north and south.

People at the bus stop pull up their coat collar and cross their arms. It is a cold, windy day with white fluffy snow-flakes that melt and turn into water. One time, Adda asked me if it was raining outside. I told her that it was raining and the sun was shining and there was a rainbow. She said that was impossible. She said it was either raining or the sun was shining. I looked again and just as before, I could see the sun, raindrops, and the rainbow. I didn't tell her she was wrong. I told Kata who was in her crib kicking her legs and flailing her arms. I said, "Your Mamma doesn't know everything." She just stared at me, smiled, and slobbered down her chin.

On this night, stores are open until midnight. Shoppers pack the streets. Red and green Christmas lights crisscross the streets. Cars and buses slosh water on shoppers, who know enough to wear boots. The wind is blowing hard and you have to be careful when you open store doors so they don't whip off the hinges. Salvation Army people with red noses ring bells, and paperboys yell, "VÍSIR, Algeria fights for independence. Read all about it!" I wonder if Algeria lives in Iceland.

The store windows are decorated with cotton batting sprinkled with star-dust. Upright in their cardboard boxes stand dolls with eyes the color of coffee and thick lashes staring at me, "can I come home with you?" They sure are pretty.

At the end of Laugarvegur (Pool Road) close to Torg (the center of town), we stop at a little shop called Stella, like my sister. Pabbi must be getting Mamma a scarf or gloves. It's all he looks at. Stella's shop smells like nice things, silk and leather. Wearing a thick brown coat, a woman in front of us keeps touching and wrapping scarves around her head and neck. "This looks beautiful on you," the sales lady coos. Scarf after scarf the sales lady continues, "Now this is truly your color. It brings out your eyes." I lean in front of her to see if her eyes are coming out. She pushes me out of the way and says, "Pleeeease." Pabbi moves me closer to him, and when I whisper that I don't think that all the scarves looked pretty on her, his eyes smile back at me.

Pabbi looks at a pair of black leather gloves. They are soft and smell like the inside of a taxi-cab. The sales lady tells us that they were made in Italy. They are hand sewn and lined with rabbit fur. They are really expensive, so she shows us other gloves that are thinner, stiffer, and not made in Italy. I tell her that we are buying this for my mother. Pabbi feels them, looks inside, and then looks at the price tag. He looks back at the price tag of the rabbit gloves. Back and forth, price tag of a different pair then back at the tag of Italian leather gloves. He must be in his forgetful mood. Finally, he hands the sales lady the good-smelling-lined-with-fur gloves and says, "I'll take these."

Riding home on the bus I fall asleep in his lap and dream of the beautiful doll in the window holding out her miniature hands pleading, "Take me home with you."

# Chapter 6
## Vífilsstaðir—Sanatorium

*This chapter is about Olive Oyl, a ghost, and buggers—1955 to 1957.*

In our first floor laundry room, Pabbi built shelves under the window for our shoes and boots. In the summer, when we left the window open, flies got caught in the curtains and flopped around trying to find their way out. By fall those that hadn't escaped were scattered around the window sill with their legs curled against their bodies. Once a neighborhood cat, black with white paws, got inside the hall and jumped up on the window sill. It pawed the flies as if it were trying to wake them up. Flies are dirty creatures, that's what Mamma said, but it was mean to toy with them like that even if they were dead.

Upstairs and downstairs families took turns using the laundry room, every other week. They shared everything except the washing machines and clothes pins. Mamma had a white cotton bag that hung at the end of one of the lines. When your laundry turn ended, you covered your machine and pushed it to the side.

Katrín Kjartansdóttir and I are lucky to be best friend and live in the same house. We visit each other without going outside—just walk across the first floor laundry hall. But my luck has run out. She's moving. Her parents, who are younger than my parents, want a bigger place. Their apartment is smaller than ours. We have an upstairs foyer, a pantry, and an attic that Pabbi is still working on. They don't. Ásta's room is done, but there is no heat in the attic yet. Pabbi thinks that's fine for now. Mamma is less sure.

In seven-year-old class, I'm the best reader. My teacher, Ása, lets me read to the other kids. When I finish, she says, "Thank you, Edith. Very nice." She says "very" louder and slower. I always raise my hand to read. It gives me a warm feeling, like the sun shining on my face.

Sitting on the floor with my feet hanging over into the laundry room cellar, I tell Mamma about Ása's complimenting me. She says, "I see." I explain in greater detail to make sure she does see and understand that I'm the best reader in the class. Now she doesn't even say, "I see." The warm feeling is cold.

A new family moves into the first floor apartment. They had three kids. One was my age; her name was Hafdís. Her two older sisters were Ásta's age. Their mother, Lovísa, walked stiff-legged and always looked tuckered out. When she did laundry, she stroked her forehead with the back of her hand and said, "Aaawwww." My sisters copied her and said they were doing the *Lovísa move*. If she saw me in the hall, she took a deep breath and asked tiredly, "Are you looking for Hafdís?"

Hafdís has dark blond hair, a round nose, and freckles. She is a little bit fat and not very nice, and we don't get along so much. I miss Katrín, who is not a little bit fat and always nice. When I tell Ásta that I don't like Hafdís, she says, "But you hardly know her at all. Maybe she'll get nicer." I hope she is right.

The new family's apartment was stuffy, and Hafdís's father, Lúter, coughed all the time. He just couldn't get rid of that cold. He was tall and skinny, and his face was white like the bleached sheet on the clothes line. After a long coughing spell, he would clear his throat and spit into the bathroom sink. Then he would cough more and spit more, cough more and spit more. Afterward Lovísa would tell us to be extra quiet so he could take a nap in peace.

Hafdís and I preferred to play upstairs in my apartment. Mamma let us play in the attic as long as we didn't touch Pabbi's tools. When Pabbi finishes the other two bedrooms, Stella and I were to share and Jórunn was to have her own.

On cold, windy, or rainy days, Hafdís and I tried to become good friends. Hafdís would come upstairs, and we'd play with paper dolls and look over our napkin collections to see if we wanted to make any trades. My paper napkin collection was stored in a box big enough to lay the napkins side by side, but overlapping. It made it easy to leaf through them without taking them out of the box and getting them dirty. We kept our most special ones on the bottom. Hafdís's oldest sister was an airline stewardess and brought her napkins from other countries. Her bottom napkins had princess pictures and came from America. She would never trade them. She said she wouldn't trade one princess napkin for four colored napkins. I asked if she would trade it for a blue, two yellow ones—I had a lot of yellow—a pink, and a white napkin with a rose, for one of her princess ones. That's five napkins for one. She said, "No, no, no, no." That's what I mean about her not being so nice. A nice person says no only one time.

More and more families were moving into Bústaðahverfi, a three-street neighborhood. Hólmgarður was in the middle with twenty houses, ten on each side. The other two streets, Bústaðavegur and Hæðargarður, had only one row. Kids of all ages lived in these poured-concrete houses with four front doors, diamond-design cement fences, and roofs in green, red, yellow, and blue. Each house had two downstairs and two upstairs apartments. City buses drove up and down the gravel roads every 30 minutes. With so many kids, a new school, Breiðagerði School, opened in 1955. However, some of the older kids, such as Jórunn, took buses to their old schools. When Jórunn turned twelve, she left Laugarnes School and went to Réttarholts High School, which was down our street, to the left, and up a steep hill.

Villi finished Samvinnuskólann, business school, and worked for BP, an oil company. He had given up on the widow from Bústaðavegur and now liked only his girlfriend, who also went to Samvinnuskólann. Mamma told him to bring her home so we could meet her. He had so much on his mind that he forgot. Mamma was good about reminding forgetful people.

The day we met Villi's girlfriend was a busy day. Her name is Guðrún; Villi calls her Gunna. Pabbi gave us a bath and trimmed our nails so we look nice. Stella, Jórunn, and I fit into the tub at the same time. We splashed and poured water over each other's hair, and when we'd gotten too much water on the floor, Pabbi said, "Now I have had enough."

We wear our Christmas dresses, pink seersucker material with wide stripes and short puffy sleeves. We get new dresses for every Christmas and Easter, and silk ribbons to keep hair out of our face. When Mamma cleaned at Feldur, the tailor woman left bolts of fabric with a note, "Dear Ágústa, use this to make something nice for your girls." Now Mamma has to pay for the material.

"Kai, you better get your shirt on. They'll be here any minute." Pabbi is not a fast-moving kind of father. Mamma's urging doesn't do much good. Putting Old Spice into his palm, he pats his cheeks going, "Aaaahhhh." White shirt buttoned up, he moves his head from side to side to make sure his tie isn't too tight.

When a cab pulls up, I head down the stairs. Mamma had polished the stairs extra good so I hold the handrail tight. A tall lady in a light blue coat comes through the door, "You must be Edith." Before I can answer, Villi scolds, "You should wait upstairs. Act like a ..."

He never finishes because Olive Oyl says, "She is a beautiful young lady." I could tell that she is the kind of a person who likes little girls.

New Years Day, 1954, Adda married Valli. She and Kata moved to Lokastigur 11 and lived downstairs from Valgeir's mother. He was her only child, and she didn't want him to move away. Their house was close to the middle of town, Lækjartorg, where the city buses started and ended.

Old Katrín—that's what Adda called her—was thin and short with giant ears and long gray braids. Her eyes were small and her Santa cheeks red and skinny. Old Katrín's hands were covered with wrinkled parchment skin dotted with brown spots and blue veins that pushed up like tunnels. Even though I wanted to push them down, it wasn't good manners.

Mondays through Saturdays, at quarter to eight in the morning, Old Katrín went to the milk store and waited for it to open. There was plenty of milk and *skyr*; the store was not going to run out, but she wanted to be early. "It's her way," Adda said, a habit she stuck by like butter on bread.

Old Katrín attended church infrequently. "But," she explained, "just in case, it's best to show your face once-in-a-while." Walking through their gate, she always made the sign of the cross. Adda had no explanation for that behavior.

Mamma missed Adda. She told Pabbi that Old Katrín this and Old Katrín that. She was worried that Valli's mother was not being nice enough to Adda. It didn't sound like a big deal to me. What I didn't want was Adda to come back with Kata. Kata should be with her father and grandmother. Mamma would tell us to dial Adda's number, 14827. We didn't want to. Adda's house phone was upstairs in Old Katrín's apartment. Yelling down the steep, narrow, treacherous steps, "Adda, it's for you," she sounded grouchy. Mamma told her sister Margrét that Katrín had hoped that Valli would marry into a better family.

Ásta worked at a bakery one street over from Lokastígur, so she could eat lunch at Adda's house. Mamma asked her about Adda; Ásta shrugged.

I hear mother moving around. Smell of coffee signals that it is time to get up. I look over the rim of my bed to see if Pabbi is still in bed. I sleep in my parents' bedroom, but one day I'll have a bedroom in the attic. I'd slept all night, but even so, I'm tired and my teeth chatter. Finally, I have to get up, and it is hard, harder than going to the dentist even when he's pulling a tooth out. My clothes are draped over the upright heat register and too far to reach from my bed. I undress in the bathroom, leaving my pajamas on the floor. Quickly I slip a wool T-shirt over my cotton one and then put on my sweater, pants, and socks. My body just doesn't want to warm up this morning. Jórunn heads for the bus, yelling good-bye. Pabbi yells back, "Watch the stairs." By the time I get into the kitchen, Mamma has already left for work.

After breakfast of coffee and French bread with butter that taste like soaked newspaper, I leave for school. Hafdís has left without me. A morning wind pushes against me wanting me to go back home. Running, I take ten minutes to get to school.

If you walked, it was longer than ten minutes. Trudging takes a really long time.

Breiðagerði School was a gray cement building with six separate entrances and stairs to individual classrooms. Each classroom had a square hall area where we left our coats, schoolbags, shoes, and boots. Front entrance doors at the end of the building led to offices and special classes. Above and behind the roof of Breiðagerði School was Mount Esja, today hidden by grayness.

Around me, kids race across the field, some jumping over puddles splattering dirty water. Cling, cling, cling of the school bell could be heard all over Bústaðahverfi. Ahead, kids line up in front of classroom doors waiting for the teachers to come. Door after door, they disappear into the cloak room. Suddenly, the field is quiet, just the ice-cold wind and me trudging. The second bell rings and the cloak room empties. Ása sticks her head out the classroom door, "Edith, you're late." I knew that.

Outside for recess, in a corner by the cement stairs, I hide from the wind. My friends ask me to play, but I say I don't want to. They leave me alone. My body hurts. Back in the classroom, I put my head on my desk and sleep.

Back outside, I returned to my shelter. Ása won't let me stay in for lunch recess. She reminds me that it is her break. My legs keep shaking and my face feels hot and soft like dinner rolls just out of the oven. I keep my back to my friends and don't care that my best school friend, Svala, plays with Margrét, who is not even a friend.

Back home, climbing the thirteen steps to our apartment, I hear Stella and Jórunn arguing. Mamma and Pabbi are still at work. Dropping my coat next to the closet, I stagger into the girls' bedroom and collapse like a limp noodle on a divan that used to be Villi's bed and fall asleep.

It is hard to tell if I am sleeping or awake. I hear Mamma calling my name. When I open my eyes, the walls move towards me. They get bigger and bigger. Now I'm floating around the room like a seagull looking for prey. Mamma's voice gets louder and I fight my way through the fog and back onto the divan.

"Edith, wake up. Can you hear me? Wake up." Mamma stops my hand from pulling off a cold damp washcloth she'd put on my forehead. I don't want the shivers to come back. "Don't!" Mamma orders. She asks me if I'd felt bad all day. She says that I have a fever and that the doctor would come tomorrow. She then makes me stand up and takes off my clothes and replaces them with clean pajamas. Standing takes all my concentration, so I don't talk to her. Svala said that tomorrow, she'd bring her jump rope. Right now it doesn't sound so good.

Mamma kept waking me to drink. "It's red currant juice." She is not going to leave me alone until I take a sip. "Is that the best you can do?" Instead of lying back on the divan—a reward for drinking—she says I need to go to my own bed for the night. She walks me down the hall to her bedroom, past the light brown buffet where our phone sits. She helps me climb over the side of my yellow wooden bed with its headboard covered in stickers. "I know you feel cold, but your body is trying to cool you down. Covering yourself up will only make the fever worse." She tucks the duvet around my legs, strokes my forehead, and leaves.

Perhaps it is the sip of juice or walking, but I am wide awake and feel better. No school tomorrow. I'm glad. Lying on my stomach, I bury my face in the pillow breathing in the clean scent, stretching my body on top of the ironed sheet. Maybe the doctor won't have to come. Mamma will stay home with me, and Sigga will go to work for her. She will go to the store and get me a banana and maybe even a Coke. It will be a good day. Little by little, the phone stops ringing, my sisters go to bed, and the kitchen door closes for a grown-up talk.

Sleep comes, sleep goes. When it goes, I listen to the night sounds, rhythmic sound of water flowing through the registers, Lúter coughing, a car driving by, and raindrops slapping the window. Pabbi snores; from Mamma there is no sound. Even in her sleep, she doesn't want to bother anybody. Then sleep returns.

Lub-DUB, lub-DUB, lub-DUB. I wake up to a pounding inside my chest. Lub-DUB, lub-DUB, lub-DUB. I turn to the side and pull my knees into my stomach. My sheets are damp and I feel perspiration running sideways from my forehead to the pillow. The sickness has returned. But something worse has also come. A deep chill tells me. My mouth tastes fear. My hair sticks out on the back of my neck. I slide my feverish body under the duvet, pulling a corner of it close to my chin. The radiator under the window continues making a swush–swush sound. Dad's snoring is louder. But there is a new sound in the room. No, not a sound, a feeling, a sensation that grabs and holds tight, like thin music pulling at my memory. I am afraid to open my eyes. I know I have to. I know I will. I do.

An old woman stands in the doorway looking at me. Her dark floor-length dress has buttons down the front. Her thin gray hair is pulled up in a bun. A scream comes out of my mouth, a scream without a sound. She is holding a skein of yarn and knitting needles in one hand, with the other she reaches for a chair sitting at the end of my bed. Like a wave on the ocean before it crests, she floats towards me—chair in one hand, knitting in the other. I push myself to the back corner of my bed, as far from her as possible. My feet push the duvet in front of me to create a barrier between the two of us. With the chair by the headboard, she sits down and runs a hand over her lap to smooth out her dress. Picking up her knitting—it was a green sock—she smiles at me.

Lub-DUBs are coming fast and hard. My heart is trying to jump out of my chest clear through my drenched pajama top. I'm not like regular afraid. Afraid is when you see a spider in the bathtub and your pabbi has to come and kill it. This is more like crazy scared. I have never fainted, but now I think I might. Waiting is out of the question. It could take her all night to finish the sock. Staying on the side far from her, I crawl to the end and put one leg over the bed frame. I push my hand down into the mattress and heave the rest of my body out of bed. Can she hear my heart? She just knits. I see that her hands and head shake a little bit. To reach Mamma's side, I'd have to walk by the old woman. I opt to wake Pabbi.

"Pabbi, Pabbi, wake up!" I shake his shoulder. "There is an old woman in the room." Pabbi blinks and blinks, trying to wake up. He looks in the direction of the old woman now floating out of the chair. She wraps up her knitting slowly like she was one of Mamma's sewing club friends. Pabbi and the old woman with the shaky head look at each other. Then he lifts up a corner of his duvet, gets up, and tells me to crawl in. After the night visitor glides over the threshold, out of sight, he turns his attention to me.

Pabbi, who was that?"

After my sisters leave for school, Pabbi carries me to the divan in the girls' bedroom, so I am closer to the kitchen. My teeth rattle in my head like a tin box full of marbles. Staying awake is an effort. Our grandfather's clock ticks … ticks … ticks … Dr. Albert comes, feels my wrist, listens to my chest, and asks me questions. The room is spinning, and Dr. Albert is upside down, but he doesn't fall. He unbuttons my pajama top and listens with his stethoscope. The cold air pricks my skin. Finally, he leaves me alone and I fall asleep. When I wake, men with a gurney are lifting me up. Mamma says she is riding in the ambulance with me. I am going to a hospital. I hope it's warm in the hospital.

Days passed and the doctors still didn't know what was wrong. I was feeling better and asked Mamma to take me home. Mamma said I wasn't better yet. Then a mean thing happened. Doctors and nurses came into my room and helped me take off my pajamas. You shouldn't call that helping when you didn't even want to take them off. They told me to lie on my stomach. Next to my bed they set a tray with long needles, scarier than our attic in the dark. They told me it wouldn't take long. They didn't say what IT was, but I knew it had to do with the long needles. They surrounded my bed and held me down. They said, "Be still." They stuck needles in my spine. I told them it hurt. They said it wasn't so bad. I told them it was hurting worse. They said they were almost done. They weren't. Afterwards, my pillow soaked from tears, I slept for a long time.

Mamma came and said they were taking me to a new place, Vífilsstaðir. "People that have tuberculosis go to this place," she said. This time the ride in the ambulance was more fun, and I stayed awake for the whole trip. They didn't drive fast or put the sirens on so I knew I wasn't very sick.

Vífilsstaðir was a big white building out in the country. Mamma said she would come to visit me on Sundays. I asked her if I could go home with her next time she visited. She explained that it would take a little while to get better, but then I would come home. So that's how I knew for sure I'd get better.

Third-floor patients on Vífilsstaðir were mostly wrinkled women older than mountains. They sat in the hall smoking, crocheting tablecloths. They said they were killing time before time killed them. I told them that Mamma was coming on Sunday to take me home. Older-than-mountain women said that the only way out of Vífilsstaðir was in a long rectangular box. I didn't even know what rectangular means.

Vífilsstaðir's smoky halls were like our apartment after a party. It made your eyes burn. At home the best place to clear the stinging was in our pantry in the hall across from the stairs to the attic. It was cold with no heat and a little window you could open. It was where Pabbi stored boxes of apples and oranges from his brother Svend and Coke bottles for Christmas Eve dinner.

Mamma said Vífilsstaðir was not a hospital but a sanatorium. A sanatorium is for people who are just a little bit sick. My floor was for women only. Now it was for women and one girl. There was another sort of girl; she was fourteen. She was sicker than I was, and she died. I'm glad I didn't know her well. When you know people, like I know my family, you miss them, especially when you are trying to fall asleep at night.

Most of the people were nice. Ólöf, the boss nurse of the third floor, was not in the most group, but Hanna, who was learning to be a nurse, was super-nice.

I shared a room with Jónína, who had little kids at home. She had short brown hair, freckles across the bridge of her nose, and small teeth. Jónína spent most of her time in bed. "I'm just a little tired today," she'd say.

"Jónína, you are tired every day," I told her.

She didn't like the food, not even the desserts that she gave to me. Pabbi was right about the children in China; you shouldn't waste food, so I ate her desserts.

The food at Vífilsstaðir was pretty good except for the oatmeal. They didn't know how to make it. You put a piece of butter in the middle, sprinkled sugar over it, and poured milk around it. That's the right way. Theirs was thicker than whale blubber, and they used brown sugar and no butter. Ólöf left it in my room until I ate it. After a while it got cold and crusty. Nursing students tried to sneak it out, but Eagle Eyes-Ólöf would catch them. Jónína said I should plug my nose and just gobble it down. But Mamma said that animals gobble, people eat. It was just that it tasted so bad in my mouth that I gagged and had to spit in out. Taking another bite after spitting when your mind tells you that the food was bad, now worse, made it impossible. So I sat on my bed and waited for Ólöf to go home to her family, who probably never ate oatmeal.

Nighttime was unlucky time. Inside I felt sad. Stroking my legs and counting sheep helped, but sometimes tears just came. Jónína talked to me from her bed. She said my thinking made me cry, so I should think of happy things. But Mamma said you should find work to do to chase away sad thoughts. But I wasn't allowed to get up and sweep or clean. To chase them off, Jónína talked about the women on our floor and how long they'd been here, about their families and who they were before they were TB patients. She also told me not to listen when they said that when I left Vífilsstaðir, it would be in a rectangular box. I told her I didn't. I told her that soon my mother would come and get me and we would go home in a cab that smelled like Italian leather. She laughed until she coughed. Then she took out her white metal container and cleared her throat from down deep and ejected the phlegm. Phlegm and spittoon are two new words I learned from Nurse Hanna. "Edith," she said holding up a white metal container, "use the spittoon to spit out the phlegm." I bet Stella doesn't know those words.

Freyja, another patient, was not old. She was a young grownup, like Adda. She was an artist and played cards with me. We played crazy eight and gin rummy. Sometimes she brought paper and art pencils and taught me to draw. She showed me how to draw a house with a fence, a chimney with smoke coming out, and curtains in the windows. To draw a flower, Freyja said that first you draw a circle and then make little hearts around it, each touching the circle. With two or three lines inside each heart, they looked like pretty flowers. Jórunn and Stella could draw really good. Jórunn could make faces with eyelashes and freckles that looked real.

One thing Freya didn't like was my scaring her. Walking down the hall, turning a corner, I jumped up yelling "Boo!" She'd grab her chest and turn whiter than new fallen snow. Catching her breath, "I don't like when you do that," she'd say. It was kind of funny to see a grown up so scared. It was too much fun to stop. She got more careful, and it was hard to catch her off guard.

Our Father, which art in heaven, hallowed be thy name ..." Every night, after I said my prayer, I asked God to let me go home. Then I lay still to hear His voice. I told God that I would hang up my coat and eat rutabaga and carrots. I said I would quit dropping my bread crust in the space next to the kitchen register because I knew it didn't fall to China. As the months passed, going to sleep got harder. A feeling inside my stomach like a flutter showed up, and the only way to get rid of it was to cry into my pillow—so Jónína couldn't hear me. I also missed being outside. From the window of my third-floor room, grass, little trees, and flowers looked so nice. Every time the doctors came to see me I asked them if I could go outside. They said soon. Mamma said I'd go home soon. Soon was taking too long.

God was too busy to hear my prayers. He was probably listening to hungry China children.

Mondays were x-ray days. Bare on top, I was put behind a big cold plate, and doctors twisted my shoulders forwards and told me not to breathe. My chest was pushed up against the cold plate, and the back of the machine shut me in like a sardine. "Don't breathe," x-ray doctor would say walking out of the room while everything went black. I held my breath until I heard a click and felt the back of the machine move away making mmrrrrr sounds. It was hard to hold my breath. Sometimes I would start coughing. He'd say, "OK now, this time let's work together." I wished we could change places and I could do his work.

I was allowed to call home, 33615, but not very often. Vífilsstaðir's patient phone was on a landing between the second and third floors. It was up high, but if I stood on my toes, I could reach it and turn the dial. On the phone I heard my sisters laughing, doors closing, pans rattling, or the radio playing. Some days I heard all of it. I talked and talked to keep them on the phone. But then I ran out of things to say, and so did they. When I hung up the phone, I had bad thoughts that I'd never see or talk to them again. Afterward, on my bed with my head against the wall, I pleaded with God to let me go home. His phone line was busy.

X-ray doctor said my lungs were getting better. Pills and shots helped my lungs to heal. Every day nurses gave me four shots in the buttocks, which looked like pin cushions. In my opinion four shots were too many. Soon I recognized the sounds and sights, preparation to sting patients. I hid. Sometimes it took so long for them to find me that I got only three or maybe even two shots. Dr. Garðar said it was important for me to have four shots. He was too nice to be a doctor. I told him and he laughed loudly. I told him I was serious, so he didn't laugh and promised to "give this some thought." I explained to Dr. Garðar that I got too many shots and my butt hurt. He said he'd make a deal with me. If I cooperated with the stinging-bees nurses, I could go outside on nice days. I told him, "That's a deal."

That night I was feeling better about God. Maybe He misunderstood my prayer to leave Vífilsstaðir and thought I just meant to go outside. So He thought he was answering my prayers. "Now, God, please let Hanna be the one to give me the shots and not Ólöf the boss nurse." I also told Him thank you for letting Hanna learn to be a nurse on my floor. For good measure I told Him she was doing real good. Anybody who could nurse old mountain-women was doing good work. I had the feeling He was listening, so I continued: "You see, God, Hanna talks to me when she gives me a shot. She looks for skin that's not met the needle, and then it hardly hurts at all. Ólöf storms in, leans me against the bed, wipes any spot, and rams the needle in pushing the liquid in so fast that it burns my leg down to my toes. When I told Mamma that she was not a nice nurse, she said that maybe Ólöf has a hard life. Well if hurting me improved her life, she must be having some good days, I thought. Sleep that night came without tears.

Mamma came on the two o'clock Sunday bus. She brought coloring books, crayons, Coke, and candy. She sat on a chair next to me, and I told her about my friends at the hospital. She said that the kids at my school were all tested for my sickness, and nobody had it. It would have been nice to have just one girl here to play with though. Stella and Jórunn were not allowed to visit because I could give them tuberculosis. She told me that Villi and his girlfriend would be getting married on April 21, so she would not visit me on that Sunday. They were building a basement apartment on Rauðalækur 38. Visiting hours were short, and she had to catch the 3:30 bus to go home and cook dinner. I asked her if I could come home. She said soon.

I told the older-than-mountain ladies that Mamma said I would go home soon. No, I didn't know the date yet, but soon. They said they were happy to hear that and wanted me to come and visit them sometime. I told them that I would come and visit them many times, and I'd bring Prince Polo, my favorite chocolate bar. They said that seeing me would be better than Prince Polo. They said nothing about the rectangular box.

Finally, a day warm enough for me to go outside. I had on Stella's old coat over my pajamas and exchanged slippers for walking shoes. It had been more than five months since I'd been outside. Stepping over the threshold was like stepping into a movie I'd watched out my window for months. The air was full of sound, smells, color, with insects flying around. Blue sky above had a few fluffy white clouds that looked like gigantic cotton balls. Oh, but the smell! The smell! It was sweeter than Pabbi's roses on the side of our house. It was sweeter than crepes sizzling in the crepe pan. I breathed in as deeply as my lungs would allow. Then the cough came, and I had to swallow the phlegm. I should have brought my spittoon. I knelt down and pulled out a blade of grass and wet it with my tongue. Placing it between my thumbs, pressing against my lips, I blew as hard as I could. Instead of the high pitch sound, what I expected, I coughed again. Throwing away this experiment, I looked up at the third-floor windows to see if Boss Nurse was watching. All clear. I removed my socks and shoes and walked barefoot in the grass. Had it always felt this nice?

Outside, workers wearing boots and *lopi peysas* (wool sweaters) stood by a cow barn down a ways from the hospital. They were laughing about something. It gave me a good feeling to see happy people who could laugh without coughing. Behind the hospital was a large open field covered in daisies and dandelions swaying in the breeze. Bees everywhere. Sparrows, starlings, wrens and other birds whose names I didn't know chirped, hopped, and sang. This must have been what Eden looked like except there was no apple tree and, I hoped, no snakes.

Slipping my feet back into my shoes, I picked flowers to keep on my bed stand. Instead of a vase, which I didn't have, Hanna would get me a clean spittoon. Sitting on the ground, I picked white clover stems and weaved them together. Clover, with its long leafless stems, is the only flower I can make a crown with. Finished, I placed it on my head and practiced taking deep breaths for Dr. Garðar.

"Hi, are you a patient?" Her name was Halla. Her father was a doctor, and they lived in one of the houses, "over there," she said. "It's OK that we play. I go inside the hospital all the time. I can't get sick."

She told the truth about coming to the hospital. When she came, it was around lunch-time. I'd meet her and we sat on the stairs talking. Every day I went to the stairs hoping she'd show up. I brought my coloring books and shared my candy. Halla liked candy as much as I did. She said I should ask my mother to bring licorices. I wished I had my napkin collection to show her. One thing I did not like about Halla was that she picked her nose and smeared it on the stairs. I had to be careful when I scooted around so not to slide into a green bugger.

Saturday visiting hours were quiet. Most visitors came on Sundays. Older-than-mountain women seldom had visitors, so on these day, I read them fairy tales. After I finished, they'd light a cigarette and say, "Edith *mín* (dear), that was a good story." Down the hall, a lady guest came hobbling. She looked like someone I knew. My goodness! That's what Hanna says when she gave me a shot. My goodness, you are a brave girl! It was Lovísa, Hafdís's mother carrying a gift.

"Hi," I said, wondering who she was visiting. She handed me the gift so I knew. "Do you want to see my room?" I asked. This was a big surprise. We walked to my room. I brushed tiny black bugs off my bed and sat down wondering if we should talk about laundry because that's where we usually talked together.

"You can sit on that chair," I pointed to a chair next to my night table. Inside the package was a porcelain tea set with a tea-pot, creamer, sugar container, four tiny cups, saucers, dessert plates, and teaspoons. Each cup had pictures of fluttering bees, butterflies and dragonflies. The saucers and dessert plates had tiny purple flowers. "Thank you," I said to Lovísa. "It is really beautiful."

Lovísa left her coat on. She asked me how I was feeling and said that Hafdís missed playing with me. I told her I'd be home soon and we could play again. When she left, I watched her through my window as she hobbled down the driveway to the main road. It took Mamma ten minutes to walk from the hospital to the bus stop. It would take Lovísa much longer. She sure was a nice lady. Halla will want to play with my tea set.

Mamma said that the tea set looked nice. Through her shopping bag, a string tote with short handles, I saw two bananas, Prince Polo, and an *Applesín* (an orange drink). She said it would have been better if Lúter had gone in for his TB check ups as he was supposed to. Lúter was at Vífilsstaðir? Imagine that. That must have been how Lovísa knew her way here.

Mamma asked if I'd seen the doctors lately. That interested her. She wanted me to repeat everything they said. Sometimes I told her they had when they hadn't. I'd tell her that they said I could go home next week. Then she got quiet and didn't ask any more. But this time I didn't want to talk about doctors; I wanted to talk to her about little black bugs in my bed, mostly on my pillow. She said it was nothing and brushed her hand over my pillow. I told her that they moved. And another thing, sometimes the dirt under my nails moved. She rummaged through her purse and found her reading glasses. She read the newspapers with them every day, but not books. It took time to read a book, she'd explained. Leaning over me, she lifted up the duvet and picked up my pillow. Then she did a weird thing: She threw the pillow on the floor. "Edith, get out of the bed." She must have been in big cleaning mood. She tossed the duvet on the floor and ripped off the sheets. Jónína raised herself on her elbow and watched. Then Mamma tore out of the room, madder than a bee without a hive and came back with Nurse Ólöf looking scared.

When Mamma left, two aides took me into the bathroom, stripped me, and poured water over me. They put foul-smelling soap in my hair and scrubbed and scrubbed my scalp until it felt tingly with rawness. They poured more water, and I saw hundreds of little black specks flowing over my body, down the drain. The aides squealed in horror or delight—I don't know. After a few more stand-up baths, the black moving specks were gone and I was allowed to play with Halla again.

Halla liked my tea set, but she was more interested in Mamma's treats. "What did your Mamma bring you on Sunday?" I told her that I didn't want to share my treats with her any more. Just in case she came to my room, I hid them behind the spittoon. She told me that if I didn't give her my candy, she'd put buggers on me. After that I stopped playing with her. That's when I met Vilhjálmur Jónsson from Ferstikla in the Westfjords, a patient from the second floor.

Vilhjálmur liked to read books. "We don't talk about books," he said. "We discuss them." He asked really good questions. He was the nicest man and told funny jokes. "I'll have to bite that sour apple," was his favorite expression when the nurses told him it was time for him to leave my room. He said visiting with me was his favorite thing to do. That was really nice. He wrote children's books, and one of the stories in his next book was going to be about me. After the book was finished, he'd give me one.

One morning, Jónína's coughing stopped. I looked over at her bed. She looked comfortable, sleeping peacefully. I slid off the bed, put on my robe and slippers, and went to the bathroom. When I returned, she hadn't moved one inch. I tip-toed to her bed and touched her arm. It was cold, rubbery, and heavy. "Jónína, wake up." She was gone. That's how the old-mountain women said it when a patient died. Only her body remained. Her children would never get to see her again. I went to the nurses' station and told them.

Vilhjálmur brought me lots of books and stayed with me while they took her body away and Hanna and a helper changed the bed linen. He asked me to read to him and said that I was a good reader. I knew that. He told me that he thought Hanna liked him. She heard him and laughed and told him to stop it. He laughed too and said the he was going to keep believing that because the world was brighter when somebody cares about you.

Although I'd talked to Mamma yesterday, this was important enough to make an extra call. Mamma would want to know about Jónína. Pabbi answered the phone, "Hello."

"Hello, Pabbi."

"Hello, who is there?" he asked.

"Pabbi, it's me, Edith."

"Who is there," he asked again. Then he said to Mamma, "It's nobody—it's a prank."

Yelling, "Pabbi, it's me." My stomach flipped over. Then all I heard was the dial tone. They were tired of me. It was hard for Mamma to come on the bus every Sunday. Jónína was gone and I told God that I didn't like Him.

Sunday, April 21, 1957, instead of visiting me, Mamma went to Villi and Gunna's wedding. My whole family was in Garðar where Gunna's parents lived. Mamma had told me that she and Aunt Sigga were going early to help Gunna's aunt with the preparations. Stella and Jórunn would be wearing their Easter dresses, and I didn't get one. My pink one from last year with the stripes and puffy sleeves wouldn't fit me now.

Back in my room, I wouldn't eat, talk, or get out of bed. Now I was like Jónína. God didn't listen, and Mamma's promise was not true. Just as when I was sick with fever before they took me away in the ambulance, I wanted to be left alone. I turned to the wall and slept.

Dr. Garðar said that if my parents could find a place for my sisters to stay, I could go home for one night. My part of this deal was to eat my food. Dr. Garðar didn't know that my family was having a good time without me and that Mamma was tired of me. I quit saying the Lord's Prayer, and I told God, "You are a mean God. You don't listen. I'm not going to talk to you any more." Ólöf said that I didn't have to eat the oatmeal if I didn't want to. I wasn't going to anyway. She asked me if I liked Corn

Flakes. I didn't answer. When I coughed up phlegm, I didn't spit it out like I was supposed to. I swallowed it. Freyja brought pictures she'd drawn for me, but I didn't look.

Hanna gave me Monday and Tuesday shots. I told her that I missed Jónína. I missed her talking about her beautiful Akureyri. Jónína always said my Akureyri. She told me about the church that stood like a crucifix higher than any other building, with a pipe organ and a ship suspended from the ceiling. When I asked her why they hung a ship inside a church, she didn't know. She described summer evenings and festivals and houses with roofs in all the colors of the rainbow. She'd walk down to the harbor with her husband when he went off on a fishing trip. I wondered if her kids had forgotten her. No, I didn't think so. You never forget your mother.

"Edith *mín*, I know you miss her." Tears were coming down Hanna's face. I asked her if she got tuberculosis in her lungs. That would make you cry. "No, no, no, I just want you to eat your food." I told her I wasn't hungry, but I'd try. An orderly brought my evening tray and removed the untouched lunch tray. It smelled like rotten potatoes. Remembering my promise to Hanna, I took a forkful of the pound cake. It tasted like oatmeal.

Vilhjálmur said that he was not going to leave my room until I talked to him. I didn't. He said that he had it in his power to grant me one wish as long as it was not to go home. I thought about that. So I sat up and told him that my wish was for a Coke. He left and came back with one. He wouldn't tell me where he got it. He said he couldn't share his secrets of power. I sat up and drank it slowly. He asked me about a book, *Blue Troll*, on the nightstand. I told him how Trygg the dog chased Snodda to bite his feet. I started laughing when I thought about the naughty dog and the poor troll mamma trying to protect her dog. Then the nurse came in and said that all gentlemen had to leave the women's floor.

During visiting hours Wednesday evening, I was reading my book when one of the evening nurses stuck her head in and said, "A handsome man and a beautiful woman are coming down the hall to see you." Vilhjálmur? Who was the beautiful woman? I used my fingers to comb my hair when through the door comes, not my writer friend but Pabbi and Mamma, on a Wednesday! Mamma put clean pajamas on my nightstand and a bag of goodies inside my bed stand. She had embroidered EA on the pajama top. Pabbi, grinning from ear to ear, told me to get out of bed. "We have a surprise for you." I'd not seen him for months, and I think he was sorry for not talking to me on the phone. Outside, waving like two crazy birds, were my sisters Jórunn and Stella. They jumped up and down, yelling something, waving, waving. Behind them was an old car, Pabbi's car. Pabbi had bought a car! That's why they could come on a Wednesday.

My last week at Vífilsstaðir was long, like waiting for Christmas to come. Each day slower than the day before. Twenty-eight shots and I could go home. There was the last x-ray day, last walk outside the hospital, the last phone call home, last linen change, and finally the very last time that I lay in bed listening to the night noises—nurses scurrying, patients coughing, bells chiming, and staff whispering. On this last night, I tried to stay awake to make sure I didn't die like Jónína, but I fell asleep and lived.

Knowing I'd probably never see the older-than-mountain women again felt weird and sad. Freyja cried from happiness for me and asked, "Now who's going to scare the bejesus out of me?" She shouldn't say that in front of Mamma. Vilhjálmur told me to look for his new book in the mail with my story. It was about our visit together the night Villi and Gunna got married. He named the chapter "A Visit with a Lady." He said that I was the lady. Hanna left a week earlier to practice nursing at a hospital in Reykjavik. She'd cried and hugged me and told me to be a good girl. She's got to stop all this crying. It makes patients feel bad.

After months of wearing pajamas, clothes didn't feel comfortable. But still, I liked them better. Strutting down the hall flanked by my parents, wearing a blue jacket with a fur around the hood, I turned around and waved to my friends. Then I walked backwards and waved more. It was going so well that I jumped up and down and waved both hands.

Back home, our apartment looked tiny. I'd told my friends at Vífilsstaðir that our hall was almost as big as the hospital corridor. "Mamma, our home shrunk," I said.

"You've been in a big place, so it just seems that way to you. It's the same size as it was when you left. How about some crepes with whipped cream?"

When my sisters came home from school, we were shy with each other. All the things I was going to say to them were gone out of my mind. We looked at each other.

"Did you like being there?" Stella finally asked.

"Don't ask her that," Jórunn's sensibilities were offended. "Of course she didn't like it there. Would you want to be away from your family for many months and your family can't visit?"

Stella ignored Jórunn and continued. "You look really white." She paused leaned towards me and whispered, "We are never going to be mean to you again."

Dinner was *buff* with potatoes and rhubarb soup. My favorite meal. Mamma should teach the cooks at Vífilsstaðir how to cook good. Their food doesn't taste as good as Mamma's. Most of the patients were skinny; I bet that's why.

However, even on a perfect day there can be bad news. The bad thing was that I could not go back to school this year. I'd miss all of eight-year-old class, and I had already missed most of seven-year-old class. That was bad, I missed my friends. But my news was not nearly as bad as my cousin, Ástþór's news. He had cancer inside his leg so the doctors cut off half of it. Dr. Garðar would never do that. They gave him a fake leg so he could get better. That was the good news. But then they found cancer in the other half of his leg. He died. To die when you are 16 is way worse than bad news. Aunt Margrét had lost three kids and her husband, Leifur, drank more and more. One day

after Aunt Margrét visited, Mamma said, "Death of a child is a lonely place." I didn't know what that meant.

September 30, 1957, Gunna and Villi moved from Hólmgarður to Rauðalæk 38. They stayed up all night, not to organize their apartment, but for their first baby to be born.

# Chapter 7

## Family Gains and Pains

*This chapter is about swimming, brain tumor, and do a rond de jambe—1958 to 1959.*

Pabbi's first new car was a Trabant. It was made in East Germany and had a small engine. So small that going up hills it huffed and puffed like the wolf in the "Three Little Piggies." Kids made fun of Trabants because Communists made them. They were cheap and ugly, and you could outrun them. But it wasn't true; well, the last part about outrunning them wasn't. In their opinion it was only a step above riding a city bus. Some said that they'd take the bus before they'd be seen in a Trabant. I wished Pabbi had bought a different car. But that was like wishing that I didn't have to go to swimming classes.

Stella, Jórunn, and I moved into our attic bedrooms with icicles hanging from the skylights. Jórunn had her own room. Stella and I shared. Ásta moved out, but her bedroom was there if she came back. I didn't think she would. She was unhappy at home and always in a bad mood. Jórunn now 14 years old, told Stella and me that Ásta was a real dish. Stella was lucky that Mamma didn't hear her talk like that. We didn't know where Ásta was. Then one afternoon Mamma saw Ásta downtown.

She was pregnant. Mamma and Pabbi had many kitchen talks. That Sunday we drove to Hveragerði, a small village at the bottom of a chain of mountains, to look for her. Mamma had an address of a summer cottage where Ásta and Agnar lived. We found the place, but not Ásta. It was nothing like I'd pictured a summer cottage. Dirty dishes piled in the sink, clothes strewn around the place, just one room. The stench, probably because they didn't have a bathroom, convinced Stella, Jórunn, and me to go back outside and wait. A dark heavy feeling rode back home with us.

Hafdís and I walked to school together even though we were in different classes. After missing a year and a half, it was fun to be back in school. In nine-year-old-class, we began learning Danish. We had gym twice a week, needlework and music once, and swimming twice. Except for swimming, school was good. In needlework we were knitting a cover for a coat hanger, crocheting washcloths, and sewing patterns on a cross-stitch canvas. That was the year we learned to play the flute.

Swimming classes were held at the Sundhöll by Leifsgata where we lived when I was a baby. The school gave us free yellow bus tickets. You could also drop money into the coin machine next to the bus driver—ping. Bus drivers had a good job. Buses were warm, people were happy to see them, and they wore blue uniforms with a cap that had a visor to keep rain out of their eyes. I had started wearing glasses and considered this an advantage.

Shine, rain, or rainbows, my class showed up at Sundhöll for swim lessons. We showered under close scrutiny of washroom attendants who checked for toe-jam and under-sole dirt. Next, we stood at the pool edge waiting to be allowed in. It was like being in a freezer turned to the lowest setting. Our teacher, in pants and a sweater, took his time. He went over the rules for the umpteenth time. "Don't run. When I lift my hand, you listen. You can go on the lower diving board, not the high one." That rule I would never break. He droned on and on and the three boys who would break the rules, always the same three, were busy snapping swimsuit straps of unlucky girls standing in front of them.

Sundhöll had a shallow pool separated from the deeper pool by a rope. Mamma said that I should not say that I hate this or that. I should say I didn't like it. On the other hand, she said that I should speak the truth. The truth was, I hated swimming. Well, that's not exactly correct. You can't hate something you can't do. So what I hated was having to go there, each time thinking I'd drown. This relationship had started in six-year-old class and had not improved.

When I returned to the pool, after the sanatorium, there were only a few kids left in the shallow pool. Now that I was back, there was one more kid in the shallow pool. There were many differences between the shallow and the deep pool that had nothing to do with the depth of the water. For example, the kids in the shallow end were fitted with black angel-wings on their arms. Deep end—bare arms. Shallow-end kids spent most of their time thinking about drowning. Deep-end kids wished they had swimming every day, well, maybe not Christmas and New Year's Day. Both ends kept looking at the big clock hanging on the light-green tiled wall but for different reasons. But I knew, just as spring follows winter, that I had to learn how to swim. We, the drowning ducklings in the shallow end, knew that by the end of twelve-year-old-class we had to swim 200 meters without stopping—in deep water.

Margrét was the youngest of Mamma's siblings. In addition to coming together at family celebrations and at difficult times, the four sisters talked on the phone. When Margrét was diagnosed with a brain tumor, my Danish-speaking mother went with her to translate and look out for her. Margrét's husband, Leifur, whose red nose revealed a vice unpardonable when you had a wife and children, could not be trusted.

Adults in my family smoked. They drank on holidays, at parties, weddings, and at confirmations. But two people drank all the time. Leifur was one. Helga, married to Mamma's brother Magnús was the other.

"Jórunn, go to medicine cabinet and remove the rubbing alcohol." Before a party, Mamma took precautions. At parties Helga was said to have a weak bladder. Removing the rubbing alcohol improved her bladder. That's how Pabbi phrased it. They must be wrong. I couldn't fathom how anybody could drink that stuff. Dabbed on a wound, it hurt worse than getting a fishbone stuck in your throat—Mamma mia!

When the guests came, I kept my eye on Helga. Sure enough, she would go to the bathroom. But so did everyone else. When people drank, they got happier. It was as though all worries were lifted off their shoulders, and they talked about happy things, they joked with each other, and said kind things to us kids. Was drinking such a bad thing? But parties meant burning eyes and sore throat. To clear my eyes, I visited the hall pantry that was cold, fresh, and clean of smoke. There was nothing to do about my sore throat. A wool sock wrapped around my throat was Mamma's solution. After sleeping with Mamma's solution, I'd wake up the next morning throat still sore now with an added red, scratchy neck.

April 20, 1958, Adda had a boy and named him Bragi. What kind of name is that? Nobody in my family has that name. He had the biggest head I'd ever seen on a baby, and if that weren't enough, it was covered with red fuzz. It's poor manners to eavesdrop, but when Mamma told Sigga about Adda's labor being difficult, I accidentally overheard it. She said Adda's hands had to be pried off the bed-post. It must have been a great disappointment for Adda to see Bragi after all that suffering. When Pabbi and I visited her, and she acted all happy. Then she said, "He's not much to look at." I didn't think you should say such a thing about your baby, even an ugly baby. Then she slobbered all over him. She was going to make the same mistake with him that she did with Kata.

The previous year Villi and Gunna had a boy with a normal-sized head. He had blond hair, and was now starting to walk. He was very cute and Villi could make him laugh so hard that his whole chubby body shook. Mamma held him for the sprinkling of holy water. He was named after my parents, Jens Ágúst.

While Mamma went with Margrét for her brain surgery, Adda did her work, cleaning for a dentist in Hlíðum. She towed Bragi along, who did not last too long away from her breast. I hoped that breastfeeding didn't make babies' heads grow bigger. Valli knew nothing about babies. He laughed at Adda's cuddling—encouraging this behavior. Even Mamma noticed, "I don't know about all this cuddling and carrying," she'd lament to Pabbi who had no opinion. I, on the other hand, had an opinion. Her kids would grow up and be monsters. Adda can't say I didn't warn her.

With Mamma away, I went to stay with Villi and Gunna. Gunna had an oval face, a beautiful smile, and short dark–blond hair. If she wasn't cooking and cleaning, she was reading the newspaper. When it was nice outside, I watched Jens, who sat in his baby carriage at the back of the apartment building.

"Gunna is good for Villi." That's what Mamma had to say. She said she herself couldn't have picked a better wife for my brother. I don't think Villi would have wanted her to. He continued working for BP doing computer work. Computers are machines that can think and do work faster then people.

While in Denmark, Mamma stayed with her friend Tante Lára. We called her Aunt, but she was just Mamma's friend. Mamma told me that Margrét had her skull opened and they took out the tumor. Margrét was in a room with other patients who had only a sheet covering them. "They laid there shivering asking for covers," she told me. "It was difficult to watch."

Mother was the most tender and attentive when someone was sick. She had stick-to-itiveness was in her blood. She was a great cook, she made beautiful clothes, and she kept our home cleaner than any other home I visited. Mamma told me that when she was young, she'd wanted to be a nanny. I was surprised. I never thought of Mamma wanting to be anything but our mother, the kind of mother who believed that you pull yourself up by your own bootstraps and solve your own problems.

Leifur went to Denmark and came to the hospital to borrow money from Mamma. He belonged to a men's organization, Oddfellows. They had a lodge in Copenhagen where Leifur also went to borrow money from the members. He said he needed it for his wife's casket. This wasn't true. She was doing better than expected. Certainly better than her husband thought. Maybe he just had to drink to forget about his dead children and sick wife. Drinking made him happy. I knew that from the parties. But I also overheard that he was not working or taking care of his family. That's when you should stop. You can't spend money on alcohol if your family needs food and clothes. I decided that drinking to be happy was bad if it made you forget your responsibilities.

Ásta moved back home before her baby was born. Her bad moods were worse. When my parents were away, the brunt of Ásta's frustrations landed on Stella and Jórunn. Stella yelled at her and called her a crazy woman. Ásta yelled back. It was horrible. Pabbi spent time with Ásta behind the glass kitchen door. It didn't help. Ásta was angry, unhappy, and sad. Nobody wanted to remind her of our family motto: "If sad or bored, clean."

When Ásta's time came, Adda took her to a midwife, who had room for three duvet-women. That's what they called women who took to the bed to have a baby. Ásta's labor was hard and relentless, but the baby didn't come. Adda asked the midwife to call the doctor, but the midwife said that first babies were the most difficult and took the longest. Besides, the midwife shared, the doctor was at a party way on the other side of town. Short time later panic set in. A phone call was made, and after a good long time, a woman doctor rushed in ordering Adda out of the room. The baby boy came out blue with no signs of life. Ásta went back to live with and support Agnar Jacobsen, who read no-good magazines. My request to move into her room? *Soon.*

Stella went to Stóravík Farm by Selfoss for that summer. This was a big farm run by three brothers, two sisters, and their children. Including Stella, they had five summer kids from Reykjavik.

The farmer's wife whom she worked for followed Stella around. My sister would wake up and find her standing over her, staring. At other times she'd hide behind a door with a knife waiting for Stella. By then Mamma was back from Denmark, and Stella called to tell her she wanted to come home. Stella, who was not afraid of anything, said she was scared. Mamma didn't believe her and told her to make the best of it.

However, since it was only ninety minutes away and she fretted so, Stella was allowed to take the bus home for a week-end. She counted the days. A couple of days before, sitting in the barn on a three-legged stool, an unwelcome fever was growing inside her. Farm chores, feeding the pigs, and watching the younger children while her fever flushed her face red was not easy. When she got a fever, it was always a high fever. If the farmers knew, they'd not let her go home. Finally, bus day came with Stella onboard. Three burning days paid off. Instead of a week-end, she stayed home for a whole week.

By the end of the summer, she had earned a few hundred *krónur*. It went into the family *budda* (purse).

My lungs were stronger, and the coughing was gone, but I had a constant sore throat, especially after family parties. For months I went to see an ENT doctor, Dr. Skúli. He was old, like the old-mountain women. When Mamma was nine or ten, she lived with his family as a kind of a house girl. She scrubbed floors, dusted, brushed their shoes, and ran errands. Anyway, Mamma's home treatment, wool sock around my throat while sleeping, helped the most when I got out of bed and could take it off. Phew, what a relief! The sore throat? Getting worse.

After school, on non-swimming days, I took the bus to see Dr. Skúli. He wiped my throat with a thin stick, cotton on the end, soaked in an antiseptic solution. I gagged and fought the urge to push his hand away. I pleaded with Mamma not to send me. But I also complained about my ever–aching throat. Finally, he got tired of seeing me and proclaimed that my tonsils should be removed. A different doctor was assigned this chore.

In the backseat of a taxi-cab, Adda said, "When we get back home," me without tonsils, "Mamma is going to have ice cream for you."

I don't know how they take out your tonsils, but my stomach does and at this moment it is alive with butterflies, no—big yellow moths. Waiting for the nurse to come for me, Adda rubs my back. She is treating me like her babies. A bad sign. I ask if she can come in with me. She says it isn't allowed but that she will be right here waiting for me. I can tell that she wants to. Another bad sign.

The ENT doctor is a taller than most men I know and wears a white uniform with no stains. Mamma will like to hear that. He has narrow eyes that make him look as though he were peering into the sun except he is looking down. His nurse smiles and pats the chair, "Come and sit right here." There are other chairs in the doctor's office that I prefer. Like Adda, she has no wrinkles, a smooth skin, and a nose that fits her face but a heavier body. Everyone is heavier than Adda.

Never will I complain about shots in the butt. Shots down my throat—a thousand bee stings. I stare into the doctor's eyes, trying to tell him that something is wrong; it shouldn't hurt this much. Then he uses a metal scraper to detach my swollen tonsils from the side of my throat—they cling unwilling to let go. Inside my throat feels as though he were taking a dull saw to it, working it back and forth, back and forth. I need more numbing, but talking is not possible. The nurse holds my hand, rubs my arm, strokes my bangs away from my forehead, but the scraping continues and continues. I watch the clock on the wall, twenty minutes, thirty minutes. Even tears refuse to come out.

"We are almost done," the nurse whispers.

"We are almost *half* done," the doctor's eyes are hard and reprimanding.

Eternity later, "OK, then, we are done." He takes off his gloves and walks to the sink. His nurse reaches out for me and eases me out of the chair. She is talking, but I don't understand what she is saying. Kaleidoscope of colors and shapes dances around the room. Then I am floating away from me and the nurse. Bloody instruments, the chair, the phone that prolongs the pain when the doctor takes a call seem harmless. I drift into a soft blackness and everything stops.

"Hey, Edda *mín*, are you OK? Can you open your eyes? Wake up Edda *mín*. The cab is here. Let's go home." Adda wipes strands of sweaty hair out of my face. Her face is white and tense. She is probably anxious to get home to her kids.

Mamma gets me ice cream to eat, and I stay in bed for a few days. My throat hurts like hate. In a few days, maybe a week, it should be better. The thing about shoulds is that they don't always do. My throat heals from the invasion of the instruments then returns to its normal every-day hurt, especially after parties. The wool sock—I refuse.

February was still my least favorite month, but what made it bearable were Punchky Day, Explosion Day (Sprengidagur), Ash Wednesday, and increased daylight. For Punchky Day Mamma baked pastries, éclairs filled with jam and whipped cream. You could not eat too many of them, that's how good they were. They awakened every taste bud on your tongue as they melted in your mouth, airy, creamy, a fruity sweetness. Explosion Day we had salted lamb and pea soup, which was pretty good, or about three steps below *punchkies*. A week before Ash Wednesday, we started making little cloth bags from pieces of fabric that Mamma gave us. We sewed them by hand and put a long thread on top with a pin bent so the bags could hang. All day we would sneak up on people and hang them on their backs. If they already had one, you would pin yours on the bottom so that little by little they would have a long tail of bags. In the olden days, they put ashes in the bags. The teachers kept telling us to quit, but they were not mad for real.

In 1959 I celebrate my first double–digit birthday. We don't do anything special for our birthdays, but Mamma makes hot chocolate and cake and she says I can have a party and invite a few friends. I invite Hafdís, Selma, Hildur, and Anna. I wear my Christmas dress, and we are allowed in the living room. Kids were not allowed in that room except on holidays and for parties. This is a party.

"Shouldn't you ask Labba?" Mamma asks. I don't want to. Labba lives across the street and I don't like her. She has bad breath and brown teeth, and kids make fun of her. "Don't you think you should?" Mamma asks. "I see her out there playing with you kids." It surprises me that she pays attention, but she leaves out that most of the time, unless we are desperate for another player, Labba just watches. Our conversation ends without a resolution.

My friends give me a book, a jump rope, new mittens, a coloring book, and a twenty-four-pack of Crayola crayons. When I let them in, I see Labba playing *kilo* (a street softball game) with the neighborhood kids. I show my guests my napkin collection. I have a 130 napkins. On the bottom I have a white one with tiny red roses and green petals. I also have some white ones with gold letters that spell "cocktail." Hafdís traded them with me for three napkins, a green, blue, and yellow. Her sister Stína, an airline stewardess, gave them to her. She told me they were very expensive.

We play cards and each of us gets one sheet from my new coloring book to color. The pictures have houses, animals, farms, flowers, and people. Hildur shows us how to trace the flowers and the lines in the leaves with a brighter color. People's hair, you make it darker closer to the head and then lighter as you move away from it. I have never colored this well before. We put our names and date on our pictures and hang them on the wall by my bed. They cover some of the holes in the Donald Duck wallpaper.

After they leave, I show the gifts to Mamma. Instead of paying attention to my gifts, she pulls a chair to the kitchen window and climbs up on it, resting her knees on the window sill. Opening the small horizontal pane on top of the window, she yells out, "Labba, come up and have some birthday cake." Then she turns to me and says, "Get the door for her."

This turn of events is not to my liking. Before I can object, the bell rings. I walk down the stairs and let her in. "Happy birthday," Labba says as she takes off her shoes and walks behind me up the stairs. Mamma is making more hot chocolate and asks Labba about her family and if she likes school. Then she adds, "You are a good babysitter. I see you walking your brother in the carriage every day." It is as though they are friends. I leaf through my coloring book, but Mamma's look persuades me to close it. Labba is ruining my first birthday party.

Labba asks if I like school. I say, "No." Then I get another look. Labba finishes her cake and hot chocolate.

"Thank you, Ágústa. It was really delicious." Putting her arms in the sleeves of her coat, she starts walking down the hall.

It's polite to walk your friends to the door." Mamma's voice is unfriendly.

When Stella and I shared a bedroom, we never agreed on whose turn it was to clean it. We agreed that it needed cleaning. So neither one of us cleaned it. Instead we hoped our parents stayed downstairs. Jórunn was partly to blame. Her room was such a stark contrast to ours.

At night, instead of going to sleep, we played the good-night game and who do you love? Our parents were blissfully unaware of what went on in the attic, and we preferred it that way. At night, when our giggling crossed Mamma's threshold of patience, she chased us upstairs, "*Nú er upp á ykkur typpið*" (now your penis is up). We laughed our way upstairs, closing the nine-glass-pane hall door behind us segregating the upstairs and downstairs.

The good night game was simple. The last one to say good-night won. "Good Night, Stella." She'd respond in kind. This would continue for an hour and usually end with Jórunn saying, "Be quiet!" This always struck Stella and me as funny. Little by little, the good-nights became less frequent and we surrendered to Mr. Sleep.

Who do you love? involved Stella and my crawling into Jórunn's room after she fell asleep. We'd heard somewhere, so it had to be true, that a sleeping person was a truthful person. We had a hunch that she liked Höskuldur from down the street. Stella didn't like Höskuldur. She told Mamma that Jórunn liked Höskuldur and that he was a thief. Jórunn, in a sassy voice, goes, "Oh yeah, so you are saying that he stole everything in our living room?" I guess that was enough to prove his innocence. By then, Mamma asked if they didn't have something better to do.

So once Jórunn was asleep, we'd inch our way into her room and take her hand. If she woke, she told us to knock it off and go to our room. Sometimes she wasn't even sleeping and when we reached for her hand, she grabbed ours hard scaring the gasooba out of us. Then she laughed and laughed.

At night was when Stella and I told each other secrets. She told me that when Mamma was a child, she'd had a dream. In the dream Mamma's mother was lying in bed holding two numbers, 6 and 5. Years later she died at the age of sixty-five. This was scary stuff.

In the mornings none of us laughed much. We were in a constant state of exhaustion from our penis sticking up for too long. If we really pushed it, staying in bed after the first wake-up call from Pabbi, we'd hear his heavy steps on the stairs. This got us up quicker than a newspaper on its way to squash a housefly. So fast, in fact, that in the time it took Pabbi to climb eleven steps, I could be fully dressed. What heat was supposed to be in the attic radiators that Pabbi installed did little to warm our spaces. So Stella, in the cold of winter, draped her duvet around her body and walked down the stairs, looking like a made bed moving.

Pabbi did most of the disciplining. "Now I has enough" would come just before he banged the kitchen table for emphasis. Although we were used to Pabbi's Icelandic grammar errors, there were moments that they just made us want to laugh more than anything else. Of course, to give in to this urge would have had a dire outcome. We didn't know what, and that frightened us even more.

Pabbi believed it to be his right to have his daughters wait on him. For the longest time, he always called for Jórunn to serve him. Stella and I didn't mind. Jórunn complained to mother, which she shouldn't have. Mamma talked to Pabbi. Now it was "Edith (or Stella), hand me a spoon, answer the phone, get the mail, and take out the garbage." Sitting in the kitchen with the silverware drawer behind him, needing a spoon for his oatmeal, he'd yell for me from another room. Jórunn should have thought this through just a bit better before going running to Mother.

During meals we were expected to be quiet while he ate, read the newspaper, and listened to the news on the radio—all at the same time. If we talked, he put the paper down, looked above the frame of his eye-glasses and said, "Shush!" That was usually the end of it. But sometimes a chuckle leaked. His head came from behind the paper, his left hand took off his glasses, and he would point to the door, "Out with you." This left two of us, tears running down our cheeks as we held inside a blast of a deep belly laugh, screaming to be freed. After a while our ribs hurt, and at all costs we avoided looking at each other.

When Pabbi used a plural pronoun, such as *we*—as in "We need to sweep the floor for your Mamma,"—it meant that his daughters did it. At first I thought it was his bad grammar. Then I considered the possibility that he had a mouse in his pocket and the two of them were going to sweep the floor. Not so. Mamma also waited on him then instructed her daughters not to follow her footsteps. Adda took mother's advice. If Valli asked her to get him milk she'd say, "What? You don't have feet to take you to the refrigerator?"

About the ongoing saga of our bedrooms, of course it had to happen. Mamma came up to change our linen. She was aghast at the condition of our room.

"You can't live like this," she stated. That wasn't factual. We could. We did.

Stella insisted that it was my turn to clean. Mamma reminded her that she was older and she should do most of it. She got mad and snapped, "How would you like to live in a room that is papered with Donald Duck?" I thought Mamma would slap her across the face for being rude. She didn't. It was rare, rare like a day without wind, that Mamma slapped us. But when it happened, it was for sassing.

At our local bookstore, I'd seen a picture of a ballerina on the cover of a German magazine. Her pink outfit, white tights, ballerina shoes, and tiara were beautiful. I told Mamma that I wanted to take ballet lessons. She said that starting at ten might be too old. I pleaded, I begged, I pestered. A new friend, Katrín, took ballet classes—she could do the splits. My goal was to learn to do the splits. Mamma relented and bought the leotards and tights, but the tutu would have to wait she said. Classes started, and our dance instructor taught us to bend at the knees, plié, and, while holding onto the barre, point our toe forward and circle our foot around. The shiny wood floor was flanked by mirrors on every wall. By the end of the first ten minutes of class, I knew one thing and remembered another. I knew this was a mistake, and I remembered that Mamma had already paid for the class. I would be doing pliés and do *a rond de jambe* for ten more weeks.

Pollyanna, the protagonist in a book with the same name, made the best of everything. Each week I came in with a Pollyanna attitude; Edith, you can do this. Think of the poor children in India, I said to myself, they have never had this opportunity. A little Indian girl would give much to have white tights. This Pollyanna attitude could have worked if not for the mirrors on every wall of the dance studio. Mirrors show no pity. Removing my eyeglasses helped, but I wished my eye-sight was worse. In every mirror, I looked like a handicapped ballerina with poor coordination and balance, and without an ounce of grace. Frankly, I looked like a student in the wrong class.

After a while, a good thing showed its face. I was getting the hang of the do a rond de jambe, pointing toe forward and circling the foot back. This unexpected result was a ray of sunshine in my bank of hope. On the bus I practiced my do a rond de jambe. Even when there were empty seats on the bus, I remained standing pointing my toe forward and circling my foot around. After I kicked a couple of passengers, I confined my practice to the kitchen holding onto the countertop for support. It surprised me that my family was not noticing the improvement. Stella copied me making ooohhh-aaaahhh sounds and flailing her hand in the air. Jórunn laughed and Mamma ignored us.

Just as I was starting to look forward to dance class and doing the do *a rond de jambe,* the rules changed. We could no longer hold on to the barre. Just like that, I was back to my handicap status.

The seventh week I took a break, skipped class, and took the bus all the way to Torg. Adda's house was within walking distance, but she would ask me what I was doing downtown. She and Mamma never lectured long, but they gave you a look that made you wish they'd lecture longer and drop the piercing stare. Adda wouldn't tattle, but that didn't make it any better. She made this grunt or huff of air with her throat to express displeasure. By the time I reached Klapparstígur, the street below hers, I had concluded that walking aimlessly for another twenty minutes was better than visiting her. When I got home, to make up for skipping class, I did a plié up every step to our apartment. After a snack I would start for real on my splits. After all, that's why I was talking ballet.

Upstairs, alone in my bedroom, I extended a leg in opposite direction sliding my bottom to the floor. Ooohh la la! I worked on it for days and days. Finally, I got all the way down. It was painful. I said, "Ow, ow, ow, ow" the last couple of inches. For the nanosecond I was in the split, feeling like two burley seamen were pulling my legs north and south, I thought I was stuck. Falling backwards pulling my legs together I yelled, "Ow, ow, ow, I did it!"

Moving closer to my eleventh birthday, ballet behind me, I knew what I really wanted to do. Girl Scouts wear uniforms and get patches to sew on them. Mamma said Girl Scout uniforms cost too much money.

A girl in my class was selling her uniform for almost nothing. Mamma said that 35 *krónur* was not almost nothing. Then she said I could go ahead and join. She didn't know what a good decision she was making and I would prove to her that I would be an ace scout. That night I went to Guðný's house. Walking home, I wondered if there would be enough space for all the patches I'd be earning.

Our first meeting, I earned a round welcome patch with green letters and an Iceland flag pin. You earned it by showing up. We learned how to make knots and talked about patches that we could earn. The ones I decided to work toward were an art patch and a healthy patch. After I earned them, Mamma sewed them above one of my breast pockets. The "Being my Best" was pink and maroon.

Mamma told me to quit Girl Scouts. "You don't go to your meetings," she reasoned. When I explained that none of my best friends were Girl Scouts, she said that I should stick with things I start. Well, I was sticking with my friends. We sold my uniform, and I told the girl she could keep the patches Mamma had sewn on it.

Mamma was probably right that ten was too late to start ballet, but she shouldn't have given in to me about the Girl Scouts. I might have gone to some meetings. There was another thought that kept visiting my brain. The thought said, "Edith, you could be a famous pianist." Actually, it made sense. First, we owned a piano. Second, I had long fingers. Third, there was no special clothing requirement. Fourth, a piano teacher lived on the street south of ours. She was my music teacher, Hannes's wife. Finally, I knew I'd found my true calling; I kept it to myself—for now.

Winter returned. Mother worried about Ásta and Gunna and Villi had a baby girl, Kristín Andersen. She was named after Gunna's mother.

# Chapter 8
## Neighborhood Families

*This chapter is about Old Mrs. Dýrset, those
damn stairs, and a shoe shine boy—1960.*

Hólmgarður 26 and 28 were in the same building. Like
other buildings on the street, it had four apartments, two
upstairs, two downstairs. Like us, the Dýrsets lived upstairs but
on the east side of the building, number 28. Einar Dýrset and
Vilborg had five kids. He was from Norway, and came when he
was 25 years-old to marry Vilborg whom he met in Norway. He
was a builder for a living and a singer for fun. Einar and Vilborg
had four daughters and one son, Gunnar, who was in dental
school. I didn't play with the Dýrset kids because they were
older. Although we knew the three youngest girls— Sigríður,
Ragnhildur, and Jórunn.

Jórunn and Stella, for some reason, seemed to know a lot
about this family and told me. It was a secret, they said, that
Einar's mother was dead and now living in Iceland. Specifi-
cally, she lived in Reykjavik, on Hólmgarður 26, upstairs in my
room. By then, I'd moved into Ásta's room. "She hung herself,"
Jórunn confided. At night my sisters, the torturettes, painted
a vivid picture saying, "Old Mrs. Dýrset hangs around your

room."—Really hangs—as in dangling from the beam above my bed. At night I was sure that I heard choking and fretful sounds of someone trying to breathe. Air brushed my skin, the kind you get from a hanging body struggling to free itself. Of course I knew you couldn't be a living dead, or that's what I told myself. You are either dead or you are alive. Even so there was a tiny place inside me that entertained the possibility that my sisters were right. My nightmares started.

The ballerina wallpaper Mamma had put up in my bedroom was cheerful in daylight, but at night the ballerinas turned into skulls with no teeth, laughing. Pink tutus turned blood red. My room became a Cimmerian cavern. Their relentless stories of Dýrset's fate took up more and more space in my bucket of dread. Darkness of winter filled me with fear big enough to devour me. At dinner-time I'd start worrying about having to go to bed and the subsequent results—falling asleep.

After closing the door to the apartment and turning left down the hall, we climbed the stairs to our attic rooms. At the top of the attic stairs, a string hanging from a light bulb was the only light between the apartment and our bedrooms. In winter we scaled the steps in blackness and prayed that when we reached the string, the light bulb hadn't burned out. I tied an extension on the string and let it hang down to the floor below, but no matter how I pulled and pulled, it wouldn't click on. "Mrs. Dýrset," I'd whisper into the darkness, "if you are there and I see you, I will faint."

In my nightmares I was always trying to get away. Sometimes everyday monsters chased me and at other times it was old Mrs. Dýrset, rope around her neck, reaching, reaching, "Jeg vil berøre deg" (I want to touch you). In my dreams, unfortunately, I understood Norwegian. On a good night, instead of being chased, I dreamed that we were going to be bombed into oblivion by the Russians.

There were times that I knew I was dreaming and could influence what was happening. Instead of running, I stopped and faced the beast—then nothing happened. To wake up I'd pinch my arm or leg as hard as I could. Once awake, drenched in sweat, I had to undo my mummy state and free myself of the duvet and bottom sheet. Sitting up on the divan, my bed, exhausted, I could feel the blood running through my veins and thumping, ba-Dum, ba-Dum.

Before returning to sleep, I found a way to calm my heart and mind. I'd open the attic window, stand on a chair with elbows on the window ledge and head outside, and breathe deeply the arctic coldness. Above, stars winked from a black canopy. Unlike inside, outside blackness was soothing. Stars dim and bright, tiny and large looked nonthreatening. There were thousands of them, bluish white, some bright, some a mere hint. Sensation of wind on my face and the feel of cold metal, the window frame, cracked the spell of fear. After a while, confident that I would live to see another day, I returned to bed. Pulling my duvet up to my chin, I wondered if there were people on other planets. Did they know about us? Could they see us? Were they like us? For a second time that night, I'd recite the Lord's Prayer.

In late May, muddy streets dried and I am allowed to take my first bike, a Christmas gift, outside. Standing next to the bike on our patio, I think it looks colossal. This is the first day of many, I imagine, where I will ride it up and down the street like a princess on a white stallion. But first, I have to learn how to ride the steed. I walk it through the gate to the gravel area.

I knew that when you are scared out of your wits, learning is hard. Unlike with swimming, with biking, breathing shouldn't be an issue. This reminded me that I had one more year of swim classes, and if I couldn't swim 200 meters in the deep water I couldn't go to the next grade, which was high school. In all honesty, my progress was regress. I tried. I did the Pollyanna. I had a one-on-one with the Lord, and I still couldn't even float on my back. Whenever I try, I start thinking that I've drifted over into the deep pool and panic. Swimming class now has fifty kids in the deep pool, practicing different strokes, laughing, cheering each other and three of us, two boysand I, in the shallow pool. Our instructions are always the same, "OK kids, time is ticking." After that our swim-teacher spends the rest of the class with the kids in the deep pool who can swim, while the ticking time bombs practice drowning.

Walking my stallion through the gate, it tips left and right showing no inclination to remain erect long enough for me to get up on the seat. Climbing up on the concrete fence, I slide onto the seat and sit. Of course, the bike is held up by the fence. I wave to Mamma, who is watching me from the kitchen window. Shouldn't she be cooking potatoes or something? I get off the bike and pretend to be looking at the tires. Yes, they are round all right. Of course, that's part of the problem. With Mamma out of sight, I get off and walk it to an area that looks pretty flat and mount it putting one foot on a pedal and pushing off with the other foot. After a few tire rotations, and then a few more, it gets easier and I've not fallen yet. A couple of hours later, I'm riding from the top of Hólmgarður to the end each time looking for Mamma in the window. She should take more interest in her daughter's progress. By the time I finish, many neighbors have seen me and I think this is a sport I could be really good at.

Kids ten and older worked during the summer and played outdoors at night. Free of heavy coats and walls of cold wind, rain, and ice, we ran around like colts getting our legs under us for the first time. Grassy areas, although not many, were covered with wildflowers. After particularly difficult nights when Mrs. Dýrsethad been unusually active, I'd nap on the hill in the backyard with a handful of midges and flies for company. When I listened, really listened, I could hear the quiet. It filled up my ears with glorious peace. It was the sweetest sleep ever.

Before getting up and leaving my Sanctuary Hill, I'd watch white fluffy clouds meander across the sky in shapes of animals, flowers, and people's faces. The sky was bluer than any eyes, bluer than the ocean, the mountains, or blueberries. Whimbrels, plovers, skuas, and small birds with light brown chests flapped their wings, floating effortlessly, like a kid going down a slide.

After short rain showers, gigantic rainbows stretched from side to side over our neighborhood in red, orange, yellow, green, blue, and indigo. No matter how reachable the beginning or end seemed, my bike never got me there. Our winter northern lights were different, more like misty beams from a lighthouse that lasted for hours.

On weekends, Hafdís, Gréta, Magga, and I biked to Elliðará, (Old River) to rock walk and catch fish. Rock walks inevitably ended with one of us falling into the less-than-a-foot-deep river and the fish getting away. After a few cupped hands of cold river refreshment, we headed north to the Atlantic where we could see Viðey, a long skinny island, and Mount Esja behind.

Summer was my favorite season. After work we played until ten at night. Impatient to leave the dinner table, not one to learn from experience, I'd rush down the stairs. Always a mistake. Wool socks have no traction and don't stand a chance on Mother's polished stairs. As the number of falls added up, Pabbi became vocal about his dissatisfaction at seeing his offspring slide at a speed greater than his Trabant could muster, down the yellow linoleum stairs. Gravity didn't kick in—didn't have to. I flew, bouncing off every step, landing on the hall mat bruised and battered.

The day of the bad spill, after my back slams down a few too many steps, I land with the breath knocked out of me. Commotion upstairs, and Mamma and Pabbi are next to me. Mamma tells me that all is well. Pabbi has had enough.

"Why you keep polish these damn steps?" he hisses. "It a death trap for us." Hearing him cuss was such an unusual occurrence that my breath returns. However, I have their attention and decide to cry for good measure. After all, stairs, just a little less dangerous than the lower diving board at Sundhöll, are no laughing matter. Mamma continues to say I am fine and Pabbi goes back upstairs in disgust. Mamma says that I should hold the handrail around the bend, steps three and four. Pabbi continued to call it a deathtrap. Mamma continued to polish the stairs.

Speaking of death, there was Nonni. He lived on Hólmgarður 23 and was the biggest baby on the block. When the neighborhood kids played *kíló*, between his house and mine, his mother brought him out and told us to include him. We didn't want to. But that wasn't something you said to an adult.

In *kíló*, we divide into two teams. Half of the kids, team A, line up on home base behind the hitter, who is also on team A. We go for a few minutes and switch. The hitter holds the ball with one hand and punches it as hard as she can with the other hand and then runs to base two, three, four, and home. If you make it all the way around, we earn two points and you go to the back of the line to wait your turn to hit again. Otherwise, we earn one point for getting on a base. Team B in the outfield has to catch the ball or chase it on the ground and tag the runner with it or throw it to a team mate on first base, who throws it down inside the base. If they catch us, they yell, "You're dead!" This is when Nonni goes "Gaga goo goo."

"I'm not dead," he cries. "I'm telling Mamma." This is a given. This is what he always does. Then she comes out and yells at us.

"Who said that Nonni was dead?" She has a take-no-prisoners look, and the culprit, the one who announced the death sentence, now scared silly, won't fess up. So all twenty or so of us stand there, shoulders hunched, heads hanging, mumbling into our chests. Magga from 22 downstairs tries to explain that dead just means that he was out. His mother says that he is not "out" and that our behavior is shameless. At this point, some of the kids leave and those of us who live close to Nonni play half-heartedly for a while then make excuses and leave as well.

Hildur, Gréta, Hafdís, Magga, and I were the neighbor-hood juggling queens. Hafdís had a set of juggling balls that

Stína brought from America. They were striped and hard and bounced better than our old ones did. We juggled three balls at a time, against the house. First, we'd toss one under-hand and catch it. Then two over-hand; three under; four was three under and one over. This continued until we could do all ten sequences without dropping a ball. Nine was two under, one over, three times. It was easy to do it with two balls, hard with three, and almost impossible with four.

On other days we watched Magga pull earthworms out of the ground. "Ugh, double ugh," we yelled. It wasn't pulling the slimy creatures out of the earth, it was what she did next. Without wiping the dirt off, she put a worm on her tongue and let it slide down. If it tried to escape out of her mouth, she pushed it back in. Having Magga was like having a neighborhood circus. She had acts for houseflies, ants, and her younger siblings when her parents were out of sight.

In our family Stella was the one who pushed the boundaries. She was far more daring than Jórunn and I were. She also stood her ground, right or wrong. Like the time she peeked into a tin can on 22 that belonged to Sigfús, touching other people's stuff without permission. We didn't know much about Sigfús except he lived in the upstairs apartment and had a wife who was really fat and a daughter who never came out to play. He owned a carriage, an axle, and two wheels he stored inside his yard. Anyway, Stella, her upper body hanging over the fence, reached the can and flipped off the lid. She told me that it was chock full of worms.

That evening Sigfús came over and complained, "Stella let all the worms out of my can. These were worms," he explained, "I use for fishing."

"I'm very sorry. I will talk to Stella."

"My wife saw Stella leaning over the fence."

"She will not do this again. We are sorry." Mamma told Stella that she shouldn't be touching things that don't belong to her.

"They were just stupid worms," Stella barked.

Sigfús on the other hand, who happened to live above Magga, would never know that my sister had done a kind act. Otherwise, the worms could have ended up in Magga's circus act.

That fall, before school started, Mamma planned a trip to Glasgow, Scotland, and took me with her. Mamma's plans were shared on a need-to-know basis. She got an idea, planned, plotted, and delivered it to the surprised family a day or two in advance.

In 1955 when she decided to leave for a summer with me in tow to work in the kitchen of Red Hill (Rauðhólar), a place for troubled kids, Pabbi asked, "You are going where?" Before she could answer, he followed up with, "When was this planned?" They didn't fight about it. Actually, they had words only over money.

We sailed across the Atlantic on the ship *Gullfoss,* reaching Scotland in four days. Our hotel, Mamma told me, was close to a shopping district, a park, and a street from the Glasgow Central Rail Station. This was a shopping trip, but it didn't keep me from hoping that an amusement park like Tivoli Gardens in Copenhagen was on the to-do list.

On the sidewalk next to the Rennie Mackintosh Hotel entrance, a shoeshine boy, about my age, had a two-seater stand, each seat occupied, and was popping the rag so fast that his hands were a blur. He was a lot faster than my kindergarten teacher was showing us how fast the Earth moves. His two customers, men reading newspapers, paid him no attention. Maybe I could do that on Torg. Mamma told me to stop staring.

Mackintosh Hotel had a large foyer and high ceilings with chandeliers four times the size of ours in the living room. The entry had a marble floor and a large rug with a fading rose design. There were cracked leather couches, high-back armchairs and photographs of city streets. It was the kind of place I'd seen in movies although the smell didn't fit the decorum. At first it was just musty, but the sixth floor hallway where our room was smelled like someone's old aunt mixed in with cigarettes and sweat.

People at the reception area had a hard time understanding Mamma. Mamma had a worse time understanding them. Finally, she showed them her passport, and a woman in a green suit started shaking her head up and down. We got our key and lugged our suitcases to the elevator.

Our room was sparsely decorated, had two beds, a dresser that Mamma said we wouldn't use, and a private bath. "While I nap," she said, taking off her coat and brushing off invisible dirt off the bed, "you can go and buy postcards." Standing by the window, she pointed to a shop across the street in a building smaller than our hotel. "Go out the front door and cross Union Street at the light. Then come right back." She gave me two shillings, brushed the bedspread again, and lay down for a nap.

Outside the hotel, the shoe shine boy had different customers. I walked down the sidewalk, large paved blocks, past a phone booth to the corner light and crossed with a sea of people. Women around me wore dark coats, scarves, and nurses shoes; the men wore wool jackets and caps. A piercing note of a horn startled me. Then the click-clack of a train explained the noise, and I calmed down. I crossed at the Union and Gordon intersection.

Glasgow streets were wide with tall brick buildings on each side. At street level there were small shops with awnings. Wood doors between the shops led to the floors above where people lived. Tall arched apartment windows looked as though they'd never been cleaned. In the distance I saw I gigantic chimney spewing black smoke. I thought about Skúlagata, where the wind off the Atlantic was fresh, cold, and salty.

The gift shop had cards, teddy bears with kilts, small bagpipes, plaid wool blankets, and British flags. After picking two cards, one for Pabbi and the other for Sigga Páls, I handed the store girl my two shillings. She returned one along with a three-pence coin.

Back outside, it looked nothing like I remembered it. I walked to the corner and the street sign read Gordon and Mitchell Street. How did that happen? I wanted Union and Gordon. I kept looking up at the tall building to find our hotel. I paced up and down different streets; still nothing looked familiar. Standing at the curb, a cab driver pulled over and asked me a question. Inside the cab, I said, "Rennie Mackintosh Hotel." He took off, and we drove and drove. Clearly, he was going somewhere else. This was it. I'd be stuck in Scotland for the rest of my life. What would my life in Glasgow be like?

Finally, the dark-skinned cabby driver pulled up by a train station, turned to me, and said something. I stared back at him. I didn't want to get out of the cab. He kept talking and talking. He had a lot to say, and he pointed at the train station. I wondered if he had a family and if I could live with them.

Few long minutes later, he handed me a paper and a pencil and said, "Blah blah blah blah." I printed the name of the hotel the best I could remember and handed it back to him. Throwing his hands up, smiling, then tapping the palm of his hands to his forehead exclaiming, "Ooohhhh, blah, blah, blah blah." We were off again, and this time he took me to our hotel. The shoe shine boy was still there. When I handed the cab driver a shilling and three six-pence coin, he pushed my hand away, "No, no, no, no." That I did understand.

Mamma woke up when I came into the room. "What time is it?" she asked. "You were gone a long time." I left it at that.

On the following day, we went shopping. Mamma looked at the clothes carefully, sometimes turning them inside out to see the finishing. If there were threads hanging and the hem was uneven, she'd talk aloud about how poor the workmanship was, or she contemplated redoing some of the seams because the price was so good. In the kids' department, she pulled dresses off the racks. She chose a few, and a sales-lady pointed to the fitting room. In my eleven years, I'd tried on many dresses made by Mamma. I'd not imagined ever having a store-bought dress. I tired on a blue dress fitted at the waist with a checkered front. It was to Mamma's liking. Not mine. It felt tight at the waist, and in the mirror I looked like a barrel. It's not that I was fat or anything. It's just that I had no waist, and I looked like Suðurlandsbraut, the straightest street in Reykjavik. That's what Jórunn and Stella said. I didn't want to be ungrateful, but couldn't Mamma see that the black-and-white tweed dress with the black bow looked a hundred times better?

Finally, after trying on five or six dresses, the blue one twice, Mamma handed the blue *and* the black-and-white dresses to the lady. My mouth dropped and Mamma laughed. "Yes, we are getting both of them. They look nice on you." I loved it when Mamma looked happy. It was the best feeling in the world.

Crawling into bed, Mamma was still checking her passport. She took it out of her purse along with the travelers checks every hour. She counted the checks, looked inside our passports, then slid them back into her purse and shut it closed. That night she told me that when she was young, she'd wanted to continue her education but dropped out after a year. She'd encountered a hurdle she couldn't conquer: working full time, helping her mother at home, and going to school. Spontaneous conversation with my mother was rare. I sat up in bed and listened. She talked to me about when she was in Copenhagen working in an orphanage and the time she met Pabbi. She told me how handsome he was and a great dancer. The she said, "He liked Magnea best."

I must have heard wrong. Leaning towards her, "Mamma, Pabbi liked your sister?" Mamma didn't say things like that. "Pabbi wanted Magnea to be his wife?" Of all my aunts, Magnea was the bossiest. When she came to the house, she'd order us girls around.

We called her Magnea the Priestess because she preached to us. "You girls should clean your rooms instead of having your mother do it." Well, Mamma didn't clean our rooms, and it was none of her business. Although we didn't obey, we were obligated to go to the attic and pretend we did. Now Mamma is telling me that she was almost our mother.

135

"Mamma, why do you think that?" In my mind this conversation was just starting. Her silence told me otherwise. I sensed she regretted telling me, but the cat was out of the bag—and there it remained.

# Chapter 9
## Höfn in Hornafjöður

*This chapter is about Labba Louse, Rhubarb, and Arctic tern—1961.*

In 1961, I got the whooping cough, and Mamma discovered that she'd omitted many of my baby inoculations. This illness almost ended with my becoming an angel. Mamma was angry with herself. This mishap was rectified, and I got the shots I missed. Consequently, instead of working the summer of my twelfth year, Mamma was determined to find a setting where my scarred lungs could heal, some serene setting away from the city.

In early May farmers placed ads for kids to help with haying and farm work. Mamma found an ad from Farmer Jón in Höfn in Hornafjöður. She told him, "My daughter Edith has been sick and needs fresh air and rest. Will you consider letting my daughter stay at your farm? Of course, we will pay you for her keep." Jón was sympathetic to my sick troubles and enthusiastic about the money. Mamma told me that there would be other children to play with, streams to wade, rides on a hay wagon, horseback riding, and of course fresh air and blue skies, a YMCA camp with a different name.

May 1961, on my first airplane ride, I am off to Höfn in Hornafjörður. From May to late August, I rake hay, pick potatoes, milk the cows, haul water to the farm, wash wool socks on a washboard, set the table for our meals, and clean the kitchen. After a while the blisters from the rakes go away just as Magga said they would. Magga is Farmer Jón's wife. She has a round face, high cheek-bones, and brown hair kept short so she doesn't have to brush it. She says that the cows, pigs, chickens, and horses don't observe the Sabbath, so neither would we. She was raised on a farm, so she was used to the animals. She senses my fear of them and tells me not to show it. It makes the animals uneasy. Knowing this makes me uneasy. After the first week, sharing a bedroom with two smelly summer boys where we sleep on sheepskin and horse-hide spread around the room, I conclude that Mamma had paid enough for the fresh air, not the part that called for rest.

When another Reykjavík girl comes to help Unnur with the children, what a surprise! It is Labba from Hólmarður 23. We call her Labba Louse. Her parents and three siblings are also dirty. Her breath is so bad that you have to hold yours when she talks to you. She stands close when she talks to you so you see her yellow and brown decayed teeth. I remembered how Mamma invited her for cake on my tenth birthday. I never played with her after that and still didn't like her. Hafdís is mean, but she is clean. But Labba is the only girl on the farm my age, and my friends at home would never know.

Magga's farm has two houses. Magga and Jón live in the big old one. Unnur, her daughter, Bjarni, and five children live in the newer smaller house that has electricity and an indoor bathroom. My farm has kerosene lamps that we use in late August when light fades to semi-darkness. The outhouse, at the back of the farm, houses more flies than our laundry room window and fish store combined. Before you sit down on the toilet seat, you have to brush them off. After you are seated, you can feel them on your butt looking for escape. Disgusting. It's not like you can stand up and brush them in the middle of a bowel movement.

In the kitchen, an iron coal stove, recessed in the far corner, is the source of heat. Next to it is a washtub with a hinged wooden cover. It takes many buckets of water to fill it for a bath. I was there for four months without a bath. Flies like Magga's kitchen as much as they like the outhouse. At dinner, they are the first to be seated at the table, on our plates, glasses, silverware, and food.

Unnur and Bjarni aren't married. They have been so busy with all the children there hasn't been time. They have been waiting for the priest to come. Magga says they should wait until the kids are grown when they'd have more time. Unnur has a big round belly. Another baby is coming.

Spirit and Tracker, female sheepdogs, slept in the barn with the cows. Spirit's two front teeth are missing and her tongue hangs out the side of her mouth. They are black and white with bear-like heads and jaws that remind me of scissors. Spirit's missing teeth don't make her any less menacing. As soon as they see me, they come running, barking, and waving their tails. I stop, hold my breath, and wait for them to bite me. After poking my legs, they sit down and watch me play statue. Eventually, they get bored and run off. Phew! Run doggies. Run far across ditches and fields.

Each morning Magga gets us up off our skins and hides for *skyr*, buttered bread, and milk from the barn cows. Jón is the last one to get up. He is tall and thin and wears lopi peysa, pants that are too big for him, and suspenders. He changes his socks religiously, not his clothes. One of my jobs is washing everyone's wool socks with lye soap on a wooden washboard partially submerged in icy water. Afterward I use the water to wash the kitchen floor. Hauling the water inside is hard work, so water is used sparingly and repeatedly.

Farmer Jón is a good eater and a good sitter. After dinner he drinks his coffee through a sugar cube held between his teeth. Burping, not saying excuse me, he gets up to retire on the floor with his legs crossed and back against the wall. Fishing his pipe and tobacco out of his pants pocket, he fills it with tobacco and lights it. Then he talks to us. He knows a lot of things even thought he doesn't have a radio.

Jón does one rude thing: He farts. He lifts one butt-cheek and does it. Magga says nothing, and I don't think his old mother hears it. In my family we hardly fart at all. If we do, it's silent. We never say the *fart* word. If Mamma accidentally farts, she's embarrassed and apologizes right away. After Jón farts, instead of apologizing, he looks at Siggi and Palli, the summer boys; they laugh.

In the mornings, Jón's mother helps me clean the breakfast dishes, and Magga takes the boys out to the fields for a day of raking and, later in the year, pulling potatoes out of the ground. I join them after I finish house chores. Old Unnur helps me—dries the dishes and washes the kitchen table. She wipes the table slowly, carefully, beginning with a big circle around the edges. Then smaller and smaller circles until the crumbs are piled in the middle. She folds the sides of the rag over and drags the crumbs to the edge then over the edge into the palm of her hand. Walking to the sink, she opens her hand and shakes the crumbs out of her hand onto the floor for me to sweep. She wipes her hand on her apron.

"Unnur, I'll wipe the table," I offer.

"They are in the *tún* (homefield)," she responds. "Jón needs to replace the posts on the south end. They are rotting away. Bah! The wires are sagging on the ground." She can't hear me, so we end up having two conversations. It's easier just to sweep the floor, but it makes no sense to me to wipe a table and throw the crumbs on the floor.

Bjarni, who is married to Young Unnur, has a deep voice and the skin is of a person who spends more time outdoors than indoors. Muscles on his neck are thick as a bull's. He and Magga do most of the work. Bjarni takes charge of fieldwork: scything, raking, collecting, baling, and storing the hay in the silo.

With callused palms and fingers, fieldwork is my favorite. It is easy to keep up with the line of people, raking in front and in back of you as long as your rake doesn't get clogged up or stuck in a mangle of brush. Lunch—we sit in the hay and eat sandwiches and drink milk. My appetite has grown like Heidi's when she went to live with Grandfather in the Swiss Alps. She slept in the attic looking through a roof window where bright stars blinked at her. That sounded better than sleeping with two smelly boys.

On sunny days the color of the sky above the farm looks like oceans or wild pansies. By evening when your muscles want you to stop, the sky above has a glow of a washed–out, faded blue, making it look the way I feel. On these summer days, I can take deep breaths, my chest rising as I fill my lungs with air. No coughing. When the world is this beautiful, I decide, God is in a good mood.

Höfn in Hornafjörður is a peninsula east of Reykjavik south of Vatnajökull, our biggest glacier, on the Atlantic. Surrounding mountains are bare, gray, with grass and fans of rocks that spread out towards the bottom like a skirt. When the sun shines on the mountains, I can see the little hidden people coming out of it. Then they moved closer, they look suspiciously like grazing sheep.

On the far side of the tún beyond the wire fence, horses and cows chewed grass. A fence divided the field from the cows' grazing area. Home-fields were manured and watched over. Without grass, there would be no food for the animals. Closer to the farm, pigs sat in puddles and dogs chased each other. The main road that led to the town, Höfn, was far from the farm, so instead of car and bus horns, all we heard were sounds of animals and the wind.

At the end of a day, grass was loaded on a trailer and pulled by two horses more interested in eating it than pulling. When Labba hayed with us, Bjarni let the four of us city kids ride on top of the hay as he led the horses back to the barn. Exhausted, yet we jumped up and down, fell on top of each other, full of happiness.

One day Palli found a lamb stuck in a crevice outside the fence that surrounded the *tún*. Magga quizzed about the mother's whereabouts. Sheep had been herded and taken to the mountains—his mother must have strayed. Bleating loudly, the lamb tried repeatedly to get up on its legs and raise itself upright. "Ewes are very good mothers," Magga told Palli. "It's rare that one takes off like this."

There were no markings on it, so no way to tell what farm it belonged to. Magga wrapped it in a big towel and handed it to Palli to take to the barn. After he left she showed me how to fix its food. It would be my job to feed it, she said. "But Palli found it, and I think he'll want to feed it," I objected.

"I want you to do this," Magga was clearly not going to relent. "It needs to eat four times a day. After *réttir* (sheep gathering), it will go back with the herd." It was a male lamb. She showed me how to put small pieces of butter into the milk, warm it, pour it into the bottle, and stretch a plastic nipple over the spout.

"Here, little lamb, come and drink." It was my first time alone with the black lamb that was housed in a fenced-in area at the end of the dairy barn. He looked smaller and cuter when Palli held him. "Come and drink, come and drink," I chanted. The upper half of my body hung over a wood railing, arm outreached with a full bottle of milk and a fake teat. He wouldn't budge. "It's good, yum, yum." He bleated and lay down. Fine then, I thought. I took the nipple off and poured the milk out. Next two attempts met the same success.

After dinner that night, Magga asked, "Did you forget something?" Of course I didn't, but I wished she had. This time I asked if Labba, who had turned out to be a nice not-so-clean girl, could come with me. Unnur said that Labba was busy with the kids and after that she had to clean the kitchen. A lot of words to say no.

Back in the stall, the black furry thing looked up at me—then put his head back down into the hay as though he wanted to sleep. At Vífilsstaðir I selected sleep when all the goodness, all the happiness had gone out of my body. If only Vilhjálmur was here—no, Pabbi. He would do it for me. Bending down, I held the bottle between the wood planks and whispered, "Come here, Rhubarb." He looked nothing like rhubarb, so I don't know why I called him that. "You don't have to eat the oatmeal; instead I have warm milk that you will like. It's dessert." He looked lonely and leaving him alone and hungry for the night tasted wrong.

Quietly, slowly, I climbed over the fence and sat down in the hay. Rhubarb didn't budge. Inch by inch I crawled closer until I was sitting next to him. I watched him closely ready to run if he turned into a hostile ram ready to attack. But that didn't happen. His sad eyes looked like he'd lost his mother. He had. Carefully, right next to him, I reached out and stroked his back. Magga told me to stroke him like the female tongues her young ones. I told Rhubarb that all was well in the world. I told him not to worry about the Russians. Next to him, I put my arms around him and he seemed to like it.

Feeding him took many tries. When I put the nipple by his mouth, he just moved his head. "Come on, Rhubarb; you will like it. All sheep like it. For sheep it's better than chocolate." I squirted milk on my index finger and put it next to his mouth. He licked it. After a few more licks, my hand stopped shaking, and he was willing to try the teat. I heaved him into my lap and stroked him while he drank. Next time I should bring a bigger bottle.

Now Rhubarb bleated whenever he heard me enter the barn, "Hi Rhubarb," I yelled. He would come toward me, still bleating, as if I were his mother. Holding him made my insides feel mushy. And even though others disagreed, he was the smartest animal on the farm.

After you live on a farm for awhile you get used to farm smells, sour hay and manure. In one of those odorous places, the barn, Jón showed us how to milk the beasts, that's what he called them. You learn quickly that cows' tails move constantly. They flick away flies gathered on their backs. If you get smacked with the swish or swoosh of a tail, it hurts like fury. You have to tie their tails to their hind legs. Jón said we should always sit on the cows' right side. "They can be cranky, like a chicken with a toothache," he laughed, and added, "That's what they are used to and they are not open to change."

First, we rinsed their swollen udders with a wet rag. With a pail under the teats, tails tied to their back-legs, we'd get comfortable on the three-legged stool and lean against their warm stomachs. To milk them, you place a bent thumb on one side of two teats, circle it with the rests of your fingers, and squeeze while pulling down alternating teats. It felt good to sit with my cheek against her warm hide, listening to the drum sound of milk hitting the pail, letting the rhythm empty my mind. Up and down, up and down, and warm frothy milk streamed into the pail. Every so often I'd send a squirt into my mouth. After a while the stream thinned and you switch to the other two tits. Lastly, you smeared greasy ointment on the udder.

The chicken coop and the pigsty were not on my list of responsibilities. However, picking feathers off chickens that minutes earlier ran around headless until they realized that the head was gone and collapsed was. The job of singeing the hair off sheep's heads—that was mine and Labba's. We stuck a stick up into the head then used a small torch to burn the hair off. We liked working together.

Sometimes when Magga fed the chickens and collected the eggs, I'd go with her. The chickens went crazy, but she ignored them. I watched from the other side of the fence close to the door of the coop. On a shelf I saw eggs with baby chicks pecking their way out of the shell. Magga explained that you should never help them. Pecking helps them grow stronger before they come out. Helping them would hurt them. Loud clucking chickens scared the bejesus out of me, but the babies were adorable. Magga promised that at the end of summer, I could take one home with me.

On the farm whale meat is stored in wooden barrels filled with brine. They called it meat, but it was blubber. It was blubbery blubber that still had hair stuck in it. That summer I learned that food can grow in your mouth. The more you chewed, the bigger the piece got. You had to swallow while you could still breathe and hope like a pig hopes for puddles on warm days that you can keep vomit from coming up in your mouth. Horse-meat was better except Magga put so much salt on it that I could hear the sea call for its return. The other food that threatened an untimely upchuck was birds' eggs from the cliffs—after the chicks' bodies had started to form. Jón scooped the head off and ate it. At the dinner table, I was hungry but never that hungry. Siggi and Palli actually hoped for an egg with a chick forming. They said it tasted like a regular egg, even better. I didn't take their word for it. Fortunately, we had big bowls of potatoes, dairy curd twice-a-day if we desired, and carrots that I was starting to like, especially dipped in sugar.

Labba and I spent time together when we could. She was different, not like she was in Reykjavík. Neighborhood kids had no idea of how considerate and thoughtful Labba could be.

At the back of the farm is a beaten dirt path that leads to a field by the ocean where birds nest. On this particular day, Labba and I walk it. It's wet from an earlier rain squall, but the sky is clearing. We stop often to pull up our socks to keep them from sliding to the toes of our boots. As we near the ocean, a shadow above turns out to be a great black gull. With a scolding squawk, it swoops down around us. Bjarni, who collects eggs from the cliffs, says that gulls feed on other birds' eggs, so they are no friends of his.

Just before we reach the home of the *kría* (Arctic terns), we cross an area covered with meadow buttercups, ferns, cotton grass, dandelions and poppies. Rocks covered with gray-green moss sit next to some tiny bell-shaped pink flowers. Plants everywhere, even in small cracks between rocks and stones and down the sides of a ditch that divides it from the bird field.

We pick up long sticks to protect our heads from bird attacks. At first we can't see the nests, only brownish and greenish eggs, usually two together. What is supposed to be nests look more like the parent birds had just scratched the ground and called it a nest. We didn't stay long because these are some crazy birds. They circle us, crying loudly, and dive at our heads. There are so many that some get past my stick and peck my head. Ouch! Let me tell you, you can feel that poke.

Returning home, we see in the distance close to the mountains, a group of wild horses eying us, inching closer. We are some ways away from a fence that will deliver us from this danger—if need be. Need is. We start running, but horses outrun twelve-year-olds. Labba uses a wooden post to heave herself over the fence. I, whose waist has grown this summer, doubt a successful outcome and instead squirm between barbed wires tufted with sheep's wool. I feel and hear my clothes tearing. There is snorting. They poke at me with their noses. They are stronger than Spirit and Tracker are.

Labba comes back swinging her stick and shouting, "*Láttu okkur vera. Farðu í burtu!*" (Leave us alone. Go away.) But I am still stuck, and the horses don't understand Icelandic. Then she climbs back into the danger zone and helps me get untangled. Now the horses poke her while she helps me crawl through.

"They wouldn't hurt us," she says. It is good to hear that but even better to be on the other side of the fence. I've torn my pants badly, and my other pair is dirty. I wonder if I would have climbed back in there for her.

As I walked to the barn on another evening to milk Carmella, Daisy and Rose, my three responsibilities, the sky was pale pink, striped with long high clouds in lavender and reds; the pink around the setting sun on the other side of the valley was the brightest. "Red skies at night, sailors' delight," a familiar proverb. This time of year the sun meanders around the horizon without setting. After dinner we'd return to haying. Frost could come any day now. The silo was filling up It had been a good hay season, they said.

I was resting my head against Daisy's flank listening to her it's-about-time moo when Labba came into the dairy barn. Labba worked harder than any of us. In my family being a hard worker was a mountain compliment. Mamma would say, "Gunna is a hard worker." Then there was always a little silence, and my sisters and Pabbi said nothing. Hearing any compliment, even thought it wasn't directed at us, was not a moment to be taken lightly. Also, we were thinking that we'd heard Gunna praised more than enough.

Anyway, before I could say anything, Daisy's poop splatter hit both of us. I laughed. Labba didn't. "I burned myself," she whispered for the benefit of my ears only.

"What happened?"

"The iron fell off the table while I was ironing and I caught it." She showed me her left hand with large bubbly purplish blisters covering the palm of her hand. Her face was pained and she had to work hard to keep the tear faucet shut.

"Labba, oh, no!" My involuntary cry caused Siggi and Palli to look in our direction. Lowering my voice, "You have to tell Unnur." I stopped milking. My sister Ásta, burned her back and shoulder when she was little and now the skin looked like red puffy crocodile hide. Labba squeezed her wrist with her unburned hand. Her knuckles turned white. "You have to rinse it so it doesn't get infected." Daisy looked back at me and mooed unhappily.

Scooping out clean water at the wood supply table, I poured it over her hand.

"Ow, ow, ow," bent over at the waist, Labba tried to shelter her hand from water and air. A long low moan escaped through her lips.

"What's wrong, Labba" Siggi yelled. While she waited for it to dry, another blister popped. I dabbed Vaseline on it, but it hurt her so much that I stopped.

"Labba, you have to tell them," I urged.

If I tell them, they won't let me iron again," she said. Her face was crunched up and she was taking short breaths. That didn't sound like a good reason to me. Besides, Unnur was a lot like her father, Jón. They both liked to sit, he on the floor with legs crossed smoking a pipe, she staring at the coffee pot like it were Aladdin's lamp.

We hayed until eleven o'clock that night. When we got back, it was too late to go over to Bjarni and Unnur's farm. When I finally saw Labba again, her hand was bandaged and she told me that Unnur was still letting her iron.

Old Unnur didn't iron, but she talked to herself. When you've lived as long as Old Unnur had, you probably had a lot to say. Nobody listened. When I tried to, it often didn't make sense or it was hard to believe. She told me that her father wove horsehair into strings that they used to tie the hay into bales. "You never threw things away. If you broke a saucer or a dinner plate," she told me, "you make little hole close to the edges and tie them together." I didn't say it to her, but this was a terrible idea.

Sundays, Old Unnur made crepes. The smell of the fried butter and the sound of sizzling and bubbling batter made me think of our kitchen with the electric stove, sink, and running water. I was starting to get homesick.

At the end of summer, men on horseback and dogs on four legs brought the sheep down from the mountains. Bjarni, Jón, Siggi, and Palli along with Tracker and Spirit, took off early in the morning. The dogs' work was to find sheep that had strayed and bring them back in the flock. Our dogs had been trained not to bark while gathering the sheep so as not to scare them. Way up in the mountains they can trace, smell sheep that had been covered up with early snow and dig them out. Labba, Magga and I join them later in the day. It was the first time we'd met kids from surrounding farms.

Réttir (sheep gathering), dogs running circles around the corrals, and people catching up with news continued for hours. Some older kids set up a horse-race. Labba and I sat on our horses and watched from the sidelines. "I wish we could race," Labba lamented. That made one of us.

Our summer boys were in the line-up. A farm boy or a city boy, I don't know which, rode to a ravine a few hundred yards away and held up a stick with a handkerchief. This was the finishing line. The starting signal was a loud smack on a pail. "Get ready," a warning came.

"Clank," and the kids and horses were off. My brown mare, Comatose, raised her head curious-like. It would probably have ended right there except the overly eager starter continued hitting the pail, screaming, "Go, go, go". This was simply too much for Comatose. She started running. My body rocked from side to side. I grabbed the reins, hugged her flanks tight with my thighs, yet feeling myself slipping. I grabbed her neck. The ground was a blur and the button on my last pair of pants popped off. I heard hooves clomping nearing Comatose. Bjarni's voice, "Hold on, Edith. It's OK." It wasn't. My body met the ground before Bjarni had Comatose under control.

"Are you hurt?" Bjarni wanted to know. Rubbing her mane, "Hey, girl, we have to change your name to Wide Awake." Stupid is a good name.

That was embarrassing. If only I had been hurt. A broken ankle would've done nicely. I got up to find out that people were far more interested in the race, now in full fury, than a twelve-year-old with a red face holding up her pants.

Then it was time to return to Reykjavik. Magga, true to her word, gave me a soft, fluffy yellow chick. I played with him on the plane.

It had been twelve weeks since I'd seen or talked to my family. Mamma, Pabbi, and Jórunn came to meet me. I was wearing my blue jacket, unzipped out of necessity. The waist on my pants was tight enough to hold them up without a button. Comatose probably ate it. The boots would last another year. As I got nearer to my family, I held up the little chick like a trophy, my pay for the summer of rest.

My chick took naps on Pabbi's chest, and Mamma cleaned up after it and said we had to get rid of it. Then Pabbi said that the cuteness would fade fast and that I should take him to a house on Bústaðavegur, to a lady who had a chicken coop. It's hard to take something you love and leave it with strangers. Pabbi said that the chick was better off with his own kind.

# Chapter 10
## Christmas Countdown

*This chapter is about a book flood, bus tailing, and a watch—1961.*

Christmas was an enchanted time. It was in the air long before we sat down for Christmas Eve dinner. Early hints were Christmas cards amidst daily mail. Often, Christmas was the only time Pabbi heard from his family and they us. Families thanked each other for the year about to pass, informed each other of special happenings, and added that they hope to meet in the near future. But the first sure signs were the store windows that made even the dullest store a winter wonderland.

In the kitchen Mamma hung up a Christmas calendar with little windows for all the days leading up to December 24th. One by one the windows opened, revealing wondrous gifts and Santas. Waiting to open our presents and celebrating Jesus' birthday was torturous and sweet all in one.

Outside, December house roofs turned fluffy white—like whipping cream piled on a cake. Our egg lady ran out of bags. Lines of people at the grocery store buying flour, sugar, baking powder, and vanilla extract got longer as the days and daylight got shorter. The sun peeked above the horizon before noon, disappeared mid-afternoon.

Thirteen days before Christmas, Grýla, an ogre, comes from the mountain and is back on the prowl. Her husband, Leppaloði is bed-ridden, so she has to go from house to house begging for food. In the old days, people didn't have enough food for their own family, let alone strangers. So Grýla kidnapped children, boiled them, and fed them to her family, which included thirteen goblin sons and a black cat.

Grýla's goblins are the worst-behaved little people in the land. Dressed in red, the Yule lads come into town and steal candles and food and play tricks on the people. Sheep-Cote Clod, with his stiff peg-legs, comes first. Bowl-Licker comes on the seventeenth. He hides under your bed hoping you will put down your plate so he can lick it. Of course, I know this is just a legend, but even when I know, my mind says, maybe it isn't, and then what?

Superstition thrives in my country. "Don't open an umbrella inside the house," Mamma admonishes. She believes that it means that someone will die. If your palms itch, you will receive a gift, was another one.

I pick and choose superstitions to believe in. Looking in a mirror in a pitch-black room, you will see your future mate. That's one I believe. When I fail to see anything and have a hard time finding the mirror in the darkness, I ask Mamma if my inability to see means that I will never marry. She looks up from Morgunblaðið ready to make an unwanted suggestion so I make a quick exit. I also believe the superstition about itchy palms and gifts.

Parents told unruly children, "Grýla is going to get you." Eventually, the Danish king banned the story. Perhaps his mother the queen had threatened him with Grýla. People unwilling to abandon this fine family folklore started telling a different tale, making the goblins carriers of gifts. Just like that, we went from unruly delinquent Yule lads to gift bearers. For the thirteen days leading to Christmas, they brought gifts to children and placed them in children's shoes resting on window sills. However, if you had misbehaved, the Yule lads put a potato or a rock in your shoes.

The Andersens are not buying this version. Besides, the idea of putting dirty shoes on our windowsills was inconceivable. Mamma believed that cleanliness was well before godliness. Even when Stella and I challenged it, we quickly learned that it was a rule not to be toyed with.

For the most part, our bedrooms were protected under a Switzerland covenant that protected it from hostile outsiders, Mother, Father, but not Magnea. Aunt Magnea, who Mamma said Pabbi liked the best, ignorant of this unwritten treaty, violated it every time she visited. "Ágústa, the girls should clean their rooms! They should be helping you more." In fairness to my aunt, Stella and Jórunn had more free time than they needed. There was some merit to this part of her argument.

Days leading up to this holiday of all holidays, Mamma sat hunched over the sewing machine, and new Christmas dresses, like our brother Jesus, were born. At night the whirring sound of the machine traveled to the attic, soothing my restless mind, keeping Old Mrs. Dýrset's spirit away.

Christmas time, our pantry should be renamed Cornucopia. Uncle Svend sent wooden crates of oranges and apples kept in the hall pantry. Inside the crate every piece of fruit was wrapped in tissue paper, ripe, and ready to eat. On the way to bed, it was easy to make a quick stop in the pantry and make off with an orange or an apple. Evidence, peel or stem, was thrown out on the roof the way Mamma threw stale bread to the birds in winter.

Bottles and bottles of red currant, bilberry, and rhubarb juice sat on the top shelf. Jars of rhubarb and bilberry preserve on the shelf below. Source of this wealth? Currant bushes that line the west side of our property line. August bilberry picking out in the country was a family effort, scooping them up using a round rake with a cotton bag. At the foot of our yard, we had a vegetable garden with carrots, potatoes, rutabagas, rhubarb, and cabbage.

Crates, each with twelve 8-ounce Coca-Cola bottles, were off limits. To take one would be too obvious, leaving a hole that screamed, "Look at me. I was robbed!" A second crate was a mix of malt and orange drinks. Pop was so much better than milk, and we never drank water. Your first sip of a Coke, sweetness and a prickly feeling going up your nose, a wonderful moment. Coffee was in the fourth seat ahead of milk. After Christmas and New Year's Day, our pantry was open season, and we feasted it to its bare bones.

Stella, Jórunn, and I start bantering for Christmas gift clues. Stella tells me that if I tell her what she is getting, she will tell me. Jórunn insists that neither of us know. She is the keeper of this information. She tells us that we are getting underwear, towels, or socks, all things we don't want. Then she laughs and leaves.

Jórunn has finished school and is learning to be a hairdresser. She gets on my case about brushing my hair, washing my neck, and other hygiene. Now she takes baths twice a week and spends a lot of time in the bathroom. Jórunn has thick auburn hair and a thin face with freckles across the nose. Her dream is to get a tan and ooohhhs and aaahhhs when her girlfriend—Gunnhildur, an airline stewardess—comes back from America with a tan. Few days later the tan is gone and they claim that getting a sun tan in America is like buying clothes from there, neither lasts long.

On the radio, followed by the noon news and weather, Christmas ads take over. I listen to the announcer describe new books. This is the Christmas book flood. I've been downtown to look at books in the teen selection—I'm almost a teen. You are allowed to pick up the books and look, but they are in cellophane so you can't peek inside. This year I'm hoping to get *The Story of Ester Costello* or *The Adventures of Albert Schweitzer*. I may not get them because they are expensive. I console myself with the knowing that Mamma has never picked a Christmas book I didn't like. Stella, Jórunn, and I share our Christmas books, so it's really like getting three books.

Impatient for Christmas, I decide to spend the day in town. Bus 7 is packed full, standing room only. Getting off at Torg (Town Center), I fell gale winds from the ocean push against me making forward progress a challenge. Sleet pounds my face. It's impossible to look into it so I hunch my shoulders and lean my body into the gale.

Eymundsson Bookstore is downtown on Austurstræti (East Street) and Mál og Menning (Language and Culture) on Laugarvegur (Pool Road). As I make my way up Bank Street towards Mál og Menning, I stop to use an underground bathroom, women on the right side of the street, men on the left.

An attendant in a white uniform comes out of a small warm room on my left and I give her 2 *krónur*. She is old and talks quietly as though she's overseeing a church instead of a public bathroom. She hands me a towel to wipe my hands so it's hard to skip it. Noticing my skates she tells me, "Put your skates on the floor, not the bench."

Back outside, climbing Bank Street, I wonder if it's my imagination, but the winds always seem to blow against me no matter what direction I walk. You listen to the weatherman droning on and on with "Faxaflói and Breidafjördur, (two bays on the west side), winds at 37 to 44 mph predicted and intermittent snow in the south, freezing rain in the north, temperature 26°F." In Iceland we have ocean currents, the North Atlantic Drift that moves northeastwards and another one—the Irminger Current—that sweeps around the south, west and north coasts. The cold winds come from Greenland and Pappi says that our temperature comes from these wind currents. Today, it feels like Eskimo winds.

The Language and Culture Bookstore is packed. The store was started by the Communist Party with money from the Russians, and the store-owner sends the profits to Russia. But it is just a rumor, and looking around, I see nothing that looks Russian—at least not how I see things in my mind's eye. What

I see are long lines at the cash register of regular Icelanders even though it is only December 20th. Stores stay open until midnight on the 23rd, Þorláksdagur, and it's crazy busy. After that everything closes for three days. The *Adventures of Albert Schweitzer* is sold out. It's disappointing. Even though I might not get it, I wanted to see it. There are several copies of *The Story of Ester Costello*.

Before I leave, I go downstairs to the school section. Wooden pencil boxes with designs have tops you slide on and off. Crayons are in packages of twenty-four and forty-eight. If I get to keep some of my earnings from this summer, I want to get the forty-eight-crayon–box. Bookstores and libraries are my favorite indoor places. Favorite outdoor place next on my list is Tjörnin, a home to ducks and swans.

I leave the bookstore and take Bergstaðastræti to Skálholtstígur that takes me to the big pond. There are really two ponds, a large one with an island and a smaller one separated by a road bridge. The pond has been frozen for a few weeks, and the ice is unusually smooth. In the twenty minutes it took to get there, the winds have died down, and I can't wait to put on my skates.

In summer mothers bring their little kids to the pond to feed *bra bra*. That's baby talk for ducks, geese, and swans. Swans and geese are aggressive, so people fling bread far in an attempt to reach the better-tempered mallard ducks with their green heads and white neck ring. Females are brown. There is not much to say about geese except they poop everywhere. Swans, on the other hand, are graceful and faithful; couples stay together for life. In Hans Christian Andersen's *Wild Swan*, the princess has to spin and weave material from stinging nettles for eleven coats with long sleeves for her brothers whose wicked stepmother has turned them into swans. So in my book, swans on Big Pond are heads and feathers above geese.

To warm up I skate circles around the perimeter of the safe area. There are Do Not Go Further signs on the south side of Big Pond. Now with my arms outward making a V, I lean forward increasing the speed feeling a light wind on my cheeks. Before long, I'm so warm that I take off my hat and stick it into my coat pocket. Avoiding a collision with a smaller kid, I fall down on my side. Unhurt, I put one foot between my hands and use the toe picks to push myself upright. After a few more rounds, I do the backward wiggle with predictable success—that is, I'm mostly standing still wiggling my butt. After a while my toes move from cold to hurt, so it's time to leave. Sliding my feet into my boots is lovely. I run to Torg. Bus 7 is already there, warm, humming, ready to take me home.

Dinner that night is fried fish balls, boiled small potatoes, and cocoa soup with breadcrumbs for garnish. I watch Mamma who seems to be moving painfully slow, but it's probably my empty stomach that missed its usual afternoon snack of buttered French bread dipped in coffee. Stella goes crazy when I do that. "Ugh! look," she says to whoever happens to be in the kitchen at the time, "she's got greasy butter floating on top. Sickotating!" You'd think that she'd quit looking if it's that gross. To me, it tastes *wunderbar*—that's German.

Jórunn and I sit on the built-in white bench facing Pabbi. I'm against the window and radiator that has a small compartment where I still drop food not to my liking. Tonight all is to my liking.

After dinner Jórunn and Stella do the dishes. "Can't Edith take out the trash?" they whine. I'm in the dining room watching Pabbi.

"Pull up your sleeves," Mamma instructs. "I don't know how you girls work with sleeves hanging down to your fingers."

"Taking out the trash comes with the doing dishes," Pabbi answers.

Mamma goes to the storage room upstairs for the Christmas ornament boxes, and I'm not going to worry my head about their complaints. Pabbi is making a church in the shape of a cross made of cardboard. He's spread newspaper on the table and, using a razor blade, he cuts rectangular holes, the windows. A big double door in front of the church has small panes, four-by-four, set up high. The steeple, or tower, of the church has a cross and two tall, narrow windows. He hums to himself, pushes his glasses to the top of his head, engrossed. Red cellophane is pasted from inside. Pabbi's hands are large and thick, so the next part—pasting strips of paper, window panels, from the inside—is time consuming. A light bulb goes inside, a layer of white cotton, Christmas snow, covers the roof and drapes the window ledges. When he lights the bulb, the church looks like it's on fire, Christmas fire.

Finished with the dishes, Stella goes to the phone, and Jórunn admires Pabbi's work. He heads for the bathroom, and we call Mamma to come to the dining room to see our Christmas church. It will sit in the hall window, right below the stairs to the attic.

Mamma takes off her glasses to look, hears Pabbi, "I wish you would hit the side of the toilet. Every time you go to the bathroom, Lovísa hears you." Mamma complains about this all the time. She doesn't want Pabbi to pee straight into the toilet. Instead, she says he should hit the sides of the bowl so Lovísa won't hear. When I pee, I try to sit close to the front so the stream hits the inside front of the bowl. But there isn't much I can do about flushing the toilet. Sometimes I turn the sink faucets on high blast to blend the sounds and confuse her. She probably knows how often the whole family uses the toilet. It's weird though that she'd care. If you happen to be in the laundry room when she is doing her wash, she looks up at you, takes a deep breath while sliding her forearm across her forehead, "Ooowwwhhh." What can you say to an adult who lets out a low tired sigh?

Mamma also doesn't like it that Pabbi walks around in his pajamas. "Kai, put some pants on. The neighbors can see you."

"Why deprive them of beauty?" he smiles, his eyes twinkle with naughtiness. "If they enjoy looking at me, it's OK with me." I agree with him but keep that little thought private.

It's time for bed, and I hope Old Mrs. Dýrsethas gone back to Norway. After all, there are only three days before Christmas Eve Day.

December 21, Pabbi has three tickets to the Danish Christmas Ball at the Independence Party's hall. Mamma has finished my blue–and–green print baby-doll dress with a white collar and short puffy sleeves. It has a big bow in the back. This year our dresses are not alike, and Jórunn is not going to the ball. Instead six-year-old Kata will join us. Ásta and Agnar are no longer together, and she's moved back home. She has a small bedroom inside the apartment.

Independence Hall is alive with kids. Clanking of dress shoes and the rustle of chiffon dresses greet us. We stick our mittens and hats in the pockets of our overcoats and Pabbi hands it to the woman tending the cloakroom. We receive a bag with chocolate wrapped in shiny colored papers— Macintosh candy.

With treat bag in hand, we walk through the colossal ballroom doors. It's like a side of a mountain opening up to mortals to a color festival of the hidden people. It's hard to breathe. This better not be a dream. Girls wearing holiday frocks in colors of the rainbow hold their parents' hands. Boys tugging at their bow ties, hair combed and shoes shined look like princes. Music brings into being a feeling of godliness. It fills the air with peace and a reminder of why we celebrate Christmas.

> Silent night, holy night
> All is calm, all is bright
> Round yon Virgin Mother and child
> Holy Infant so tender and mild
> Sleep in heavenly peace
> Sleep in heavenly peace

In the middle of the ballroom, a gigantic Christmas tree, green as the grass in July, sparkles with hundreds of miniature lights, glass balls, angels, tiny violins, satin bows, snowflakes, and glitter. On top, shining, blinking is the Star of Bethlehem. I smell sweetness and holiness and stomach deep pleasure.

December 22, an north-easterly gale brings sleet that soon turns into ice pellets that make a crisp clicking sound when they strike the cement blocks on our patio. Coming back from the egg lady at 32, I hold the brown bag in front of my face, walking carefully. Mamma is baking cakes and cookies; tomorrow she'll make ice cream.

"This is a good time for you two to clean your rooms," Mamma suggests. She is looking at Stella and me. Stella looks shocked as though Mamma has suggested that she stand on her head. Stella and Jórunn used to do that. They'd push each other from a flat on the floor position up toward the ceiling. Then they let go of each other's hands and act as if they are flying. Now they're too old for it.

"I cleaned it. ..."

Stella is trying to come up with a reasonable length of time when Jórunn, who is giving Mamma a perm, pipes up, "You won't remember that far back."

"If you start now, you'll be finished by dinner," Mamma never answers our complaints. She just keeps on talking, finishing what she has to say.

Defeated we head for our bedrooms upstairs. By the time we get to the hall, we are running to see who can be first up the stairs. Taking two steps at a time, she beats me by one, just barely, because I'm grabbing her calves hoping she'll shriek all the way up. She doesn't disappoint me.

We keep our doors open for company, and Stella yells to me, "Do you know that if you hold a lit lamp and touch a metal handle of an attic window, you can die?"

I tell Stella that I don't believe her. I push coloring books, socks, and pajamas off my bed so I can lie down and rest. Stella is three years older than I. She is taller and has bigger bones. We tease her and say that she has "Jóhanna's thighs." She has blue eyes, high cheekbones, and thick brow hair like Villi's and Jórunn's. They inherited it from my maternal grandfather. Stella is defiant and gets into trouble more than I. Even though we have been told not to crawl out on the roof, if Mamma and Pabbi aren't home, she does anyway.

"Well, it's really true." I walk in to her room to check on her as she reaches for the window handle with a lit lamp in the other hand.

"Stella, stop it."

"I will if you tell me what I'm getting for Christmas." Her hand inches closer to the window.

"OK, OK, but first put the lamp down." I have to think of something she wants. I haven't a clue. It's not that I haven't looked in every nook and cranny. Now with Mamma home every day, my parents' bedroom is off limits. Stella is enough of a daredevil to go and hurt herself. "You are getting a purse." I watch her face closely to see how I did.

"OK." She turns to me and asks if she is getting anything else. I tell her that she is getting a book. "Which one?" Skepticism has crept into her voice.

"She got you *The Adventures of Albert Schweitzer*." I should have stopped after the purse.

"No, not that one. I want *Sister Angelina*!" That's a romance novel and it cost 28 *krónur*. She's not going to get that book.

"Do you really know that," she asks, "or are you making it up?"

"No, I really know it." You can lie if it's to save your sister's life.

By late afternoon the winds have calmed and the entire street, a gravel road about half-a-mile long has frozen over. Cars are moving slowly, chains on tires. Bus 7 stops at each end of the street every thirty minutes. Coming downstairs after cleaning our room, I see that Hafdís, Magga, Hildur, and Selma are outside with their skates headed to the bus stop and I know what that means.

"Mamma, I'm going out."

"Did you clean your room? Stay where I can see you," she calls back. "Dinner will be ready soon."

Clutching the handrail, I scale the stairs-to-death, slick as the ice on Big Pond, and get my skates out of the laundry room. Lovísa is hanging up sheets, so she can't rub her arm against her forehead. I say, "Hi." She sighs.

"You kids are not bus–tailing, are you?" an old guy at the bus stop wearing a wool cap and a scarf around the collar of his coat asks us. He spits brown juice and waits for an answer.

I've already had my quota of fibs for the day and wait for one of the girls to answer.

"No, we are waiting for my brother. He's supposed to be on the bus." Magga can fib without flinching. She doesn't even have a brother. She looks him in the eye and smiles.

"Is that so?" he responds with a cold smirk, his blue eyes flicker in a face made red by wind and wine. It might be Hanna's dad who lives across the street from us, 25 downstairs.

"If I see you guys hanging on the back of the bus, I'm stopping!" Mr. Bus Driver is wearing his bad mood uniform. He's suspicious of a group of girls wearing skates. I'm losing my courage. All this interference has dampened my enthusiasm. Unlike Stella's and Magga's, my ration of courage—a scant morsel—would starve most. Nobody refers to me as a plucky girl. Ssshhh, the doors are sucked together. They close with a thud.

It takes Bus 7 a few seconds to get going because the streets is glassed over with ice. It's just long enough for us to grab the back bumper. Squashed together in the middle to prevent view from the rear-view mirror, we squat down our butts almost touching the icy street. Half way down Hólmgarður, we can't resist expressing our delight and yell "Yeah, yeah, yeah!" There are no cars behind us so Magga calls out, "One, two, three, NOW!" We let go and slide a ways, and I'm without one mitten now frozen to the bumper on its way downtown.

December 23, the early afternoon sky is one dark continuous cloud. Looking out the hall window, where Pabbi's church sits like a beacon to those braving the elements, I watch the clouds move towards the east. Reykjavík's weather report predicts light snow and gusting winds. Þorláksmessa Day, named after a priest who lived during the Middle Ages, is achingly slow. I calculate that there are 86,400 seconds in a day, slow seconds. This is a day to stay out of Mamma's way. Her head is full of bad ideas of what we can contribute to the day's work.

Our National Radio buzzes with Christmas advertisement, "Everyone eats skate fish on Þorláksmessa, The Fishstore Laxa on Grensás Road 22." That certainly isn't true and thank goodness for that. "Cooperative council of egg producers will not accept eggs after December 22." I wonder what an egg council will accept if not eggs. "Engagement rings from Hjálmur Þorfason, goldsmith on Pool Road." Whatever.

Banks and government office will be closed and city buses will go on a shortened schedule. Holiday times of church masses and a funeral service for someone named Stefán Halldórsson. What a bummer to die just before Christmas. Swimming pools are closed for three days. They should have made it three years. However, of greater interest is the next group of advertisements. *Anne Frank* is showing at New Cinema. The English film, *Circle of Horror* has a five o'clock, seven o'clock and nine o'clock showing—children allowed. Then there is an Italian suspense with Danish subtitles, nobody under 16 admitted. Darn.

When the news comes back on, Pabbi, sitting in the kitchen working on the Christmas tree lights, turns up the volume. "This year, the post office had to add 125 people to its regular staff of thirty mail carriers to deliver Christmas cards. There will be two deliveries today and one early tomorrow." Does he find this interesting? I wonder.

Pabbi inquires, "Is Stella still sleeping?" I'm happy to answer in the affirmative. "Get her up. She should be helping your mother." I'm happy to do what Pabbi asks, taking two steps at a time, thinking through how best to rephrase his request to my dear sister.

"Stella, you are so in troouubbbllleee! You were supposed to be helping Mamma, and Pabbi is a mad as a polar bear with a headache."

"Be quiet." She covers her head with a pillow. Disappointing response.

"Seriously, Pabbi thought you were in line at the milk store. When I told him you were still sleeping I thought his jaw would drop off his face." I've pushed it too far. Stella knows quite well that Pabbi expected her to be asleep. Anywhere else, running errands or doing chores, his jaw would have dropped off.

"Be quiet. Get out of here." Be quiet is as close to cuss words we can use.

If Stella gets really mad and Mamma and Pabbi aren't home, she'll sometimes use a really bad word like when she yelled at Ásta, "*Píkan þín*" (Vagina you).

"Stella, get up. Pabbi said you have to help Mamma." She turns over and pulls the duvet over her head. I might as well be yelling into the wind. She won't get up. She is the heaviest sleeper on the planet.

Pabbi's steps are on the stairs and with that my sister is out of bed with a renewed attitude, "Pabbi, "I'm coming!"

While Stella and Jórunn help Mamma, Pabbi and I go to pick out a Christmas tree. He ties it to the roof of the Trabant and we drive back on roads that have improved from the previous day.

When we return, Sigga, Pétur, Inga, and Siggi are at the house having coffee and cookies. Inga and Siggi have a car, but Pétur does not. Aunts and uncles buy gifts for us until we are confirmed. Right now, that means me. Years ago Sigga and Pétur gave us a doll sized stove with pots and pans that left us speechless. We didn't even know toys like these existed. Mamma gave it to Kata because we, her words, "are too old for it."

While the grownups visit, Jórunn polishes the silver, and Stella is irons last year's Christmas paper. Holiday music plays on the radio. Adda, Villi, and families will be here tomorrow for Christmas Eve dinner. On Christmas Day all of us go to Gunna and Villi's. Mamma thought we should skip going to Gunna's this year on account of Sigrún, who was born in September, being an infant. Also, when she was born, there were complications, and she had to have a blood transfusion. Gunna, like Mamma, never quits working, wouldn't hear of it.

December 26, Adda and Valli have us over for dinner. It's her twenty-eighth birthday. That's old. Adda, Valli, and the three kids—Kata, Bragi and Gústi—still live downstairs from Old Katrín in an old two-story house with an attic and a hall bathroom they share with Valli's mother. The entrance to Adda's apartment is through a side door. You come into a small hallway with the kitchen and one bedroom on the left. To use the bathroom, you go through a door from the kitchen across an ice-cold hall and into an even colder cement hall that leads to a tiny room with a toilet. At the end of that hall is their laundry room. The clothes lines are in the backyard. On the right side of the hallway is the living room, a large room with two big windows with white sheers and wood sills decorated with vases and statues.

Valli, tall with brown neatly combed hair and clean nails, is the only person I know, if you don't count doctors, who went to the university. Now he works for the government. When you look at his clothes, ironed and pressed, it's hard to believe that he gets much work done. He likes John F. Kennedy, who was elected president in the United States last month. He speaks English and Danish fluently, German pretty well and has studied French in school. Adda says he dreams in Icelandic. Then she grins.

December 23, going to bed is easy, falling asleep is problematic. There are unread books somewhere in the house, and the wait is agonizing. Sleep won't come; I visit Stella's room.

"What do you think we are getting?" I ask Stella.

"Whatever it is, we know it's blue," she says as she lifts her legs to the ceiling beam and pushes her feet against it. The Donald Duck paper has been replaced with yellow paper with thin orange stripes. Her pillow is under a low beam and she's punching little holes into the corners with a pencil.

With Mamma on an errand, we'd raided her sewing area and found a small piece of blue material under the radiator. Like detectives, we surmised that the lack of dust on it was proof positive that this swatch's life span had been brief. We owned no clothes made of blue terry fabric. This is what Stella is referring to. We speculate some more then Stella gets bored talking to me and tells me to go to bed.

Finally, finally, Christmas Eve Day is here. Last night, after we went to bed, Pabbi decorated the tree that now smells like a pine needle forest. Three packages wrapped in red and green from Sigga, Margrét and Inga, rest against the tree stand. A sight so divine it makes me feel religious. The rest of the packages are put out later in the day.

Christmas Eve Day minutes are excruciatingly slow. If staring at a clock wore it out, our kitchen wall clock above the white bench would have disappeared before the noon news. With my ear to the clock, making sure it's ticking, Mamma tells me to get off the bench and sweep the hall at the bottom of the menacing stairs. She would have asked Stella, but she is still asleep.

"You want me to do it *now*?" I whine. I'm dragging this out like the seconds on the clock.

"The broom is in the corner closet. Shake the rug and put our shoes in the laundry room."

"*Our* laundry room?" I ask.

Pabbi looks at me, and I can tell he's going to say something I don't want to hear. Teasing your daughter on a day like this is un-Christian. I grab the broom and dust-pan—too late.

"Whose laundry room did you have in mind?" he asks.

"Why can't Stella do it? She never does anything."

"You can't say that," he's smirking even though he knows how difficult this day is for me. "She is sleeping," he adds, "so she's doing something."

After lunch we are sent upstairs to give Mamma time to make last-minute preparations. When we were younger, we took naps we stayed awake for. Our Christmas dresses, clean undershirt and panties, new white socks and patent leather shoes for me, and nylons and low heels for Stella are ready to put on after our baths.

Pabbi shaves, splashes Old Spice on his face, and hums while he ties his tie in the bathroom mirror. Mamma dresses, and her hair from yesterday's perm is as curly as the black people's we saw in Copenhagen. Looking at us, I conclude that we are not such a bad-looking family.

Ever so slowly we are moving towards six o'clock. From the rafters in the attic to the cement floor in the basement, aroma from the pork roast with bay leaves fills your nostrils. Served with the roast will be small white potatoes browned in sugar, Orka peas, red cabbage, and creamy gravy. We start with *graut* (pudding) with cinnamon, sugar, and a staring butter eye in the middle. One almond is slipped into the *graut,* and a prize goes to the person who finds it in her bowl.

Minutes before guests arrive, I'm assigned the job of getting Coke bottles from the hall pantry and putting them by each plate. Jórunn and Stella are in charge of setting the table.

Table set, family dressed, smell of Christmas, and church music on the radio, Stella and I watch from a window. Christmas spirit in the Andersen family is alive and well.

Gunna, Villi, and crew pull up in a cab. Jens recognizes the house and sprints toward the door. Villi helps Gunna who is holding Sigrún get out of the cab. Stína's arms reach up for her Pabbi, who is paying the cab driver. Jens and Stína love being with Villi. Like Pabbi, he's easy to be with; unlike Pabbi, he's on the go all the time. Adda and her family come late; they usually do.

After dinner we eat Mamma's homemade ice cream. Mamma gets help from Adda, Ásta, and Jórunn while the rest of us walk around the tree and sing Christmas carols. Kata, wearing a yellow taffeta dress with layers that come out making her look like a dandelion, is the only one of the grandkids who understands the gifts business. The rest of the grandkids would be happy to walk around the tree for the rest of the night. That's not going to happen.

Smell of coffee and cigars signals opening time is near. Pabbi gives his gold paper cigar ring to Kata. My family of grown-ups moves so slow that you might think they'd stopped altogether. Finally, we can go into the living room. Seating determined by seniority. I'm delegated to the floor with the little kids. My aunts give me socks, a bracelet, and a white lacy petticoat. From Mamma and Pabbi, I get a pillow case and an ocean-blue bathrobe the color of the swatch we found under the radiator. Nice. But where is the special gift? My last gift from my parents is *The Adventures of Albert Schweitzer.* I'm really happy about that, but a robe for a special gift? Christmas comes with one gift that is the most special. A bathrobe and a pillow case don't fit the bill, and the task of being happy and appreciative is going to be a challenge.

Mamma, sitting on the green upholstered chair in the corner next to the piano, is telling Adda that they shouldn't have bought her such an expensive gift. I won't be saying that, I think to myself and regret it immediately. Adda smiles. Pabbi looks content looking at his new books.

When Mamma looks in my direction, I flash a quick smile. "Do you like it?" she asks.

"The robe is great, and that's the book I wanted." I'm not going to mention the pillowcase. I know it's white damask, but if I say the word *pillowcase*, tears will march down my cheeks for all to see. As is, I'm tilting my head back to prevent the flood. Blinking is out of the question.

She's carefully removing Christmas paper off another gift, this one from Ásta who watches intently. I recognize the paper from last year. Last year it was on Stjáni's gift from my parents. "You haven't seen it?" Mamma offers as a way of an explanation. "It's a small package. Look next to your chair."

It was just where she said, but it was small. For all the tea in China, I could think of nothing that small that could take me from the abyss to the summit. I was wrong. "Oh my goodness! Oh no!" I was so surprised that I didn't know what to say. It couldn't be. Did I misread the tag? No, it reads "To: Edith, From:

Mamma and Pabbi." Inside a rectangular box, under a cotton layer was a silver watch. A silver-tone beveled face with black dials and numbers in the cardinal positions and lines between. The mesh band fastened with a bracelet like clasp. Nobody in my whole family had gotten a watch before they were confirmed. In my wildest imagination, I would not have guessed this. It was outside the realm of possibilities. I couldn't wait to show it to Hafdís.

"Do you like it?" Mamma's been watching me. I give her an awkward hug. She smiles and pats me on the back to remind me not to hold on for too long.

That night I put my new pillow case on and open the window. Cold wind rattles the handle encouraging me to return under my duvet. But not yet. Above our house the North Star, named by the Vikings Leiðarstjarna (the Leading Star), shines brightly. I stretch my arms outside the window. Life is wonderful. Tomorrow Hafdís will be so jealous when she sees my watch.

# Chapter 11

## Growing Pains

*This chapter is about Mamma, sex, and a bloody slap—1962.*

L ovísa said that Hafdís is in a better class than you?" Mamma said it like a question. She couldn't have surprised me more if she'd sprouted a third eye. School was my life, my responsibility. Mamma or Pabbi never attend parent–teacher conferences or asked to see our report cards. If my report card showed a stellar performance, I'd share it with them. They had not seen it for a couple of years.

Hafdís was in twelve-year-old class D; I was in C. I told Mamma that Lovísa had this information wrong. I told her that I was in C and Hafdís was in D. She seemed pleased with this information and returned to reading the newspaper spread across the counter in front of her.

Mamma had dark graying hair, a thin pointy chin you expect in someone with a strong will, and eyes that were sinking into her skull. She was two years older than Inga but looked ten years older. She changed between two dresses and didn't own a single pair of pants. She liked having a glass of port but lately complained it upset her stomach. I'd learned about communism and socialism in school and concluded that Mamma was a socialist.

When we disappointed her, instead of raising her voice, she took off her glasses, and her eyes pierced through us. If it was something really bad, she'd add a deep breath. She spoke her mind, glasses back on nose, and returned to what she was doing before the upsetting thing interrupted her. It was her sign that we could leave to ponder our transgression.

"I'm in a better class," I repeated, wanting to make sure that Mamma heard what I said.

"That's what I thought," she said without looking up from the paper. Discussion of my educational achievement ended.

Mamma had great respect for education. Yet when it came to her daughters, she never talked about our pursuing higher education, not even a high school diploma. But as ash follows a volcanic eruption, we knew that we were expected to find a trade that could support us. She was pleased that Jórunn wanted to be a hairdresser. Soon, Stella would have to decide.

Elementary and secondary schools ranked students according to performance and the school's past experiences with the family. Students in class A were the stallions, confident and full of promise, the direct opposite of students in class H, slow-moving seals clubbed on the shores of the Atlantic.

Our three older siblings went to high school at East Side School. Three younger went to Réttarholts High School, with Jórunn as the trail-blazer. In other words, Réttarholts' teachers first introduction to our family was with someone who was well groomed, conscientious, and obedient. Jórunn took pride in her appearance, did her daily homework, and studied for tests. Her grades were 9 or 10 on a 10 point scale. The idea that you could get away with less effort failed her. I'd been luckier. I understood the law of minimal effort for tolerable results. In her freshman year in high school, she was in class A, an all-girls class. She liked all of the extra curricular classes. The mother of one of Jórunn's friends, Ingibjörg, was Réttarholts High School's economics teacher. Jórunn could swim at the age of eight and looked forward to gym classes. Sisters sure can be different.

Now that she had completed the two required years, she poured her energy into classes for cosmetology and her work at the beauty shop. Like Mamma, she wanted to get ahead. At home she acted grown-up and serious, laughed less, played rarely. I decided that reaching twenty-one is a good life expectancy. This was my last year in elementary school, and I'd start catechism classes to prepare for my confirmation in '63.

Stella was cut from the same cloth as Jórunn but a different pattern. She rarely studied but memorized, comprehended, and assimilated new information easily and followed Jórunn's footsteps in class A. Réttarholts High School did away with the all girl-class A. After Jórunn classes were mixed.

Stella's elementary school fame was her penmanship. Our ancestors, early settlers, wrote on parchment without erasers—probably not a sought-after profession. In their turf-and-packed-dirt homes, they sat around the fire writing on parchment stories of blood feuds, heroism, and love. Parchment, dry animal skin, took time to procure, and the word *draft* was not in my ancestors' vocabulary. You got it right the first time. The *Saga of the Greenlanders* takes up the skin of one calf. This, I concluded, accounted for this emphasis on penmanship. Stella's tewlve-year-old class teacher, Marino Prento, hung her papers in the school hall. Prento was not really his last name. Villi nicknamed him Prento because he sent home so much printed material.

Stella continued to challenge mother's rules. Walking home from the bus stop, Jórunn saw smoke rising from our roof. Huffing and puffing, scaling the stairs of fear, she yelled at me, "Our roof is on fire." We raced to the attic. Leaning back on the red-tiled roof were Stella and her friend Anna puffing away on Salem cigarettes. When Stella and Jórunn were little, they were pyromaniacs. They lit fires under my parents' bed. One time they put Ásta's doll on fire. Jórunn smoked liked the rest of my older siblings. However, Mamma and Pabbi had not learned of Stella's smoking, and she kept it incognito in view of birds, stars, and the Lord.

In May Villi and Gunna moved to a new second–floor apartment at Álftamýri 2. It was an apartment building surrounded by other identical buildings. Entering their apartment, you entered stepped into a carpeted hall and an open dining room and living room. Paintings adorned walls, white sheers and heavy drapes on windows. Left were a kitchen with modern appliances, a Formica table, and chairs with gray plastic cushions. Their telephone sat on a small table in the hall between three bedroom doors and a bathroom. Sigrún, who was just a few months old, and Stína shared a room; Jens had his own.

Villi worked for Esso. Gunna had taken classes with a master seamstress, Bergljóta Ólafsdóttir, and was now sewing for others. She was twenty-four-years old and had a light complexion, a beautiful smile, and three little kids. She had more energy than the rest of her family combined and often yelled at them to get them moving. When I visited, she fixed me a snack and sat down to visit. This was a far cry from Adda who greeted me with, "What do you want?" With Gunna you felt like she was happy to see you. Stella babysat for them at night and told me it was lucrative.

"Why did you tell your mother you were in a better class?" I asked Hafdís as we walked home from school. It was a gloomy day with low clouds hovering. Looking ahead through air that looked like a hazy curtain, I saw that rooftops in aqua green, red and yellow had a supernatural quality. The same did not hold true for the muddy field below my boots. Wool mittens kept my hands dry.

"I didn't tell her that," Hafdís moved from side to side and kicked rocks like a soccer player into a net.

"So your mother lied?" It was a mean thing to ask, but I said it nicely like, is your mother frying halibut for dinner? Hafdís missed the niceness, stopped, and turned to me.

"At least my mother is not old enough to be my grandmother." My mouth dropped. Did she really say that? Surprise turned to anger. Haze lifted, and my world turned flaming red, not like a rose, but like hot like lava rushing down the side of a volcano wanting to maim.

When doctors asked Mamma if she was my grandmother, she laughed, "No just an old mother." I never laughed. It wasn't funny; it was terribly embarrassing. I envied girls whose mothers were young and did things with them.

"I'd rather have an old mother than a tired moaning mother," I threw back at her.

"Your mother looks like Grýla. She's so old she scares the neighborhood cats," Hafdís yelled back. Other walkers stopped to watch.

I dropped my school bag and grabbed her collar in an effort to pull her down into the mud. "Your mother has a stick for a leg," I screamed as I hit her face with my left hand. Hafdís was bigger and heavier, and her blows felt hard, painful. Flailing my arms, I managed to hit her a few more times. Pulling her hair, I finally got her to the ground. It was raining in earnest, and her hair felt like stems of a pussy willow. My knees were in a mud puddle. Kids surrounded us, cheering for us to continue. Hafdís got her leg across my middle, heaved herself up, and sat on me. Twisting around, sticking my butt up and legs underneath, I raised her fat cow body enough to get away. If there was a dry spot on my body, I didn't feel it. Wet wool mittens weighted down my hands. There was mud in my hair, inside my boots, in and one pocket. Hate burns hot. "Your mother is a liar who looks like a hag on a broomstick," I screamed holding nothing back. Sobbing, Hafdís picked up her school bag and rushed home. I picked up a rock and threw it after her. I missed. It didn't feel good to win the fight because my mother was still old.

We stayed away from each other for a while. Hildur, Magga, and I turned our attention to more important matters, sex. After Höfn in Hornafjörður, Labba and I parted ways. That was about to change. It turned out that Labba, whose breath had not improved, was the neighborhood expert on how babies come into the world.

After school Hildur, Magga, and I went to her apartment, 23 upstairs. In our health book, page 82, it explained that a mother's egg and the father's sperm come together and a baby starts growing inside the mother. What page 82 did not explain is how the sperm got inside the mother's stomach. Labba had the answer.

The mystery of sex was of interest to me. It gave me something to think about instead of wondering if *augun hans afa* (grandfather's eyes) were floating around my room—as my sisters suggested. Mrs. Dýrsethad moved back to Norway.

Thinking was something I was good at. I thought about a lot of things. Sex was just one. I wondered why Mamma gossiped on the phone with her sisters when she said that gossip was wrong. I wondered why she told me to wash my hands in the morning because "you don't know where they had been during the night." Actually, I knew. They were at the end of my arms. She told me to stop rubbing my vagina on the corner of our kitchen table. She called it *it*. Our table was just the right height to slide onto the corner like mounting a horse. I asked her why. Instead of telling me that it was unsanitary to be sitting on the corner of the kitchen, she surprised me and said, "You just don't do that." I didn't say that it felt good, although it did. Her mannerism, the way she didn't look at me, told me that the probability of gaining empathy and understanding would be like pouring a cup of water into the Atlantic and expecting it to rise.

Pabbi said that I was an old soul. That's why I liked to think about things. He also said, "Edith doesn't think about everyday things like hanging up her coat, closing the front door when she leaves the house, or taking her schoolbooks back to school." I thought about that. But these days I wanted to learn about babies. What do women have to eat, or what pills do they take to start a baby inside them? If it was a pill, why did Mamma take so many?

To learn the secret of where babies come from, I had to go to 23, upstairs. Labba's apartment smelled putrid, and her bedroom smelled stale, like dirty clothes. Although our apartment was the cleanest place in Reykjavík, excluding two attic bedrooms, Labba's apartment needed fresh air, a bucket, and a mop badly. We scrunched together on her bed, and Labba handed us a magazine with pictures of naked women. Villi had some of those when he lived with us, but he kept them on the top shelf of the closet. I knew because standing on a chair I could reach them.

"Grownups take off their clothes and lay on top of each other. The sperm leaks out and goes inside the woman." Our attention was complete. Labba, the only one standing, spoke with authority and the confidence of a learned person. Her captive audience was girls who made fun of her and refused to let her play Paris, a hop-scotch game she was good at. This time she was in the driver's seat.

"How does it get inside the naked woman?" This was the puzzling part I wanted an answer to. The acrid odor in my nostrils and lungs was no longer important. I wanted to skip the long version. Does a sperm leak out of the mouth, ears, or where?

Labba explained that the *tilli* (penis) went inside the part of us where we pee. This was too much. I should have known that someone whose parents were alcoholics, wore filthy clothes, and had brown teeth would resort to lying. Maybe her parents, Mamma and Pabbi, no way. They would never do that to us. They care about us. I continued to listen.

"The sperm swims inside the woman into the egg that closes, and the baby starts growing." She watched us waiting for questions. I wanted to throw up. Another thing, there was no way that half of me swam anywhere. I still can't swim, so I would have drowned before any egg sucked me inside.

Hildur said she had to go home. Her face was the color of her blond hair. Magga was holding up pretty well. I wanted to stay to challenge this information and make Labba take it back. "Maybe it's enough to kiss and the sperm goes down and finds the egg," I suggested. It was a compromise. "It's a lot easier to fall down than crawl your way up," I reasoned. "I've heard that most babies just start growing like Jesus inside the mother," I lied.

Steadfast, Labba said that what she had shared is the way it is and the only way. Magga stretching her legs in front of her said, "Cool."

A nagging feeling remained inside me that Labba's truth had some merit. After that it was hard to look at my parents, especially my mother. Why would they do such a thing? I stopped visiting Mamma when she was doing the laundry.

As I looked around with the new knowledge, still hoping it wasn't so, it seemed that my whole family had gone sex crazy. Ásta married Bragi and moved to Kópavogur. We missed Stjáni, especially Pabbi who used to teach him things and feed him. Now Ásta knew how babies are made and should have known better. Jórunn was spending all her spare time with her boyfriend, Ævar Axelson. She met him September 23 when Auður and Jórunn went to Gútto, a dance place where they played old songs. This tall guy, handsome (she said), with dark hair and thin face, asked her to dance. He was from Skagaströnd, the north part of the country. He rented a room from his oldest brother, Rúdolf, a policeman, and was in trade school learning to be a blacksmith. Tuesday after they met, he called her and asked if she would come over to their house in Stóragerði, not far from us, and help him babysit his brother's kids. When she talked about him, she got red in the face and all happy. If Jórunn knew what I knew about sex, she would have thought over that offer. My family was not right in the head.

As we prepared for our confirmation, *Séra (Minister)* Gunnar said that writing down what troubled our soul would ease it. Mamma's budda (coin purse) in the kitchen cupboard was heavy with coins. Borrowing a few *krónur* would not be noticed, so I did—to buy a notebook to unburden my soul and Prince Polo to sweeten my stomach. For hours I wrote and wrote. The more I wrote about my worries, the more I thought about them. New worries came and were recorded. At this rate

I'd need another notebook. Schoolwork took a backseat to my diary although that was the normal seating arrangement. Then one day, while I was out with friends, the last day I wrote in it, Adda came over with the kids. Kata went into my room and read my private diary. I was indignant. Storming into the kitchen where Mamma, Jórunn, and Adda sat, probably talking about politics when they should have been keeping an eye on Miss Snoopy Pants, I told them. Jórunn said that my notebook was hardly a private diary, considering I left it all over the house.

On another day, I stopped at Adda's, and Kata was by herself. I took it on myself to explain to her right from wrong. She was uncooperative. A thought crossed my mind that she was a heathen, a pagan like our ancestors, or at a minimum a bad Lutheran. Perhaps it was my catechism classes, but I was moved by a spirit within to get my point across. First, I had to be sure that she believed in our holy brother and the Almighty God.

"Kata, Jesus will never forget you and always forgive you your trespasses." Diary still fresh in my mind. "Your mother would forget you before He would. We must believe in our heart that nothing is as important as our relationship with our heavenly family."

"Mamma would not forget me." She was in denial.

Anyway, it was a starting point. "Your mother is more likely to forget you, even with your clothes laying around, than Jesus ever would." She was looking uncomfortable. Good. There was concern in her eyes, concern I could have tipped to angst if Adda had not returned from the milk store. Adda gave Kata, whose teary eyes were the size of saucers, a funny look, then me a stern one. I told Adda that I best leave to catch five o'clock Bústaðabus Number 7.

After I quit recording my problems, I thought less about them. As far as where babies come from, not knowing can be better than knowing. Mamma asked if I was feeling OK. She never asked me that before unless I was physically ill, so I must not have been hiding my disgust with her probable behavior too well. Without looking at her, I said I was fine. As a last attempt to find a source to back up or dispel Labba's spiel, I spent time at the library. After a while the librarian said that I should be looking on the children's shelves, not the adults'. No help there.

Mamma didn't ask me again, but she glanced at me more often. One Saturday she invited me to go with her downtown to the fabric store that was holding a sale. Mamma had started making dresses for girls and selling them. It was a mild October day, and Mamma, usually in a hurry, wasn't. Her back was improving after breaking three ribs falling off a window ledge while cleaning a window. Pabbi was still in the bed when she came crashing down. He cursed. He said that she should leave the damn windows alone. She stayed in bed for days, doctor's orders. Jórunn and Pabbi cooked, but only Jórunn did laundry. It was the one thing Pabbi did not do. He even knew cross-stitch and how to knit.

Walking to Torg with fabric wrapped and bundled under one arm, Mamma asks me, "How about a waffle at Hressó?" It's the most popular restaurant in town. Unless we were overseas, Mamma has never taken me to a restaurant in my life. Waffles with preserve and real whipped cream are expensive. She asks again. "Would you like a waffle?" This is as good a time as any to start talking to her again.

"Thank you, yes." It is strange sitting at a restaurant with Mamma who is drinking coffee through a sugar cube between smokes. Mamma wore false teeth that she kept in a glass at her bedside. So did Pabbi. Mamma was a little over five feet tall and thick around the middle. She always said that our best features were shapely legs, our neck and thick hair. She said we were lucky for that.

We sit in comfortable silence. She breaks it. "Ásta will have a baby soon." Mamma's aptitude for small talk with me was equal to mine keeping conversation going with adults.

"Stjáni will be happy to have a brother or sister." It sounds mature. I am pleased with myself. It's something Aunt Sigga would say. Looking at my mother, I conclude that Labba doesn't know everything. She could be wrong. This moment is too nice to think about it. Besides, if Mamma and Pabbi had done those things, then other people's parents had as well. That was some consolation.

"Jórunn is planning to marry this spring. We will combine your confirmation and her wedding." This is really big news. Confirmation is the biggest party we have, bigger than our baptism or our wedding.

I don't know what to say but want us to keep conversing. "I like Ævar. He works a lot." Throwing in "he works a lot" is for her benefit. I don't really care that much. Mamma looks out the window. "Do you like him?" I ask. When she doesn't answer, I add, "Where is he from?" In Iceland people always ask what people someone comes from. If you say, he married one of the Thors girls, that's a praise. Thors people were well-to-do, out-standing citizens.

Old Katrín had higher hopes for Valli than Adda delivered. That was enough reason for her not to like Adda, who told Mamma, "Finding a girl good enough for Katrín's son is like finding an honest politician." Adda and Mamma had common views of elected officials. "Maybe a Briem girl would have been good enough." I had no idea who the Briems were, but they must have been better than our family.

This attitude, my family is better than your family, has lasted through the ages in our land. That was another thing that I thought about, but not as much as where babies come from. My sister Adda marrying Valli reminded me of Guðríður in *The Saga of the Greenlanders*. Guðríður married Þorfinnur Karlsefni. *Karlsefni* means the stuff real men are made of. He was the son of a man whose nickname was Horse-head. What-ever. But the saga says that he came from a big and a good family that had lots of money. Adda's family was big, something Valli liked about Adda, and good but not the money part. Erik the Red persuaded Karlsefni to take 130 people to Vinland, Nova Scotia. They stayed for three years, and Guðríður gave birth to the first European baby in America. Eventually, they were chased out of America and moved back to Iceland. It was like giving them Paradise and then burning it down. Þorfinnur's mother was not impressed and still insisted that Guðríður was not good enough and told her son so. So instead of living on the same thatched-roof farm, he built another one to live with his wife. Three points for Þorfinnur. Maybe Valli will build a new house for Adda so she doesn't have to live in a house with a woman who thinks she's not good enough.

Mamma puts out her cigarette and asks me if the waffle was good. She hadn't answer my question about Ævar. To find things out, I had to eavesdrop on her phone conversations with her sisters or Aunt Sigga. Then I was told it was wrong. Technically, it was also a sin. "Honor thy father and thy mother: that thy days may be long upon the land which the Lord thy God giveth thee." We had to memorize the Ten Commandments in catechism class. On the other hand, if you are sitting in the kitchen and overhear what your mother is saying, that's not disrespect. I can't help hearing. It's more of an accident and not covered in religion classes. Anyway, that's how I learned about Ævar's family.

He was one of ten children, so he had the big family going for him. They were raised in a small house-farm, Stream, that his father, Axel, built in a seashore village in Skagaströnd by Húnaflói, a large bay east of the westfjords. So *no* on the money. They raised sheep and cows and owned a rowboat for fishing. Every day Ævar took the cows to a grazing field outside of the village a few miles away and brought them back at night. You could tell that Mamma approved of his experiences with hard work. Compare that to Stella and me squabbling over whose turn it is to take out the trash. No, let's not compare.

Ævar loved being outdoors. As a kid, if he wasn't doing chores, he was at the harbor fishing with a line and hook. He got his first rifle when he was twelve and ammunition from a relative who worked at the co-op. Their house was on the shoreline, so he'd stack up a pile of books under the window in his bedroom to stand on to shoot birds. He must have grown a lot because now he was tall.

Ævar's mother, Jóhanna, told Jórunn that when he was thirteen, he shot a seal lying on a cliff offshore. The dead seal rolled off the cliff and into the sea. Ævar tore off his clothes except underpants and dove into the arctic sea coming back up with his seal. I hope he doesn't do that any more. Diving into the sea put my mind into panic.

On the subject of drowning, I was headed for high school only if I passed the swim test. Could I recall anyone who had been kept behind because they couldn't swim? Not really. Does that mean that 1,000 or so kids now in high school can all swim? Am I the only person in my neighborhood who sinks? Am I the only twelve-year-old in Reykjavík who can't swim? A voice inside my head goes, "Yes you are." I'm hearing voices all because of swimming—no, because of not swimming.

Deadline looming, determined, with a Pollyanna attitude, I started going to the pool to practice. If I asked my sisters for help, they thought I was kidding. "You know how to swim," Jórunn affirmed. Really, so sinking was all in my head?

Of course, I knew my strokes, breast and back. It's just that my body wanted to float below the surface of the water. I sank no matter what stroke I did. Also, when I move away from the wall or went into deep water, I started to panic. Extra practice didn't work. I just got better at almost drowning. It was so embarrassing to be in the shallow end that I pretended to be a foreigner unable to answer questions from rude little kids and their parents as to why I didn't go to the deep pool with bigger kids. Other times I hobbled, suggesting a crippled body.

Sex and swimming were not my only problems. In twelve-year-old class, some of the girls started their periods and grew breasts. I didn't. In gym class we were excused for those days. We said "Aunt Rose is visiting."

Page 82 clearly stated that breasts emerge, hips widen, pubic and body hair grows. "A pituitary gland produces hormones ..." How could I find out if I have a pituitary gland? Could that be the problem? Or could I be a boy with one missing piece? I really hoped not.

Looking at myself in the mirror, I saw nothing was growing or emerging, not even pimples. With hands on hips, pushing my chest out, I looked like a reverse Hunchback of Notre Dame. Weekly I measured my hips and chest. My teacher said you grow while you sleep. I started sleeping on my back so my breasts would have room to grow. To stop me from turning over, I'd pile books on my stomach so if I moved they fell off and alerted me. It took a few nights to adjust to not moving. I started calling Mamma, Mother. It sounded more mature. Mother wanted to know, "Edith, why do I have to go to your bedroom for my measuring tape?"

"You do?" I asked.

One day I think I see a hair under my armpit. I immediately put my arm tight against my body so it won't fall out. All day, I keep my arm close to my side. It was stiff by the time I got in front of our hall mirror, the one with a gold frame and a glass shelf. I look again. It is gone. I rip off my sweater and shirt and scan every inch of my arm-pit. Nothing. "What are you doing? People can see you from the street?" I'd been too engrossed to hear Mamma—no Mother—who's looking at me as though she's just seen a scrawny, underdeveloped goat with a tiara.

"Mamma, I need to buy a bra?" This is not our first conversation on the subject. She looks at my naked chest. She doesn't know that her last-born is the only one in the shallow pool and now the only one in gym class without a bra. And believe you me, not all the girls need it.

"What for?" She is picking potatoes out of a crate in the hall pantry.

I follow her into the kitchen with a brand new sense of courage. I am fighting for my future, my sanity, my any sense of feeling like I belong to the evolving human race.

"They have small bras. I need one of them small bras."

"You don't need a bra until you have something to put in a bra." At least she is continuing the conversation. I wish Pabbi weren't sitting in the kitchen.

"I will put cotton inside the cups until they grow." I'm not going to say *breasts* with my father listening. The girls," she's not biting, so I up the argument, "All the girl, put cotton in their bras. It's normal." I have stretched the truth to a breaking point. But using mother's proverb, *Neiðin kennir naktri konu að spinna* (Desperation teaches a naked woman to spin), I feel justified.

"Let her get a bra," that is a surprise. Pabbi is weighing in—in support of me. Although I wish he hadn't said *bra*. He could have said *it*,—"let her get it."

Later that week, Mamma gives me 40 *krónur* and says that I can get a bra. I am on Bus 7 headed downtown. My life is about to change for the better.

Miss sales-lady shows me the smallest bras made. Hard to believe that it is the smallest. I hook it in the back in the last loop and center it over my chest. Back home, I stuff half a package of cotton inside each cup. Immediately a problem announces itself. When I move, the cups slide up, eventually sticking out of my shoulders like horns. It's not a big effort to pull them back down, but I forget.

"Hey, Bridget Bardot, time to pull your breasts down." Stella is so not funny.

"Lord," I pray to our heavenly father, "could you help anchor my traveling bra to remain in Iceland instead of scooting up to the North Pole?"

Defeated and flat, small bra in hibernation, twelve-year-old class was coming to an end. Not to worry; I'd be doing twelve-year-old class for a few years. How I knew it was the end of the year was not the changing of the weather, that happened every day, many times a day, but my teacher, Haukur. He had black-board spring fever and had stopped teaching. He wanted us to teach the class. He and I were getting tired of each other. I was tired of being called up to work math problems and he was tired of my not doing my homework and scoring poorly on geography and history exams. The difference, as I saw it, he was getting paid. It was his job to show examples and help us.

Math was a strong subject for me, and for weeks I'd gone from feeling proud for getting picked to teach it to indifferent to frustrated. Right now, I'd moved to refusal, a scary place.

"Edith, show us (again) how to add fractions with unlike denominators." Haukur leans back so far in his chair that something good might happen. He was a tall man with a square forehead and eyes set far apart. Like some insects, flies for example, he could see from both sides of his head. He always walked into the classroom reluctantly as if an invisible leash was pulling him back. His favorite time with us was silent reading. He sat in front of us and slept with his eyes open. We argued about this, but I held out that he was sleeping because his body twitched. He was counting the days he had left with us. "Well, three weeks, two days, and forty-five minutes and you are out of here." He said "you" are out of here. His heart said "I" will be out of here. Pronoun confusion.

Haukur's favorite topic of conversation was his fishing conquests. He knew every fish—skate, silver herring, monkfish—and when he ate it, he said he could tell what lake or ocean it came from. If the fish had spent time in the Irminger Current, which flowed from the south up along the westfjords, it had a slightly firmer, meatier, taste. Another question I pondered, who cares?

I said that I didn't understand fractions with unlike denominators. Before I could walk to the chalkboard to prove I didn't, the school nurse arrived. She walked from student to student and poured a spoonful of cod liver oil into our gaping mouths, reminding us not to touch the spoon. Here is something else I pondered. Here I am, sitting in twelve-year-old class wondering how many years I have to repeat it, worrying, fretting, breaking out in a sweat, and Nurse Lady pours a spoon of cod liver oil down my throat gagging me to death. I gag and fight back an urge to puke all over my desk. It always felt as though I would, but I never did. Drinking water afterwards didn't help. A Coke and chocolate Capri would. Kids should be given a choice whether to take cod liver oil or not. I'd take my chance with rickets instead of this daily torture.

When the nurse leaves, Haukur beckons me to come to the front. My suffering cheers him up. "Come on up. It will come back to you."

Every twelve and thirteen-year-old in the room is watching. In front of the chalkboard, chalk in one hand, book in the other, I feign concentration. Yes, Teacher Man, I know how to add and subtract with unlike denominators. But it's your job to teach it to the class. Facing Haukur, whose feet have come off his desk, "Sorry, I still don't remember."

"This is enough, start writing. Do problem sixteen." I copy the problem on the board. Haukur is standing and wants to know if I'm going to do the problem. Hesitating for a moment, feeling my heart race, I turn to him and tell him, "no."

Before I can duck, his hand, cracks across my face and red fluid squirts out of my nose over the floor and my green and white sweater. "Sit down!" the tone of his voice punctuates his feeling for me.

Instead of sitting down, I run out of the room and school to home. He must have popped a vein—a stream of blood is spilling down my throat into stomach. My fingers pinch the nostrils together, and I'm not eager to face the music mother will sing. When I repeat twelve-year-old class, can I request a different teacher? For both of our sakes, I hope so.

Pabbi is home for lunch. I yell "hi" and run up to my bedroom. Pabbi comes to the bottom of the stairs asking me why I am home early. I'm already in hot water; I go downstairs to fess up. He suggests we go to the kitchen and get some lunch. His face is taut, tapping his fingers, index to little finger, in a quick succession again and again while he listens. I tell him even the ugly part of my saying *no* to Haukur. We sit in silence. The big, strong father and his wayward daughter. Tick tack, tick tack, tick tack. Our clock is the only sound. I tell him I'm sorry. Tick tack, tick tack.

"It's not you who should be sorry."

"I shouldn't be sorry?" I ask. Is Pabbi OK?

"Although you should do what he tell you, he should not slap you."

That night, my parents went to meet with the principal and my teacher. Pabbi came back and said that Haukur went around the issue like a cat circling a bowl of hot soup. Haukur was to apologize in front of the class.

Well, it did and it didn't turn out that way. In front of the class he said that what happened shouldn't have, but that we all knew who was at fault. He looked right at me when he said it. The kids looked at one another confused. Vindication came the last week of school when the class elected me for the lead in the class play after Haukur suggested Þuríður.

Summer of '62 I got a job babysitting for two children, a seven-year-old boy and a four-year-old girl. It was a thirty-minute walk, longer if I took the bus. Riding the bus, I'd have to go downtown, switch buses, and still face an eight-to-ten-minute walk. Rún, the mother, said for me not to tell her husband when certain men called. She also said I'd find food in the refrigerator for their lunches.

"If Arnfinnur, Baldur, or Geir calls, you don't need to say anything about it to Oddur," her husband. She'd put them in alphabetical order. It helped me remember their names, but how do you respond to something like that? I wondered. "They are just friends," she continued. I was confused and uncomfortable. This was not a role I wanted to play, the role of a mis-informer.

"Tell my husband that they didn't leave a name. No, no, tell him that it was Sveina. She is a good friend of mine," she added. It seemed to me that she had a lot of friends. She also explained that I would not always know where she was. It was better that way. I moved from confused and uncomfortable to perplexed and stumped.

Mamma took off her glasses and listened with interest as I explained to her Rún's peculiar instructions. She said that a child should not be put in this position. She asked me a few question. Glasses back on her nose, she returned to peeling potatoes. "You just make sure that you take care of the children. Are there playgrounds near by?"

"Why do you think she is acting like that?" I asked.

She seemed reluctant to answer. Potatoes boiled on the stove. I heard kids outside yelling, "You're dead!"

"I think that Rún is seeing other men," she answered quietly.

"Why?"

"Well, it's hard to answer that. You should not answer the phone. Besides, you should be outside with the kids."

It was a rainy summer, so it turned out that I was inside to hear the phone ring. I didn't answer it. Oddur often asked where Rún was, and I told him truthfully that I didn't know.

At night my friends and I continued riding our bikes to Elliðisá or Vífilsstaðir Lake by the sanatorium where I stayed when I was eight and nine. I never went inside, not even to see Freyja or Vilhjálmur. Not knowing if they were still alive was better than knowing they weren't.

Summer days shortened, and first day of high school arrived. Occasionally, I'd reread my report card. Nothing changed. I had failed swimming. I didn't talk to anybody about it. Instead I waited for the fall assembly where 300 or so of us filed into the gym before our first day of class. Our names would be called by respective teachers and we would line up and leave with them. Summer night dreams became nightmares. Days ticked away. Ten days before the assembly became six days, four days, and then the day was here.

Mamma made me a pair of navy slacks and bought a pair of green stretch pants with elastic that went under the sole of the foot. I had a green and white sweater and a blue one to go with the pants she made. She seemed excited for me. Pabbi asked why the gloomy face. This was my problem, not theirs. If only it wasn't so embarrassing.

After praying to my brother above, I check in with our father above about swimming and getting into high school. What can I do? I ask. No answer. My ancestors practiced infanticide, the practice of drowning babies. But at thirteen, throwing me into Elliðs River wouldn't do the trick. It's too shallow.

I could go a-vikinging, except a millennium too late. This is when men went raiding villages in other countries for wealth and fame. Joining a circus was a possibility, but wrong country. Can they keep me in twelve-year-old class forever?

When the day arrived, it was cool with a mostly clear sky. Walking down Hólmgarður, I caught up with Valdís, a neighbor girl, and we walked up Réttarholt Road. Today I would learn if I was a high schooler or a repeat twelve-year-old grader. Our gym was packed, and the podium was filled with teachers and administrators. "Welcome, everyone. Welcome to Réttarholts High." My heart was loud, beating, "You flunked, you flunked." Everything was big: big gym, big windows, big student body. The first group was class A. This is where the kids with best grades would go. Jórunn and Stella were in grade A.

"Adam Helgason." Homeroom A teacher paused to give Adam a chance to come up to the podium. "Ari Jónsson, Erna Björnsdóttir," and on and on until thirty-two kids were on stage. Two names were called twice to no response. I was not called.

Class B, thirty-two kids, all present. I was not one of them. Drumming in my ears started. I didn't feel so well. There was more room in the gym, but under the circumstance, it was not a good thing.

Class C, I heard them call Hafdís Lútersdóttir. Several friends from 12-year-old class went up on stage. Since E as in Edith is in front of the alphabet, it didn't take long to hear that my name was not called.

Classes D, E, F, G, and H were called. Class H was mostly boys. I'd rather repeat 12-year-old class than be in the lowest classes. Even the classrooms of those grades were at the end of the far hall. From day one, the school said—"we don't want you here."

Finally, the gym was empty except for the principal still at the microphone, me and two boys. I recognized one, a fellow non-swimmer.

"Anyone not called, come to my office," the principal's announcement was a cruel joke. How could I tell my parents that I'd failed elementary school. My grades were OK. Actually, I did great in math, language, and religion. Shouldn't that count for something?

Like sheep led to slaughter, we followed. His office was stuffed, windowsill, chairs, and floor. He sat down; we didn't. His desk had raised panel sides that kept stacks of folders from sliding off. He removed a stack before he sat down so he could see us. If I let myself think about my predicament, I'd start boohooing, so I concentrated on stuff he'd surrounded himself with. Bookshelf behind him had geometry, geology, geography, and gospel books. Unlike Pabbi's books stacked in no particular order, his were in alphabetical order. He had pictures on his wall of graduating classes from 1959, when the school opened, 1960, and 1961.

"What are your names?" He sounded tired, wishing that we were already assigned to a class. We told him. "Edith Andersen," he said as he looked at the class lists. Silently, pencil in right hand, he scrolled down class lists counting how many girls, how many boys. He looked up at us and said, "None of you took the 200–meter test this summer. Is that correct?" Talking to himself, "C we have 32, 16 and 16. D, let's see. D. Thirty-four, that's not going to work. E." I was going to vomit. He can't be serious. I realized that I was not going to be sent back to twelve-year-old-class; instead I'd end up with the stupid kids.

"Edith, take this note to room 18, class E. There is room for a girl there."

I found my voice. "My grades are good. I can go home and get my report card." I couldn't come out and say— don't make me go to class E. I will be humiliated beyond anything I'd ever experienced. But he knew what I was getting at.

"All the classes are full."

I took the note and left. Doors to classrooms were open. It wasn't my imagination, but as I walked past A, B, C, down, down, the cheerful sounds became more muted. When I came to the open door of my room, only the teacher, Gunnar, was talking.

Two-thirds of the class was boys. I didn't know a single kid. I couldn't even remember seeing them before. Gunnar pointed to a seat, "Sit there."

Back home, Stella was on the phone. Measuring coffee grounds into the pot, I realized that as far as my family goes, they'd never ask what class I was in so there was nothing more to face. Nothing more to face, except two years of going to school with retards, retards who all managed to learn how to swim.

# Chapter 12

## High School Freshman and Confirmation

*This chapter is about low expectations, a homely girl, and the rite of passage—1962 to 1963.*

M y first year in high school is coming to an end. One of my school friends, Anna, is in class A and another, Birna is in C, so our ways have parted. In E I hang around with a girl, Áslaug, who lives in a single-dwelling home on the other side of the *hitaveitustokk*. This is a three-foot high cement enclosure that runs east and west for miles delivering geothermal energy to homes.

Academic expectations are low for class E. When teachers walk in, they toss their briefcase on the desk and some sit down with legs stretched on top of the desk. Kristinn and Einar, religion and biology teachers, like us kids and earn their pay. In high school teachers change classrooms, not students. Our halls remain in good order.

Although I seldom raise my hand, I am often called on to answer or explain. My attitude is south of sunny. Except for

Kristinn and Einar, my teachers are full of themselves and make fun of many of my classmates, usually the boys. Right to their face, they make comments like, "Siggi, no one will accuse you of being the brightest light bulb in Réttarholt's gymnasium," or "Jón, you take underachieving to a new low." Why don't they stick up for themselves? This is so unfair.

Some teachers don't bother opening their briefcases. Some of them make Haukur look good. Instead, they have us take turns reading out of our textbooks. On good days they ask questions to check our comprehension. There have not been many good days in my freshman year.

Áslaug is smart and conscientious, struggles with reading, but is good in math, physical education, craft, and cooking class. She worries continually about being called on to read. "Who wants to read?" they ask, and Áslaug rummages through her schoolbag like she's searching for a long-lost friend.

At Christmas Mamma and Pabbi gave me a dark-brown leather schoolbag with a key. In March, at a family party, I heard Pabbi joke about how they'd given me a schoolbag with a lock and that I'd never asked for the key. Funny thing is, last year it was true. But this year, studying with Áslaug who is determined to do well in school, I spent a goodly amount of time getting books in and out of it. Even so, my interest in school had moved to Norway to be with Old Mrs. Dýrset. If not for Kristinn and Einar, it would have been unbearable. I found our neighborhood library more informative than school was and the librarians left me alone.

In school, bored to tears, I rest my elbows on my desk and place my face in the palms of my hands. I watch the second hand on the clock, click, click, click.

"Edith, sit up and quit looking at the clock."

"I'm just seeing what time it is," I give a surprised look as in, why can't a gal see what time it is?

"Look at the watch on your wrist."

"I do, Then I compare the times. Right now there is a sixteen-second discrepancy." I keep the why are you jumping all over me look on my face. It's a look they have not acquired fondness for.

Twice I'm told to leave the classroom after pointing out that the teacher was wrong. My Danish teacher is a weak-looking man whose mouth works up and down before any sound, Icelandic or Danish, comes out of his mouth. After a back-and-forth discussion between the two of us—a disagreement on Danish grammar—without a hint of authority in his voice, "Edith, if you insist that I'm wrong ..."

"I want my classmates to have the correct information. That's all," I tell him. When your teacher looks afraid of you, it's hard to respect him. He moves around the room, clenching and opening his hands repeatedly as though he is trying to resolve some internal struggle.

"Well, you're wrong. If you don't like my teaching, be my guest, leave."

OK, I think to myself, I don't like his teaching. He is wrong, so I'll be his guest. I get up and walk to the door.

"Edith, please sit down. I've had enough of this."

I turn to him and say ever so politely, "You are sending me mixed signals. Teachers should not do that to their students." My classmates clap and cheer. I close the classroom door behind me. Alone, I'm not brave. I can't believe I'd actually walked out of the room even after a teacher told me to sit back down. My rudeness—my arm pits, small stinky puddles—I'd pushed it too far. It is one thing to put on a show for my classmates; it is another to explain it to my parents.

For a few nights, nightmares deprive me of rest. Ghosts weaving up, down, under and over the ceiling beams whispered in Danish, "Du har skam gennemstegt sig nu," (Now you've really done it.) My Danish teacher says nothing about it and never asks me to be his guest again. From then on he ignores my hand waving in the air eager to make a comment on yet another Danish grammar rule mistake.

In math class, I am told to move my desk to the front row for *incessant* talking, a big word for my math teacher. We talk because we are bored. When I share this with my teacher, his face turns deep red, his body shakes and his ears quiver. We'd had other encounters, but this time heat had joined our encounter. With his hot magenta cheeks—I remembered that from my Crayola box—he was like Custer surrounded by Indians in many colors. He has to take a stand. He does. "Get the hell out of my room."

In the midst of adjusting to high school, confirmation neared. My last Christian rite was my baptism with Jóhanna and Ceasar Mar as my godparents. My baptismal gown, worn by all my siblings, must have been threadbare. Time and time again, Mamma dressed her babies in the christening dress, removed it, cleaned it, boxed it, stored it, thinking that this was the last one. Time and time again, she got more use out of it. When she was forty-three, she'd stopped menstruating. When I first heard this story, before Labba's sex education, it was endearing. Things change.

Anyway, after quickening within, Mamma went to the doctor who confirmed she was pregnant. What follows in my imagination is this. Elated with the happy news, after a dinner of *buff*, fried potatoes, and homemade ice cream, she announces the news to my family. Pabbi's eyes fill with tears, hugging Mamma he whispers, "I hope it's a girl." My siblings are ecstatic in their anticipation for their little angel sibling to arrive. "Let Our Joyful Voices Rise" plays on the radio while in the distance one can hear clacking of storks as they fight for the right to deliver me.

My imagination, fertile ground for romantic endings, had little in common with what happened. In reality—Mamma accepted this news as one would accept constipation after eating a pound of cheese for three consecutive days. She told Pabbi the news in a middle of chopped sentence, "I need money for groceries, I'm pregnant. More coffee?" Pabbi wanted more coffee, and fourteen years later his youngest is returning to the church to promise to live a Christian life.

April 20, 1963, I wake up to the biggest day of my life, confirmation day. Catechism classes had ended and daylight lengthened. Thick clouds stagger across the sky. Mr. Weatherman has forecasted a north wind, a change from the easterlies. On maps in books, the north wind is portrayed by a plumped-cheeked man with tasseled hair and strained expression blowing as hard as he can. North winds from Antarctica or Greenland can bring large icebergs with polar bears to Iceland's northern shores. Yesterday on the news, Búðardal (Camp Valley) seated on the base of the westfjords, which is close to where Erik the Red used to live, was hit with a snow storm. Several sheep had fallen into a lake and drowned. Poor things. Knowing how to swim doesn't help in glacier water.

Our weather is unpredictable, changing its mind sometimes hourly, making forecasting more of prediction than science. If not for my trips to Scotland and Denmark, and American movies, I'd think this weather fickleness normal, not just Iceland normal. Today the weatherman promises 8°C (46° F)degrees, light winds, and only a slight chance of rain. Wanting to check it out for myself, I make my way downstairs. Standing on the front patio in my blue bathrobe, goose bumps pop up; the wind feels cold. Come on, Mr. Wind, control your temper today. My hair is asking.

Christening accepts you into the community of Christians, Lutherans. Confirmation marks our transition into adulthood. Today, after months of catechism classes with our minister, Gunnar Árnason, thirty-five of us, twelve girls and twenty-three boys, voluntarily join the church, promising to live a Christian life. The service is at 10:30 a.m., in our four-months-old new church.

Kópavogschurch is an unusual looking church. It has tall arches, one above the other, with stained-glass windows—art and religion joining. This house of God stands alone on Borgarholt (City Hill), an elevated pile of rocks, offering a view of heaven, earth, and as far as the eye can see over Reykjavik, Kópavogur, and the Atlantic Ocean.

Our family is not a church-going family. My nieces and nephews were baptized at our apartment. We attend church for confirmations, weddings, and funerals. We listen to Sunday mass on the radio and never, never turn off the radio if our national anthem is playing. The National Radio ends every day with "O, God of Our Land."

Our country's God! Our country's God!
We worship Thy name in its wonder sublime.
The suns of the heavens are set in Thy crown
By Thy legions, the ages of time!
With Thee is each day as a thousand years,
Each thousand of years, but a day,
Eternity's flow'r, with its homage of tears,
That reverently passes away.
Iceland's thousand years!
Eternity's flow'r, with its homage of tears,
That reverently passes away.

Many nights I dive for the radio, come up short, and stand there waiting for it to finish.

In addition to spending months learning about Luther, *Séra* Gunnar had us memorize the Ten Commandments, the Apostles' Creed, and our national anthem. We knew the Lord's Prayer. We read and discussed the New Testament. Since we had religion classes in every grade, much of the time was spent discussing the Bible. Gunnar asked us questions and encouraged us to ask him. No matter what you asked, he answered seriously and thoughtfully.

"Why did Jesus get tempted by the devil?" I asked him.

"Tsk, tsk," from one of the Jóns—there were three of them.

"He had temptations like you and me. Like you and me, we must recognize and guard against them."

One of the Jón's wanted to know what the wine tasted like. Before he could answer, the kids laughed, saying he probably already knew. Unfazed, he asked if it was possible to make wine out of water.

I raised my hand. "How did he walk on water?" This made no sense to me, and I wanted an explanation that satisfied me. Walking on water sure would make swimming obsolete.

*Séra* Gunnar said that Jesus did many miracles, and this was one that he could not explain. Too bad.

"Is the Bible true? Did those stories really happen and can we prove it?" It was rare for Sigurður to ask, and Gunnar raised his hands again to quiet us. As I had, he'd noticed that Sigurður was a loner who kept thoughts to himself.

"The Bible is not a science book. The stories are not experiments we can reproduce. It is a guide for us to live by. We don't take it literally but focus on the spirit of the message. Treat others as you wish to be treated. In this way we live in harmony with others, and, equally important, with ourselves."

Sigurður listened intently. He wore a grubby sweater, a jacket that should have been given a proper funeral years ago, and shoes—that were strangers to a cleaning rag or polish. He was tall, thin with green eyes and a pale complexion; might have been a tenth-generation Celt. He avoided eye-contact and had a nervous habit of rubbing the back of his neck—feeling for axe scars? A premonition? He was the kind of kid that descendants of Norwegian earls like to pounce on. He was unlikely to mistreat anyone except himself.

Asking *Séra* Gunnar about the baby business crossed my mind. But embarrassment is a formidable gate, hard to open, harder to climb.

Although some of Gunnar's explanations failed to reach consensus with my previous knowledge, I believed that he was a man of no spiritual doubt. Walking home from classes, I wondered what it felt like to be so sure that when now the story is told, the end of life, you believe in your body, soul, and mind, that Jesus would be standing at the Pearly Gates. Mamma said that people who expected life after death were greedy, wanting more and more. This life was all there was. So why baptize and confirm? Pabbi's view rested on the other side of the *krónur*. He believed in the afterlife. The two of them must have agreed to disagree and never talk about it. *Séra* Gunnar left me thinking that there was another way to believe in God. He knew the way. I'd have to find it for myself.

I close the front door behind me and head upstairs. Draped over a hanger—twice I mistook it for Mrs. Dýrsetdangling from a beam—is a light blue dress with white lace, knee length, fitted at the waist. Mamma selected the pattern. She let me pick out my headband, covered in white lace. I hoped Jórunn would curl my hair then let it drape over my shoulders. That would look really good. My white Italian shoes are my first high heels. I've spent days practicing walking in them. Mamma is holding on to my white lacy handkerchief, the white cotton gloves, and the New Testament with gold lettering. She says, "Just in case." She means that in my possession things happen.

Since our celebration is catered, the apartment doesn't have the typical before party smell of delicious food, but as the morning progresses, excitement moves in. Flurry of activity centers around Jórunn, who is doing everyone's hair. Stella's thick hair takes forever to dry. Mamma is getting her hair colored, trimmed, and set. It is hard for her to sit under the hairdryer, too many things to attend to. Finally, Jórunn does my hair.

"Sit up straight," she orders. She'd brought her scissors from the beauty shop. A few weeks earlier she told Mamma that she wanted to quit doing hair. Chemicals in the perm solutions and the hair tint caused her hands to break out in eczema. Mamma said, "no."

"Cut her bangs short so you are not redoing it at every sun-rise." Mamma, a woman of few words— sometimes the few were too many. My hope is that Jórunn, who seems unusually stressed for a bride, will have pity on me. Come on, Jórunn, no short bangs. My eyes plead for mercy.

Snip, snap, the clicking of the scissors sends a chill down my curve-less body. There is no mirror in front of me, but the cold metal high on my forehead tells all. Many suns will set before my bangs greet my eyebrows. My face is now a full moon with a Prince Valiant haircut.

"I'm going to pull your hair up over the headband."

"I want it down."

"You'll see. You will like it." She is determined to do it her way.

Standing in front of the bathroom mirror, a beautiful water-fall does not come to mind. What does, is an ugly fish wearing high heals walking on rocks in Elliðsá. For the rest of the day, I decide, I will not look in the mirror.

Jórunn had suggested that we join our celebrations. It would be cheaper, she'd reasoned. It made sense to Mamma. In decisions regarding confirmations and weddings, Pabbi's role was to agree with Mamma and hand over money. He did well on the first. For her wedding dress, Jórunn bought off-white Chinese silk, and Gunna sewed and refused to accept money. Jórunn's last fitting, two weeks ago, her wedding dress fit. Now, on her wedding day, it is a little tight—the four–month fetus is growing. Jórunn borrowed a puffy layered veil from a friend, which was whiter than the dress, but you could hardly tell. Jórunn kept holding the two to the light, looking for the difference. It's baffling how people look for what they don't want to see.

Valli, who coached Iceland's girls' basketball team at Valhöll, a local community center, helped Mamma secure the hall for the evening. She hired a harmonica player and kitchen staff.

Dressing for church, I notice that my nylons are scratchy and the garter belt confining. My bangs have not grown in the last hour or so. In front of the hall mirror, already forgetting my resolution not to look, I can see that the expense and time to make me look nice on this most important day in my life has not paid off.

Coming down the stairs, Stella greets me, "Hey, Suðurland-sbraut, what's up?" Suðurlandsbraut is the straightest road in Reykjavík.

By the time we leave for church, I spill coffee that landed on the bottom of my hem, now a stain. Not an inconspicuous stain, but one in front like a trade-mark for a girl who is prone

to last–minute mishaps. I also forgot to clean and cut my finger nails. I'll just clench my hands into fists. Adulthood, here I
come!

Adda calls to say that she and Valli are running late and
will meet us at the church. They'd bought a car this year, so
Pabbi doesn't have to pick them up. "Tell Jórunn," she says,
"that I'll have her do my hair this afternoon." She makes it
sound like she is doing Jórunn a favor. The wedding ceremony
will be in the late afternoon. Villi, Ásta, and their families take
cabs. Except for Ágústa Bragadóttir, Ásta's new baby born last
year, the grandkids attend church both times and come to the
reception.

Last night Mamma told Pabbi that Ásta was pregnant
again. When I thought about my sister, it didn't seem possible.
She was so thin. Her clothes looked like laundry hanging on
a clothesline. Mamma was of the general opinion that her
daughters had babies too young. She was twenty-seven years
old when Adda was born. Mamma didn't want Ásta in particular to have more children. She said that she didn't have the
temperament or health for it. It's true she was often annoyed
with people. Life was seldom good to this sister and she not
to it.

Mr. North Wind has left and now the winds twirl around
and feel like they are coming from every direction. Overcast
skies prevail, reminding me of the stain on my hem. When we
get to the church, the parking lot is busy. Civility prevails and
people take turns getting inside the church. Kópavogs Church
seats 400 people, more than half already taken.

Confirmation kids are herded into a back room for our white
*fermingarkyrtla* (confirmation robes). We wait for people to
be seated and musicians to begin. Our organist is a woman
with brown hair in braided circle with a flat black cap pinned
to her hair. She is wearing one of Iceland's national costumes,
*upphlutur*. It's a black dress with a tight sleeveless vest laced
together through fancy gold eyelets. The top has wide straps
over the shoulders and a silk shirt with long sleeves. Bottom

edges of her skirt is decorated with metal-thread embroidery, silver gilded filigree. She looks beautiful.

Today, I want to look beautiful. I want to look like the girls in the magazines, their hair cascading around their faces, unblemished skin, and white teeth. Mirror, mirror, on the wall, who is the fairest of them all? Hall mirror chuckles.

Alphabetically by first name, we line up in the foyer waiting to walk down the aisle. Aroma of candles, fragrance of flowers, smell of new clothes mix with the wood puts me in a quieter frame of mind. Earlier busyness fades. Angelic sound of the choir reaches into every corner of the church. A spiritual hush comes over us, the kind of peace Gunnar talked to us about. He told us that real peace is not a quiet house or a quiet street, but the space inside you. When you have it, you will know it. In this moment, all that matters is this moment. This is what he meant. The good feeling that envelops me is hard to explain. It is as he would say, peace that surpasses understanding.

From the entrance hall, I watch *Séra* Gunnar at the altar. He's wearing his black vestment and the white of ruff around his neck. Procession will commence on his signal.

Finally, he looks towards his flock and nods. Like a wave, hymns from the organ replace the choir, touching every person, window, and pew. Coughing, shuffling of feet, and fidgeting stop. Our families watch us, one white robe after another demurely, angels with clean faces, fresh haircuts, pure of mind and body. I smile at my parents and they smile back.

From a high wooden pulpit, *Séra* Gunnar talks about our baptism when we became a member of the church. "Today you are not brought to the altar by loved ones. Today you affirm for yourselves the faith into which you were baptized and your intention to live a life of responsible and committed discipleship." Looking at our families, he continues, "They have completed their confirmation ministry," pauses and adds, "successfully." Family members chuckle.

"Confirmation is a church rite developed historically in the life of the church. The Lord has not told us we must do so.

There are no directives for it in the Bible. It is a rite of passage. Today they come before you, their family, the church and God, a transition from childhood to adults, and give their oath to honor and continue to make Christ a part of their lives."

To feel God's presence every day, as I feel it at this moment, is there anything better than that? Are there Lutheran nuns? My paternal grandmother prayed that my father would become a priest. Maybe I'd be the answer to her prayers. Also, nuns' habits, loose white or brown gowns, would suit me well. If I couldn't be a nun, I could be a priest. At this moment it is as clear to me that to live in harmony with the sky, clouds, stars, people, and animals made life a wondrous existence.

At the altar Gunnar lays his hand on my head, "Edith, God has called you by name and made you his own. Defend, O Lord, your servants with your heavenly grace, that she may continue yours forever, and daily increase in your Holy Spirit more and more until she comes to your everlasting kingdom. Amen."

Back home, I feel older, more grown up. Mamma puts out *skyr*, cheese, liverwurst, and dark rye bread. She lights a cigarette as she waits for the coffee. Jórunn is messing with her veil, moving it around on top of her head to find the most flattering spot. Stella has disappeared, probably reading, while I pace the floor trying to get back the church feeling. Instead all I can think about are my presents. What kind of nun or priest am I going to be if all I think about are gifts?

Jórunn has her wedding gown on when Adda shows up to get her hair done. She looks upset but doesn't say anything. Maybe she's not in the mood to do hair. Wearing your wedding gown might do that to a person. Pinning the veil on her head, Jórunn is ready to get married.

Walls at Valhöll, the place of our receptions, have paneling two-thirds of the way up; the rest is painted white. Pictures of people playing soccer and handball adorn the walls, trophies and wall lamps by every window. Tables, decorated with a small vase holding two white flowers, are arranged along the walls leaving an opening for dancing. Tonight Pabbi and I will

dance together. Next to the door gifts and cards are piled up on a small table. Yeah! Jórunn and I will sort them out later.

Dinner is chicken and potatoes. Pabbi and Mamma laugh, dance, socialize. Gunna wears a black fitted dress, cut low in the back. She looks like a movie star. Ævar, with an Elvis Presley hairstyle, wears a brand new suit with a bow tie and a white fluffy handkerchief. My nieces and nephews look cute in their Easter clothes. At the wedding church service, Gústi Valgeirsson, who is almost three, told his mother, "Let's go home. This is a boring movie. Jórunn is in it." His boredom now forgotten, he, Stjáni, and Sigrún, hold hands and dance together until they hear the word *cake*.

Mamma's siblings talk to me and tell me how pretty I look. It's hard for me to say thank you because it's not true. Aunt Inga, who has the most money, wears a short mink coat. Aunt Margrét, whose hair has grown back from her brain surgery, sits at a table with her children and husband, Leifur. Aunt Margrét is so kind and the only one of my aunts who hugs me. Sigga and Pétur sit close to our table, and Magnús and Helga share a table with their children. Aunt Magnea, the apostle, and her daughters, Dísa and Unna, sit together. Unna is married, and she and her husband, Helgi, look better than Elizabeth Taylor and Richard Burton. Seriously. Everybody thinks so.

Throughout the night Icelandic songs and foreign music play. Jórunn likes Elvis Presley, and Stella's favorite group is the Beatles. She says Beatles means bugs. Right! Sure!

My confirmation celebration turns out to be a perfect night. Everyone feels it I'm sure. I forget about my looks and stop clenching my hands to hide dirty nails except when Mamma is in sight. She says you can tell a lot about people by how they take care of their clothes and nails.

Back home, we are exhausted. Pabbi suggests I wait to open my gifts, but his eyes are laughing. Money in cards is nice, especially since Mamma says I could keep it for myself. Aunt Sigga got me a book. Aunt Inga gave me pink baby doll pajamas. She must have bought them overseas. They are the

cutest pajamas I've ever had, almost too cute to sleep in. Adda gives me a diary with a lock. Then I get more pajamas and more pajamas. After my fifth gift of pajamas, Mamma suggests I return some of them.

"You don't sleep enough to keep all of them," Pabbi kids.

"Why is everyone giving me pajamas?" I ask anyone willing to speculate, "Do I look sleepy?"

Pabbi laughs and Mamma offers, "It's a popular gift to give."

After unwrapping the last baby doll pajamas, which no longer look all that cute, Mamma says, "Your gift from us is in your bedroom."

Their gift is a dark oak desk with a matching chair. "It's beautiful. Wow! I can't believe it." It is the most handsome pieces of furniture I've ever owned. It's the only furniture I own. It fits perfectly in the alcove in my bedroom across from the divan. For sure this will catapult me to become a serious student. A gift like this is a premonition. Mamma knew that I was at the cusp of my education decision. One more year and mandatory education is complete. This is the incentive I need to become a serious student. I will be. For sure. I will make her proud. She would never learn about class E.

# Chapter 13

## High School Sophomore and Sisters

*This chapter is about what to do with Stella, I'm all wet, and fish—1963 to 1964.*

Come flurry or fog, hail or gale, rainbow or northern lights, our home is like the Grand Central Station in Glasgow, people coming and going. Adda comes home every Sunday with her kids, Ásta and Gunna less frequently. Then there are our friends, grandkids, sewing clubs and card parties.

Every Saturday I wake up to the smell of baking and coffee. Preparing for Sunday's company, Mamma bakes pound cakes, one with raisins and the other a marble cake in which she puts cocoa in half of the batter. On occasion Mamma makes a plain pound cake with six eggs and almond extract that melts in your mouth. However, eggs are expensive, so it is mostly raisin and marble cakes. By lunch on Monday, I'm eating end pieces, licking my fingers to scoop up the crumbs. During the week Mamma makes crepes for visiting grandkids or sends me to the dairy store for a four-layer cake with jam and glaze on top.

Stella has finished her mandatory two years in high school and now works in a dairy store. Mamma's hopes for this daughter are loftier than for her to become a professional dairy store clerk. But what? Stella, with more time on her hands, continues to push the limits of Mamma's patience, making the decision of what to do with Stella urgent.

In many ways Stella takes after Pabbi. She loves animals, music, reading, and spending time with friends. She's inherited Pabbi's temperament, takes teasing well but is not timid to give it right back. She has thick brown hair but has been spared inheriting his white ear tufts and gray nose hair. Their eyes are the color of *steindepla* flowers (rock speedwell), set above high cheekbones.Acne and illnesses have let her be. She sleeps generously and plays with abandonment. Unlike Jórunn, who prepares for tomorrow, Stella lives for the moment.

Three things put Stella in a bad mood. First, having to get out of bed in the morning. Second, being accused of wearing my shoes. Since her feet were wider, this stretched out my shoes—something that puts me in a bad mood.Third, my parents' insisting that she follow the rules about limiting phone use. She is outspoken about this injustice.They draw a line in the sand, she straggles it.The urgency of what to do with Stella increases.

On this subject, Stella tells Mamma she wants to be a nurse. In fact, she has checked this out. "For the first two years, I'll take classes and for the clinical part that takes one year, I'll be sent into the countryside." She's just read *Congo Nurse*. Stella has plans to nurse people farther away than the Icelandic countryside.

Learning is easy for Stella, who competed with Jórunn when they were both at the same school. She is not a steady-as-you-go student; instead she does things at the last minute, crams for tests. She claims it saves time and you can retain new information for twenty-four hours. In high school for a particularly onerous history test, she was up most of the night.Through two thin bedroom doors, I heard, "1241 Snorri

Sturtluson murdered, 1362 volcanic eruption in Öræfa Glacier, 1402 the Great Plague ..." I didn't have a restful sleep. Back home from school, she was disgusted. It turned out that her history teacher was out sick and her newly born knowledge would expire before he returned.

"Adda didn't finish her nursing program. I am not going down that road with you." That was Mamma's answer to this aspiration. There are some battles with Mamma that you just know you are not going to win. It's in her voice, her posture, her glasses removed, one hand on hip, the other on the kitchen counter. She is like a fort, the moat, the cavalry, and you are just a country goat. You stand a better chance of counting the stars in the sky twice and coming up with the same number.

So in '63 when Stella's friends Anna and Jenny, signed up for a summer program at Greyland College in Isle of Wight, Mamma had an idea. Mamma decided that Stella would go there not for a summer but for a year so she could learn English and increase her marketability for an office job.

Secretarial work was a new idea for Stella. She'd never even thought about it. She might have put up a fight for nursing school, even if she knew it to be futile, except the idea of going overseas with two good friends had an appeal to my sister's sense of adventure.

The day she left Mamma warned her not to talk to strangers, especially men from Eastern countries. "They kidnap young Scandinavian girls and sell them into slavery."

After Stella leaves Mamma takes a job working in the laundry room at a summer place, Silungarpoll (Trout Pond) for children from "dysfunctional homes." That is a fancy phrase for alcoholic parents. She tells us the night before she leaves. Pabbi will take care of the house, with Jórunn helping with dinners and doing our laundry.

With Stella gone Gunna and Villi hire me for evening babysitting. Babysitting my brother's kids has perks and pays well. Gunna always gets Áslaug and me Coke and other treats. Jens, almost seven, plays soccer outside the apartment house.

Sigrún, almost two, is adorable. She has an impish face like her father's, snub nose, and pale, almost translucent, skin. Gunna keeps Sigrún's blond hair short and clothes comfortable, fitting for a toddler who has enough energy for three babysitters. She's walking great except for up and down stairs. Stína, in the middle, has soulful eyes and silky dark-brown hair. She is more serious and bossy and informs me of any wrong doings Jens makes or is thinking of making. Unlike most kids, she looks at you when you talk to her as though she really wants to understand everything you say. This is interesting because "do you want milk" or "it's time for bed," is just not that interesting no matter what your age.

Magga, from Hólmgarður 22, and I, lunch pack in hand, take the 7:30 morning bus to Torg and walk the rest of the way. We work at a fish factory on the west side of town, close to the ocean. Actually, everything is close to the Atlantic Ocean. We wear heavy-duty vinyl aprons and knee-high black boots stored next to the punch clock. At first the smell is unbearable. After a few weeks, you wonder what all the fuss is about. Taking the bus back home, I go to the back and, like Moses parting the Red Sea, people scramble to get out of our way. Money doesn't smell. Mamma's words. At home Jórunn bellyaches about my leaving my fish clothes in the kitchen.

Fourteen-year-olds get 20.30 *krónur* an hour. Our union is trying to get a 7.5% pay increase. Also, women who clean and gut the fish receive 91 *aura* less an hour than men doing the same work. This is plain wrong. When fishing is good, we work 50 and 60 hours a week. With Mamma away, Pabbi lets me keep more of the money than Mamma would have done.

After stacking fish on shelves for a few weeks, they send me to the warehouse where the trucks dump fish right off the boats. Our boss in the warehouse is a big man with a large red nose that drips continually. He's about fifty years old with brown hair and coarse beard streaked with gray. He hovers over us like a black crow hunting.

My tool, aka machete, is sharp as the fins on an ocean perch. My back faces the large doors that roll up for the trucks to back in and unload the fish. When you hear them open, you steady yourself, balance equally on both legs so the hundreds of fish sliding down behind you don't take you down with them. Reaching behind me with my left hand, I grab a fish by its eye sockets and swing it onto my wood horse. Pressing the machete on the neck under the gills, I slide it back and forth. Decapitated bodies glide down in front of me, and I toss the head into a pile of plaice, cod, haddock, ocean perch, and halibut heads. None of the fish is attractive, but some are uglier than sin. Monkfish comes to mind. Eels come close to pulling my arm out of the socket. You start working fast, especially with Boss Man buzzing: bend, grab, swing, swish. Bend, grab, swing, swish. Then, bend, ouch!, no swing. By the end of the day, fish slime is in your hair, ears, and nostrils.

Some of us don't last long in this warehouse. It is a challenge to keep up, and the fish just keep coming. Going to the bathroom, just getting out of the warehouse is treacherous. But I like it. I like the challenge of keeping the wheelbarrow men busy, picking up my pile of headless sea creatures.

Geir, a kid my age, has worked with me for a while. We make each other laugh. Knowing he's there makes the time go faster. However, after a while, I know he won't last long. I tell him to pick up his pace. If I could have kicked some of my headless fish his way, I would have. When you kick a slimy fish, you know what happens? Nothing. That's what happens. Geir's movements remind me of a ship dragging an anchor. One Monday drippy nose Boss Man yells, "Geir, I'm moving you into the salt room!"

Jórunn's baby is expected at the end of September. She is working at the beauty shop and finishing classes at a community college required for her occupation as a hairdresser. Instead of attending classes—no time she says—she picks up the books and studies at home. For her final semester, she has to take Icelandic, drawing, and math. She flunks math. She has never failed in anything before. You'd think the sky was falling. She found out that they gave her a math book for the wrong class—an advanced class. Now with the correct textbook, she stays up way late to study. She is taking this education thing way too far. Her poor fetus must be anxious to get out. Then one night she went into my room and borrows a notebook, I am livid.

"Can't I have some privacy in this house?" I tremble with indignation. I am so angry that I yell and don't care who hears me. I am sick of Mamma's being gone all the time. I am angry that Stella left. I am sick of Pabbi sticking up for Jórunn. And I am sick of waiting for my breasts to grow and periods to start.

"Jórunn has an important math test. You know that. She just borrowed a few pages," Pabbi reasons with me.

"I'm sick of her! Other people around here work too. I take the bus every day to spend the day decapitating fish. That's not fun you know." Actually, it is. "When I wait at the bus stop, it's not to go to a party. I spend ten hours up to my neck in slimy fish. But I don't act like a Debbie Downer at her own funeral."

Pabbi taps his fingers. After my tirade the only sound in the apartment is the weatherman reporting how many tons of fish ships have brought in. Jórunn continues washing the dishes. They act as though I'm not really here. I storm upstairs to my bedroom at a loss for what to do. There is something wrong with this family.

Ævar works out in the country but lives with us when he is in town. Interestingly, when he's home, Jórunn finds time to waste with him. What about all the schoolwork worries then? Give me a break!

Mamma comes back from Silungarpoll. Thank God. School starts. Jórunn looks like a petite hippo. Adda finds a job working for an architect. She's still at Lokastígur, still hoping to move. The extra money pays to fix up her apartment. Now Kata has a bedroom upstairs, and their bathroom has been renovated. Old Katrín believes that the sun rises and sets with her grandchildren. Mamma goes on and on about what a good student Kata is. OK, I get it people. Let it go. When I see the bathroom that Adda and Mamma have talked about ad nauseam, I'm disappointed. It's still outside their apartment across a freezing hall.

Gunna visits. Two minutes after she sits on the kitchen bench, she's says, "Well, I better get a move on."

Mamma continues to sing praises for her daughter-in-law, something she spares us from. Her only complaint is that Gunna's dining room chair cushions are stained. She makes no more comments about Adda's hugging her kids too much, but now comments that her kitchen could be tidier. Napping after lunch at Adda's house, closer to his work, Pabbi is content with her house in any shape.

"Ásta *mín*" as Mamma refers to her, "is awfully thin." Pabbi visits her, bringing treats and clothes for the kids. Her husband, Bragi, goliath in size with mammoth hands and feet, tells gross jokes when my parents can't hear. It embarrasses my sister. I'm sure that's why we she's an infrequent visitor. Mamma is surprised when I suggest this and dismisses it. "Ásta has her hands full with two toddlers and one more on the way. Let's hope it's her last." She must have been thinking about my Bragi comment when she adds, "Bragi is a hard worker. Cement work and fishing are not an easy way to put food on the table."

After Pabbi sold his part of Gúmmibarðinn in 1958, he opened a small place at the intersection of Rauðarásstíg and Skúlagata. He got some new city contracts repairing tires on huge utility vehicles. I visit him when I'm in town and watch him work. It's hard for us to hear each other because the machinery is so loud. He likes being his own boss but is a reluctant bill collector. For a while, he has me go around to different city offices to remind them that their bills are past due. It is boring, and my success is not discussed at the dinner table. Perhaps I've inherited his reluctance. With Valli's help and new stationery, he extends his business, importing tires from England.

"September 15th (1963), dry weather and mostly clear conditions prevail in the north. The Westfjords and Húnaflói, significant snow, and temperature around frost mark. A cold breeze in the north-east, with slightly warmer conditions in the valleys. Öxnadalsheiði (a mountain range) is not passable for small cars. The weather Bureau advises drivers on ..."

I turn off the radio. Reykjavik's weather is about 7°C (45°F), cloudy and dry. Uninteresting. Pabbi and Mamma are visiting Sigga and Pétur. Hafdís and I play cards, *Russian*, at the kitchen table. We are no kindred spirits but hang out when no better alternatives exist. Constant hacking from downstairs ceased when her father passed away. Recently a large crashing sound from downstairs brought about some creative explanations in the Andersen household. Our guesses were way off. What happened is that her ample sister, Stína, while resting her leg in the bathroom sink shaving—,the sink caved. Mamma said it wasn't funny. Now it's just Hafdís and Lovísa living downstairs.

"Edith," it's Jórunn calling. Instead of ignoring her or making her call a few more times, as I normally do, the tone of her voice is different, urgent, so off I go.

"Where are you?" I call out and tell Hafdís to stay put.

Jórunn is laying in Mamma and Pabbi's bed—unusual—white as a ghost.

"I'm all wet," she looks scared and confused.

"You wet the bed?" This is not good. Jórunn is in our parents' bed and has peed in it? I yell down the hall towards the kitchen, "Hafdís, you have to leave. I'll see you tomorrow."

Looking at each other, we wait for Hafdís's steps on the demon stairs to fade.

"Are you OK?" I ask.

"No, it really hurts," my eighteen–year–old sister says quietly. She lifts the duvet and indeed her gown is drenched and the sheet and mattress likewise. Her eyes plead for me to help.

Quite simply, she looks terrible. She is going to die. I know this. I also know that like Mamma, she'll do it quietly not wanting to bring attention to herself. Freckles across the bridge of her nose look dark against her ashen face. I remember how beautiful she looked, just months ago, going to a dance with Ævar. She was wearing a tight green dress, her thick hair teased and twisted behind her head into a French twist fastened with bobby pins. It was a hairstyle that could withstand winds up to 20 miles per hour. She had on her dress coat and a silk scarf. She looked like a fairy tale princess. From the hall window, I saw Ævar open the cab door for her. Eager to be off, he closed the door—too soon. So instead of scooting into the cab, she turned back to the house with one hand cupped around the bleeding fingers caught in the door jam.

Then there was the time she took me to Nautholtsvík Beach and all the fun times we had as kids, horsing around sitting on each other tickling until the confinee pleaded for mercy. Sitting on top, we'd open our mouth swirling spit around threatening to let it drop unless the confined party pleaded saying please, please and whatever else we wanted her to say. Right now, more than anything, I didn't want her to die. I remembered Jónína. My stomach does flips, something my body never could.

"The pain is coming back," she looks scared. She holds her breath and turns even whiter—something that should not be possible. I've never heard of cancer coming on this fast. Mamma says that the lowest ebb is the turn of the tide. Well, my God, it was time for the tide to turn.

"Jórunn, hold on. I'll call Mamma." She didn't object. You don't call my parents when they are socializing, but with the weight of the moment and the fear for my sister's life, heck with rules.

"Mamma, Jórunn is all wet. Something is hurting her really bad," burst out of me. "I think she is dying." I whisper the last part.

"We will be right home," does that ever sound good, "and your sister is not dying; she is having a baby."

I pace between Jórunn and the hall window. My hearing at heightened sensitivity can hear cars blocks away. What's taking them so long? Chin pushed into her chest, the only sound Jórunn makes is "oooohhhhh-ooowwww." Then a deep breath and her head falls back on the pillow. She is no longer talking to me.

I phone again. Pétur says that they left right after I called. He asks how Jórunn is holding up. I have nothing to compare it to, so I just say, "Fine." But by no stretch of my ample imagination, is she fine.

Seconds stretch into minutes, minutes to five then ten. Come on, hurry! Shackleton came back sooner than this.

On the following day, Mamma and Pabbi let me go with them to visit Jórunn at the midwife's place. Jórunn gives me a shy smile and points to a crib at the foot of the bed. From her face I know she's under the impression that she's given birth to the most beautiful baby since Jesus. I look at the little towhead; yep, he actually is a sweet little thing but hardly worth what she has gone through. It gets me thinking about how he came out of her? A calf was born while I was on the farm, but I didn't see when it happened. Our health book, page 82, will never be criticized for excessive details.

Back home, it's now or never, I ask, "Mamma, how do babies get into your stomach." Mamma looks straight at me. She says nothing, she's thinking. I ask again. Understanding that this question is not going away, she sits down at the kitchen table and takes off her glasses.

"There are things you have to do if you want to have a baby."

"What things?" This is one heck of an uncomfortable moment. Mamma lights up a cigarette, and I can almost see the wheels in her head turning. "What things do you have to do? What does it feel like to have a baby?"

Mamma sees an escape route and jumps to the latter question. "Giving birth is like having each leg tied with a rope to a horse and each running in opposite direction."

In that moment I believed that Mamma was appealing to me to never go through what another daughter just endured.

Still unsure where they came out or got in, I knew my sex education with mother had ended. Sure as I am that the tide returns, I'd never have children.

Six weeks later, Baby Boy Ævarsson meets his father for the first time, and my father buys a record player. Baby Boy Ævarsson and the record player add new noises to the apartment. To operate the record player, you stack records on a metal pillar in the middle of a turntable. Move a small handle that clicks it on, the needle arm moves over the record and drops the needle into the first groove. After the record is finished, the arm automatically swings back and the next record drops down with a slap. It's amazing.

Áslaug and I are happy to be back in school, but for different reasons. It is the only sure way for me to see Ómar, the best looking fifteen-year-old boy in the school. Áslaug wants to get out of the house so as not to see her mother, who is expecting a baby. She is plain angry and makes no bones about it. She thinks the whole pregnancy thing is stupid. My seven-year-old nephew, Jens, covers his eyes when a pregnant woman in their building carrying twins walks past him. He finds it too painful to see. I agree with Áslaug that old mothers should not have babies, but why add fuel to the fire? Áslaug is outspoken to her parents—opposite with teachers or other adults.

When she comes to my house, she panics if Pabbi says anything to her. She claims his heavy accent makes him impossible to understand. It's vexed Mamma all these years. Although I can't hear any accent, I notice that he conjugates verbs incorrectly, and inflections for nouns, for Pabbi, are a nightmare.

She has two older brothers, Guðni and Örn, who work for their dad, Guðmundur, in the tile and wallpaper business. They have a single-dwelling house.

Áslaug is my height, about 5'6. Her hips are thick and waist small. She has dark-blond hair, blue eyes, a normal nose, and a habit of pulling her hair out at the top of her head. At school, she sits in front of me pulling one strand at a time. She twirls it around her finger and then pulls it out. She is getting a big bald spot and asks me to help her break this habit. I'm to slap her hand when it comes up searching for a stand of hair. Gunna does the same thing although less because she has no bald spot. Áslaug doesn't like her large hands, but she takes really good care of her nails. Both her parents are petite, especially her mother who is thinner than a dog's bone.

Áslaug has no crushes. I do. Ómar. He is nothing short of gorgeous. Boys in Iceland with a dignified Roman nose, brown eyes, and nice teeth are rare. Unlike the rest, he dresses well and keeps his thick black hair neatly trimmed. He's quiet, a thinker, and this has not gone unnoticed by other girls who follow him like pigeons looking for crumbs. I bet his name is doodled in more schoolbooks than anyone else's.

Sigurður, his best friend, tall, thin with pimples and boils all over his face, likes to talk to me. This is how I find out what Ómar is up to. Sigurður laughs at everything I say. My friends tease me about him, but it's insulting. Sigurður is an informant to everything Ómar does, likes, and thinks. Besides, I have another fish to fry. My periods started.

November 14, from deep within the core of the earth, underneath the ocean, a crack sprung open spewing magma into the air. For the first time, I crawled through my bedroom skylight walked to the chimney for a death clutch and watched a new island form. I'd seen eruptions, lived through dozens of small earthquakes, walked on *braun (lava)* and burnt wilderness left behind when lava cools, but this was big. This was the big of bigs. It was mesmerizing.

Eight days later home from gym class, Pabbi and Valli are sitting by the radio. Valli looks distraught; Pabbi, somber.

*This afternoon, President John F. Kennedy was shot as he rode in a motorcade through the streets of Dallas, Texas; he died shortly thereafter. The of the United States was forty-six years old and had served less than three years in office.*

Couple of weeks later Ásta gives birth to a girl. Her name is Margrét.

Returning home in '64, Stella had changed. It wasn't her brown suede jacket or olive green stretch pants, it was in her attitude. Her thick hair swept over to the left made her look older. That first night home I sat on her bed like I used to. My sister had tales to tell, experiences to share.

Isle of Wight, like Westman Islands, is just south of the mainland. Queen Victoria's summer home is there, the Osborne House. Bembridge, a small village, the home of Greyland College, was surrounded by farmland, cliffs, and blue ocean. Bembridge had three pubs, two hotels, bank, grocery store, three churches, hair salon, maritime museum, undertaker, petrol station, boat yard, and machinery shop. One public phone, an ancient box with a metal spike on top, was in the post office. Local kids hung around the streets doing nothing. Stella couldn't accept that. Dull life did not run in her veins. She didn't travel a 1,000 kilometers to be bored. She could smell fun miles away and days in the future, and soon she was all over it like an ant on a sugar cube.

One Sunday, Anna and Jenny still there, they crawled through their bedroom window and snaked to the ground. Destination, Bembridge Pub. As luck would have it, sitting at a table drinking Guinness, four Italian movie-like hotel workers, black hair and olive skin, sat as if waiting for three fair maidens. Soon realizing that they had nothing in common, it made sense to the Roman gods to invite them for a boat ride. With the voice of reason screaming no, no, no ignored, *consequences* was just an indigestible word adults used to stifle the teen spirit. For hours, bopping on Bembridge Bay, practicing their English, listening to rock and roll on a transistor, Stella and her friends thought this educational endeavor was working out just fine. At the end of the day, their fair skin blistered, swelled, and itched. But in Stella's estimation, for the fun, sun, and fury, it was chump change.

Stella referred to the housemother as a Great Lady. She sat with the girls at night and listened to their chatter while drinking a glass of French wine. Sitting on my sister's divan, listening, the Great Lady, I suspected, earned her name sharing her French habit with my sister.

Back home, Stella went to work for the government's water department. It was close to Pabbi's tire shop. Instead of riding the bus, she rode with him. Like Jórunn, Stella lost interest in games and horsing around with me.

# Chapter 14
## High School Rebellion

*This chapter is about Pabbi, an American, and
what to do with Edith—1964 to 1965.*

School comes to an end for good, none too soon. My requirements have been completed. No more teachers, but what?
Mamma listens without commenting when I share my flavor
of the month future plans. Áslaug intends to finish high school.
Mostly, I just don't think about it.

Sigurður has spent eight months asking me out, I've spent
the same amount of time waiting for Ómar to dial 33615.
How is he going to fall hopelessly in love with me—desired
outcome—if we don't talk? Sigurður confides in me that Ómar
prefers chicken over red meat. This kind of information is
a gold nugget. Ómar likes cars, skiing, swimming, watching
scary movies, haircuts, and clothes. My treasure chest content
is growing. True, we don't have much in common. OK, we
have nothing in common, but that is a worry for another day.
Sigurður comes by the house, and Pabbi declares, "He is a nice
young man." But the idea of dating Sigurður is like dating Hoss
instead of Little Joe.

Bonanza is an American TV series that I watch religiously without subtitles on Áslaug's television. There is no talk in our house of getting a television. My English is improving, and I'm adding idioms like if you sold your saddle you'd disgrace yourself and *a California widow is a woman separated from her husband but not divorced.* In one Bonanza episode, "She Walks in Beauty," Hoss wants to marry a mysterious woman, Regan, who has less than a pristine past. He doesn't care. She has eyes only for Little Joe. Hoss thinks Little Joe is trying to win her favors and beats him up. This is some good stuff.

With finals behind us, instead of our usual weekend movie, one night Áslaug and I decide to go downtown to a country dance. We spend hours getting ready, running up and down the stairs, and asking her mother for help and suggestions. She's nursing Þórlaug, a baby girl with a toothless grin. After having this baby, she's even thinner.

Áslaug is wearing a pair of jeans with Örn's red checkered shirt, blue bandanna, and a black cowboy hat. She tucks the shirt in at the waist, tightens the belt an extra notch, and, with a Coke in one hand, leans into the mirror looking for skin imperfections. She rarely gets pimples. She looks like a young version of Dale Evans, without Roy Roger and her horse Buttermilk.

I wear Áslaug's tight black pants and leave the waist button under the belt unbuttoned. Her mother, Svala, lends me a red sweater and a bandanna to match. My black dress shoes look fine, but the best part is a borrowed Stetson with a twisted leather band, turquoise beads, and a tassel. Looking in the mirror, the image pleases me. Two cowgirls ready to ride—a bus.

We walk up her street, Bakkagerði, cross the cement encasement, home of geothermal pipes, and run the rest of the way. It's a warm, dry, windy day, almost 10°C (50°F). "A chance of rain," the weatherman threatened. When isn't there a chance of rain?

Waiting in line to get inside a timber building—country barns are in short supply—some of the cowboys throw plastic snakes at us while others attempt to lasso the girls. Inside, wall to wall cowboys and girls meander among pictures of cacti, horses, and balloons. A red bandanna is tied around the handle to the girls' bathroom and a blue for the boys'. "Blue Suede Shoes" blasts through two speakers sitting on a temporary stage.

Standing at the side of the linoleum dance floor, I can see that there is no mistake that the boys agree with my earlier mirror image assessment. Pushing each other out of the way, they ask me to dance. Eventually, my bladder demands attention, and I trot to the washroom, face flushed and grinning. I pick up the pace and canter the rest of the way until I run head on into Ómar. Shock begins to describe my surprise— only begins. My bladder urgency disappears. When I go to say something, actually I'd memorized phrases for this occasion, I can't think of anything. As a matter of fact, I can't speak Icelandic, English, or Danish. My head has gone blank. Finally, lyrics from "The King of The Road" appear: "Trailers for sale or rent. Rooms to let ... fifty cents. No phone, no pool, no pets I ain't got no cigarettes." It's Áslaug's and my favorite song but hardly appropriate for the occasion.

Today I'd not even thought about him. But here he is, more handsome than any guy at the dance, prince among paupers. A cold breeze from the entrance door, kids coming and leaving, remind me of my bladder. Our staring match is getting uncomfortable.

"Hi, Edith."

"Say something," a voice within. I smile and hobble into the bathroom. Why didn't I say something? Looking in the mirror, i see, thank goodness, that my nose is not red. Mamma, who has little to offer in the makeup department, suggested I quit putting rouge on my nose. "You look like a drunk." That's how I learned to limit rouge to my cheeks. Looking in the mirror, I looked really pretty. My brown hair shone in the light. The Stetson gave me a healthy cowgirl look. Dabbing cold water on my forehead, I headed back looking for Ómar.

"Do you want to dance?" He'd waited for me. He was alone. And, do I want to dance!? Yeah comes to mind. Finding my voice, I chat timidly at first then gain confidence as the night progresses. Ómar likes slow dances and holds me hard-like. It feels pretty good, but it would be nice to talk more. He really is a boy of few words. Walking to the bus stop with Áslaug, I see the sun dip below the horizon, and Esja looks the way I feel. Tonight Ómar asked for my phone number. I take a last look at the sky and thank the stars that lined up to make this night the best of my life.

When Ómar doesn't call, I wonder if I'd written the number correctly.

Bouncing down the stairs, I yell to whoever answers the phone, "Is it for me?" It isn't. I'm reading Jane Austen's *Sense and Sensibility*, where Marianne ends up marrying, not her first love, the handsome spirited Willoughby, but an older quieter guy that she'd paid no attention to. Is Sigurður older than Ómar?

Summer of '64, instead of returning to the fish factory, I get a job for the national dairy company. Of all the stores in Reykjavik, mine is kitty-corner from Ómar's house, renewing my faith that we are destined to be together.

Ladling milk into customers' metal thermoses, I spill milk a time too many and am reprimanded. Keeping an eye on his house is easiest from the cash register. Ómar's mother shops here. When I wait on her, my hands shake as though I were in the last stages of Parkinson's disease or had an overactive thyroid. After a few weeks of her not paying attention to me, I rethink my strategy. My goal is for her to like me so when Ómar introduces me as his girlfriend she'll say, "Oh my goodness. You are that kind young girl from the milk store." Right now I'm as interesting as a pound of *skyr*. Her sixteen-year-old son's future wife is not on her mind.

Plan two is to be especially nice to my customers where from her periphery she'd notice. "I'd be glad to get you a Russian rye from the back!" I say to a little girl who looks ready to cry. Karla, who washes her white uniform nightly, is in charge of this store and tells me to stop yelling. She says it in front of Ómar's mother. I want to sink into the ground. Defeated, I hope she'll forget me so down the road we can have a fresh start, me with steady hands and a soft voice.

Time ticked, summer days lengthened, and shadows disappeared. On the backyard hill, I rigged up a windshield using old blankets.

"Where are you taking the blankets?" Mamma looked up from the newspaper.

"I'm making a windshield so I can sunbathe," I explained. She gave me one of her questioning looks—"did this child come from my loins?"

Jórunn spent hours on the hill wrapped in a blanket, a mummy with her head sticking out. Her freckles blossomed. Mamma and her sisters fashioned hats with large brims to keep the sun off their faces while they worked cleaning, gutting, and hanging up fish. Now her daughters sunbathed hoping to create an illusion that we'd visited countries at lower latitudes.

Pabbi planted rosebushes, pruned to perfection, on the west side of the house. In those moments smelling the roses wasn't just an idiom; it was how he lived. Engaged in his hobbies, inside or outside, his soul latched on to the moment. At times a source of frustration to mother, there was nothing fast about my father. Humming to himself, pants pulled above his waist held up with suspenders, pushing his glasses back up his nose, he trimmed the red currant bushes, demarcation between us and 24. My father believed that life was lived unhurriedly in quiet contemplation. Inside, he spent hours reading behind a closed living room door. He was a man of habits. Saturdays he sat in his favorite green corner chair where two wall lights illuminated his bald head with a skirt of gray hair. I couldn't help thinking that his head looked like a giant egg. It also made me think of diminishing strength. For the first time, something inside me knew that one day I would have to face life without him.

Pabbi grew up in a small farm community. He never said much about his childhood. His father ran the county school for children who lived outside the nearest town, Egtved. He told me how he and his brother Svend put elastic around the hem of their pants to keep field mice from crawling up their legs. He liked telling me stories that made me go, "Ooh, disgusting." Then there were days when he followed me around the house holding a dead fly—me screaming for Mother. He told Mamma he was helping me overcome my fears. She shook her head and lamented, "Why you enjoy tormenting the girls I'll never know."

In the back of his home, he played in the gentle sloping hills covered with heather and aspen and beech scrubs. In the spring the country-side woke up with white, yellow, and blue bursting out reaching towards the sun, and perfumed air draped the landscape with an invisible cloak of silk. Softness spread across his face when he spoke of his childhood. An almost imperceptible smile crossed his lips; his mind was far away from the harsh climate of his adopted country.

I wanted to ask him if he missed Denmark, but I was not sure that I wanted to hear the answer. I remembered a famous quote from *Njáls Saga* when Gunnar is outlawed from Iceland for three years. On the way to his ship, his horse stumbles and he falls off. He jumps up—it was summer time—looks back towards his farm, Hliðarendi. "Fair are the hillsides, so fair as I have never seen them before, the pale meadows and just-mown hayfields." He turns back willing to face the consequences rather than leave his motherland.

Mamma said that Pabbi's childhood was charmed. She told me that he'd learned to dance and play instruments and that he and his sibling never worked until they were grown. It must have been hard for her to get her mind around the idea of anyone above the age of nine not working.

Animals and small children took to Pabbi like teenagers to Coke and cigarettes. My chick from the farm, when Pabbi napped, so did the chick—on his chest. He listened to his grandkids; what a six-year-old had to say mattered to him. This was sainthood territory.

Pabbi's vegetable garden—carrots, potatoes, turnips, cabbage, and rutabaga—was at the southern end of our yard. Most dinners were fish and "Edith, get some potatoes from the garden. Enough for six of us." Being the baby in the family had advantages, this wasn't one.

It is a pleasant summer day when Pabbi's and my lunch is interrupted by the phone. I've given up thinking that every caller is Ómar. We are having an open face liverwurst with pickled beets on rye. "Get the phone." Pabbi might have been a director in his last life. Every female in the house is his go-fer. So I go-fer the phone.

"Can I speak to one of Edith Andersen's parents?" the voice asks.

"Who is this, please?" In my entire life, nobody has ever asked to speak to the parents of Edith Andersen. When he says Gunnar Guðröðrason, Réttarholts' principal, I wish this fact had not changed. He wants to talk about next year. There is to be no next year. I'm done, finished. I've completed my school requirements. I am a few months short of sixteen—but old beyond my years. That's what Pabbi says anyway. "Edith is an old soul."

"I'm sorry, my mother is not here," I say as naturally as I can under the circumstances. I hope Pabbi isn't paying attention. By saying *mother* hope Gunnar interprets it to mean that I have no father or he is a drunkard incapable of discussing matters of education. Perhaps he was a fisherman that drowned in Borgarfjörð or even closer to Reykjavik, in Hvalfjörð. Faxaflói Bay hit with 60 mile-per-hour gale accompanied by sheets of icy rain forced boats to flee for cover. My father's boat didn't make it.

"Who is that?" from the kitchen. Oh, thank the Lord, my father is alive again.

"Is that your father?" Gunnar's hearing is excellent.

I cover the mouthpiece, look at Pabbi in the kitchen, and half-whisper, "It's my principal, Gunnar Guðröðarson."

Acting nonchalant, shrugging my shoulders while raising my eyebrows as to say, he's confused. He dialed that wrong number. Have I not suffered enough under the Reykjavik School System? It seems that the answer to that is a big fat no. Back on the phone, "Thank you for calling. I will be sure to tell ..."

Gunnar is not done. No matter how much I want to, I can't hang up the phone on my principal. I have to ride this wave that will drop me off on a shoreline of its choice. In the meantime, my coffee is getting cold and I suspect that the only person in my gargantuan family that might give a smidgen, an iota about the temperature of my coffee is Ásta's few-months-old daughter Margrét. I pick her because she can't deny concern, granted—not affirm it either.

"What does he want?" Pabbi queries. There is no rye or herring on his fork. His hands are resting on the table. His antennas are receiving Shakespearean signals, something is rotten in Denmark. Pushing his chair back, "I talk to him." A minute ago I'd picture him a drowned seaman, now his grammar has been plopped on my plate of worries and potential humiliation—a plate that sits right next to my cup of cold coffee.

"Yes, this is Edith's father." I wonder if he will want to take that back when the conversation is over. He gestures me to go back into the kitchen.

Gunnar talks. He has a lot to say. Pabbi says "yes." A little later he says, "yes" again. Between yes'es, he nods. I wouldn't mind a *no* thrown in. But at least his grammar is not revealing itself. My mind tallies the yeses as against Edith, noes as in favor of Edith. Behind my attempt of humoring through this moment, I have a sense of a door closing behind me and a future path being assigned, one not to my liking. Kitchen clock ticks, ticks, ticks. The air is getting heavy with unknown plans. I push open the kitchen window, and the up draft bounces the valance around like a sheet on a clothes line. Outside, kids younger than I are playing ball, tossing it back and forth. Although I don't want to be younger, I also don't want to get older.

"I talk to you principal." His grammar and tense are both wrong. The pronoun is *your* and Gunnar *was,* as in past tense, my principal.

"OK," pretending that I'm indifferent is going poorly. I sit down on the kitchen bench below the sound of tick tack, tick tack. I rub my hands together waiting, waiting. I need habits. This could be one, rubbing my hands together. You can do it sitting, standing, before you go to sleep.

"He talk about what you do next year. Third year, you should go into business classes." It's clear that before this phone call, Pabbi has not given my education much thought. He's looking at me with new interest mixed in with curiosity while the radio reporter announces the number of tons of fish brought in the previous day.

"He say you are very smart but don't apply yourself." He looks deep into my eyes; I squirm.

"I don't want to do that." I really don't know what I want. "School is done with me and I it."

"School prepare you for work." It's hard to let this one go. There is much that I could say on this subject. "I'm just not interested in business. Besides, they take German." What does that have to do with anything? Pabbi is wondering the same, but neither of us is going down that path strewn with gravel, crag, and lava.

Our conversation ends not a win-win, but stalemate. Later, Pabbi and Mamma will discuss what to do with Edith behind closed kitchen doors. I've refused to go the business path but relented to return in the general program for two years. To add salt to a sore, this fall Réttarholts High School opens a new addition, a swimming pool.

As I think more about it, there are some positives. Áslaug is continuing in the general studies program. Ómar will be in his fourth year. It gives me breathing room—what to do with the rest of my life. It isn't a lot, but it is something. Also, I know that my attitude about school has been *south of the border*, a Bonanza line. That needs to change.

Stella, back on Mamma's radar, is dating a service-man. Rumor has it that servicemen leave Icelandic girls with child but without a wedding ring. Icelandic girls find out at the altar that last night's confessor of love ever after has returned to America to his wife and children. Icelandic families are not inclined to understand this kind of nonsense, as Mamma would say, or in a mood to forgive and forget.

Norman, Stella's sailor, fell in love the first time he saw her. He'd walked into Naustið, a popular dance club, while Stella was on stage playing the guitar and singing "Leaving on a Jet Plane."At the same time, his time in Iceland was up, and he was sent back to the States.As soon as he could, he reuped to serve another tour in Iceland. He explained that he'd met a girl he wanted to marry. He was sent to a chaplain.

Weekends, servicemen come into town prowling for maidens. In uniform they stick out like parrots among pigeons. It makes them an easy scapegoat for my countrymen full of confidence and self-importance—compliments of whiskey and vodka.With the animosity towards Americans, drunkards see it their duty to protect Iceland's weaker sex. Less–brave countrymen find an outlet in calling their sisters derogatory names. For the sailors confrontation with the natives or being caught out of uniform results in a thirty-day detention. For some the risk-reward ratio, young women whose English vocabulary is four words, *yes* and *I love you,* is worth it. However, nobody tells the brave out–of–uniform testosterone chaps that their white socks are a dead give away. Operation camouflage goes bust.

Norman has a quick temper.When two Icelanders call my sister a whore, they see a flying Greek and feel a flying Greek as he lies on top of them. Sirens blaring, red lights flashing, he escapes through the back door of Naustið.

Stella speaks English and, no doubt, has more to say than yes and I love you. Like Jórunn, she shows all the symptoms of being in love. When she couldn't be with her American, she was on the phone with him sequestered in our bathroom.

Jórunn pleads, "Stella, get off the phone. These long distance calls are expensive."

When Norman comes into the city, cops shake him down to see if he's bringing cigarettes that cost $.25 on the base and $3 in Reykjavik. "Nei, nei, nei," the cop tells him while shaking his head to make sure Norman understands *nei* as he removes a pack out of his breast pocket. They let him keep gum he brings for kids who continually beg for treats.

When they take his cigarettes, Norman feigns disappointment and defeat exclaiming, "Oh no, don't do this to me." In this game the cops get a pack of cigarettes and Norman keeps three packs he carries in his white socks and back pocket.

Watching the suspense of my sister opposing the establishment, taking risks in hope of compensation, in other words, testing fate, adds elements of mystery and romance that I'd only experienced reading romance novels.

The national objection for women to have servicemen boyfriends, doesn't make sense. Visiting Adda, who greets me with the usual, "What are you doing here?" I ask her. She makes some throat noise and continues eating *skyr* and toast and drinking coffee. This sister of mine can take an hour to eat a piece of toast She mostly just moves it around on her plate. Anyway, Adda explains that during WWII, we lost—that's how she put it—we lost—300 women who married their soldier boyfriends. Our surgeon general was concerned how their actions would affect the nation's moral–character. So he declared that these dating relationships were a dangerous disease or a plague.

Fjallkonan, is a symbol of the nurturing mother and guard of national identity, morality and culture. Our Ministry of Health's propaganda, using the image of Fjallkonan, reminds Icelandic women that like Fjallkonan, women have a responsibility and obligation to their small nation to stay and bear children, endowing them with the language and culture. In other words, stay put.

Stella announces that she is getting married. Mamma is upset. She tells Stella that she is doing this because she is

pregnant. Stella hurt by this accusation, insist that this is not the case. Pabbi, out of Mamma's earshot, eases the sting when he tells her that Mamma married a foreigner and she *was* pregnant.

Nevertheless, the thought of having one of her daughters living in a country of crime where Mafia hit men own the politicians is upsetting. But there is no talking Stella out of it. She is in love with a Greek American navy man, an Eagle Scout with an olive complexion, black curly hair, and the restlessness of a high-schooler watching the classroom clock on the last day of school.

Although I don't understand everything he says, two years of English allows me to get the gist of the message. When he is invited to dinner, I want to make it a memorable occasion for him.

"Norman," I'm about to convey a long message in English and I need his attention, "you should know that we pray before dinner. We put our head down, way down into our chest and whisper a prayer to the Lord. Don't do it loud. But do it loud enough so we can hear you." He looks confused. Hurriedly I add, "We all do it." He seems relieved. I explain that when Pabbi says, *Allt í lagi* (OK), it's a signal to start praying.

Pabbi sits at one end of the table, Mamma the other. I'm fairly certain that Mamma has never said grace or prayed at any table, and if Pabbi ever did, half a century has passed. Eagle-eye Norman watches Pabbi waiting for the signal. Mamma sets the gravybowl on the table, Pabbi rubs his hands together and says what he always says, "Allt í lagi." Norman is a quick one. His head drops into his chest like someone has hit a button. My family stares at him, especially Stella who looks like she is seeing him for the first time. "Thank you, God, for food. Thank you for letting me have food to eat. Thank you for good food." He is so bad at this that I want to laugh aloud.

His prayer is growing on Mamma. Norman, chin in chest, is still thanking our heavenly father for everything short of his white socks. We, heads up, stare at him. Mamma pipes, "We can wait for the young man to finish." By now God's son looks up and catches on. He gives me a look that says the war is on, sister.

June 25, 1964, in the *Morning News*, an announcement reads: Last Thursday (June 18) Stella Andersen, Hólmgarður 26 and Norman Briggs, 2830 Lillian Road, Ann Arbor, Michigan USA announced their engagement.

August 8, the apartment is alive with preparation for the wedding reception. Jórunn and Mamma are the labor force and I'm the go-fer to Ólabúð, our local grocer, and dairy shop for last-minute items. Stella is wearing Jórunn's wedding gown.

Dressed and of no use to the kitchen crew, I keep one eye on the clock, the other out the window for the groom. Stories of young women left standing at the altar run through my mind. This won't happen to my sister—we are not going to the church until he shows up. When a taxi pulls up and spiffy Americans pour out, I'm not sure if I'm relieved or disappointed. Pushing nay-saying thoughts aside, "Norman is here!" I yell. A shiver of excitement flows through the apartment. Those opposed to this marriage keep a stiff upper lip.

Her wedding day is a bright sunny day. Skies above are a perfect blue, the kind other skies should be compared to. White cumulus clouds are sparse, and the wind is light so as not to flick off the bride's veil blowing it into the Atlantic Ocean. *Séra* Gunnar Árnason, our parish priest, resides over the ceremony at Kópavogs Church. Bruce Dixon from Ohio is best man, a friend from the ship *Saratoga*. There are other Americans present, all dressed as civilians, special permission granted. Anna and Jenny, two friends who'd been at Isle of Wight with Stella, are there along with her friends Selma and Hrafnhildur.

It is hard for me to believe that Stella is getting married. She looks beautiful. Her white veil contrasts her brown hair. Her blue eyes are full of excitement and nervousness. Smoothing foundation over her unblemished face, she brushes rouge to accentuate her high cheek bones. She'd purchased two lipsticks, and on her wedding day she chooses Lilac Sky. Coffee Bean eyeliner is applied with success on the third attempt. As she walks down the aisle, pew after pew, family and friends get a whiff of jasmine and May rose with an aura of sandalwood and vanilla, Mamma's Chanel No. 5.

Last time I was in church was in 1963 when I was confirmed. I should come more often. In churches and alone in nature, your mind goes quiet. Sitting in church, I hear this silence before the music starts, it's a noble silence that fills me with goodness towards mankind. Stella's day is turning out perfect. Now the sound of the organ suffuses the church as "Pachelbel's Cannon in D" reaches every crevice of the church. Playing, the musician chooses a slow pulse, holding the damper down well into the next phrase, repeating the bass and harmony each time with a slight change in tempo and volume. I'd played this piece many times on the piano, but today, under the spell of the occasion and the organist's aptness, it was as if I were hearing it for the first time. Finally, Stella takes her place next to Norman. "Cannon in D" returns to a simpler structure. The organist holds the last note until it fades into the past.

I turn my attention to the navy men, looking sharp and clueless. For all they know, this could be the Devil's service. With glazed vacant looks, they stand still, frozen cadavers in perfectly polished shoes while the Icelanders sing:

*Jesus, joy of man's desiring,*
*Holy wisdom, love most bright.*
*Drawn by Thee, our soul aspiring*
*Soar to uncreated light.*

Leaving the church, Bruce, moved by joy or foreign spirits, takes it on himself to pull the bell rope and ring the church bells. We are stunned. In my country certain things you just don't do. It must be different in America. However, his hands get stuck to the rope so for a while Bruce goes up and Bruce comes down while the bells clang a sound akin to elves' chuckles.

Back at the house, after refreshments, Stella, her new husband, and their friends pile into three taxis for Hotel Saga for a night of dance and drink.

Stella will never be a Congo nurse, but she is going to a country thousands of miles away. America is the home of the Sears and Roebuck catalogs filled with clothes, household appliances, jewelry, anything you could want and more. You could even buy tires from the catalog. On the tire page, is a picture of a guy smiling pointing to a small motor that opens a garage door automatically. That is a bit far-fetched. So is the machine you put dirty dishes in and minutes later they are clean. Until I see it for myself, I'm a non-believer.

Famous movie star Stephanie Powers models in the catalog. She is in a movie, *If a Man Answers*, with Bobby Darrin and Sandra Dee, who is gorgeous.

Besides Norman, the only Americans I've met were Jóhanna Mar's grandchildren. Her daughter married an American army officer and lived somewhere on the east coast of America. When they came to Iceland to see their grandparents, Jóhanna brought them over to our house to visit. Atrocious how they reached over people for a slice of cake, talked with food in their mouths, didn't wait for their turn, and left the table without saying thank you. Mamma told Stella and me to take them downtown, entertain them for a few hours so she could visit with Jóhanna. She'd had enough. On the bus Billy didn't stand up for an older man, and they talked and laughed loudly. People stared at them. "Don't be loud," barked my sister earning louder laughs from them for her effort. We were glad to return them to their grandmother who sent them back to America.

Hollywood is in America. Rich people with beautiful white teeth live in America. Everyone owns new cars. Most families have televisions in color, not a colored plastic cover in front of the screen as Áslaug's parents have. It is the most powerful country on the planet. They stand up to the Russians. Mamma puts a damper on my rosy opinion of American life by reminding me that this is true for some white people, but black people are treated like lepers. That's the Socialist in her, insisting that money and power should be distributed according to how hard people work instead of large corporations owning everything. She says that every person, if they were willing to work, should have a decent life. She adds that there is a lot of crime in America. Mafia bosses run the big cities. Unlike in Iceland where we don't lock our front doors, in America danger lurks behind every rock, paved street, and corner. Why must she mute my enthusiasm with facts? Anyway, I heard on the radio news that President Lyndon Johnson has signed a bill to outlaw racial segregation. So that problem is solved.

After the wedding our home returns to a predictable hum. Stella leaves for America in February of 1965 and will live with Norman's parents and two siblings until he comes home from the service and they can afford their own place.

August 16, 1964, Jórunn and Ævar put an ad in the *Morning News* for a lot and a building permit in Reykjavik or Kópavogur. They are looking to build a place between 800 and 1000 sq. feet. The ad states that it must include a building permit and that they'll consider a roughed-in apartment.

Stella works during the day and talks to Norman on the phone at night. Mamma stops turning to her for help with autumn work. With Jórunn working and taking care of Arnþór, who is cute enough to make angels weep, she has me to help her, which probably makes her want to weep. Eating blueberry preserve on toast, a glass of red currant juice, a thick slice of blood pudding—nothing like it. This I do without protest. When she suggests I help her with canning and making blood pies, I protest, "I'm starting school soon."

"You have a week before school starts. Canning starts tomorrow." She has that annoying don't-argue sound in her voice. When I persist, arguing that daylight is waning and all my friends have this time off, she ignores me. Appealing to her is like Mozart playing for a deaf man.

The next morning, a Saturday, "You come down and help your mother." I'd stayed up half of the night rereading *Sense and Sensibility*, a fact of no interest to slave masters downstairs pouring their second cup of coffee. Jane Austin was only 19 when she wrote this book. Maybe I should be a writer. Sometimes I read the same book three and four times. *Sister Angelique* I've read four times.

Marianne's love for Willoughby—in Austin's novel—is like my own for Ómar. We are kindred spirits dealing with unrequited love. Willoughby and Ómar are much alike, their athleticism, looks, decorum, even how they express themselves. Granted, Willoughby rode a black licorice like stallion and Ómar rides a yellow city bus, but times change.

Marianne, talking to her sister, "Elinor, did you see him? He expressed himself well, did he not? And [with] spirit and wit and feeling!"

"And economy, ten words at most," Elinor responds.

I took some issue with Elinor on that. She made him sound dim-witted. Then I started thinking about talking with Ómar at the country dance. Economy of words prevailed. He was more interested in crushing me into his chest. That was OK, but now, thanks to Elinor, I wanted to hear him speak in full sentences. However ...

"You want me to come up?" I'm not sure how much time passed between Pabbi's first announcement and the follow-up threat. Spending the day doing housework or reading the rest of the book, life could be so unfair.

"I'm coming, Pabbi."

Pabbi's voice sounds impatient. He is not looking forward to this day any more than I am. He is of the opinion that Mamma works too much. Especially, I think to myself, when she involves me. Jórunn is of the opinion that when it came to helping around the house, Mamma and Pabbi let me off easy. She's been wrong before.

"I wait for you to come down," this is a rare turn of events. What's up with Pabbi? I crawl out of bed and pull my pants on. Everything else I slept in. What about his you are an old soul theory? Don't old souls need more time?

"I couldn't find my socks." When your father is standing in a hall watching you come down the stairs, it calls for you to say something even if it's not true.

Mamma reminds me to wash my hands. I've turned the faucet on before she can even think to say, "You don't know where your hands have been." I really wish she would quit saying that.

After hours of boiling jars, bottles, and lids, she has me inspect them for cracks or chips. Large bowls filled with red currant berries and others with bilberries are strained through a cheesecloth and poured through a funnel into tall glass bottles. Two deep drawers left of the stove are our sugar and flour drawers. Making preserves, Mamma goes through most of the sugar, cup by cup. Mamma suggests we stop for lunch before making *slátur* (blood pudding). Pabbi and I plop ourselves down before she changes her mind.

Pabbi and I carry gallons of sheep blood from the hall pantry to the bathroom. We pour it through a sieve into a gray metal tub inside the tub. Mamma mixes it with salt, rye flour, and gobs of white lard. With sleeves pulled up, Mamma uses her hands to stir it until the consistency is a medium thick pudding with chunks of white lard.

"I don't know how people work with sleeves hanging over their hands," Mamma's favorite mantra. Pabbi is done for now. One mother, ready to dispense more mantras, and a reluctant daughter remain. We pour the concoction into sheep stomachs. My job is to hold the stomach open —inevitably, she scratches my hands and now my blood is mixed with the sheep's. "My family will eat my blood for dinner," I think to myself. It's vampiric. I complain that she's hurting me. "Keep your hands out of the way."

"I'm trying. You scratch them anyway."

"We will be done soon," she offers. Soon by no stretch of my imagination means soon. I use a large curvy needle with twine to stitch the stomachs closed. Finally, the *slátur* is stored in a wooden barrel, soured in *mysa* (whey). Tonight we will have warm blood pudding with boiled potatoes and yellow turnips for dinner.

Arnþór, the youngest member of the household, a talcum-smelling Lilliputian, is almost a year old. We watch him play and freak out when we think someone has left the door between the apartment and the hall open. It is enough that the siblings spilled down the stairs like bad milk, little ones like Arnþór could meet his maker if he hit the radiator at the bottom of the steps. Arnþór seldom fusses and is fed often and walked daily in his carriage. "You want to go outside?" He becomes animated like a dog waiting for his leash, walking in place reaching up asking to be carried down the stairs. The outdoors agrees with babies, and from birth regardless of weather, babies are hauled outdoors, sometimes left in their carriage tied to a fence to keep the wind from taking off with it.

School starts, my first year beyond compulsory education. The teachers march into the classroom ready to bark at us for another year. "You don't have to be here, you know." We know that. We also know that they complain about class sizes. Quickly, English and geography are unbearable. My earlier intentions to approach this year with a renewed spirit of cooperation wanes early.

Anna—her father a grumpy German—and I start hanging out together. Anna was a take-charge girl, with reddish hair, pale skin and a big smile. Unlike Áslaug, she was outgoing and laughed a lot. With her by my side, my junior year became more palatable.

Botany class was rowdy. Openly, kids made fun of Einar. In a way it was too bad because he was knowledgeable, had traveled extensively, and told good stories. It was just that he lacked common sense and lacked classroom management skills. Kids threw paper planes, did homework for other classes, and slept. He was a short thin man in his sixties whose passion was the study of plants. He got so engrossed explaining concepts and showing us pictures, that an occasional snore went unnoticed.

"What plant besides potato, rice, and wheat is a staple diet for the world's poorest countries? It's Latin name is Manihot. By what name do we know this plant?" Zombie eyes looked back at him. Thank goodness for Pétur, who is destined to end up a science teacher.

Anna and skip botony class once-a-week and run down to the candy shop on Bústaðarveg for a Coke and Capri chocolate. Returning before the end of a class, Einar has had enough and refuses to let us inside. He comes to the door and says, "No, you are always coming late." He has noticed. Usually, he just thought we were coming back from the bathroom. "You go to the principal's office and tell him. I don't want you back in my class." He closes the door. An uneasy development. The kids must be giving him a terrible time for him to be this mad. We have hit a brick wall camouflaged in kudzu, a leguminous vine from Southeast Asia. Unwilling to accept Anna's prediction that getting back into the classroom isn't going to happen on this side of Judgment Day, I contemplate our next move.

On a trip to the Middle East, Einar witnessed thousands of men go into a mosque to pray. He explained how these zealous Muslims, five times a day, at the sound of a bell, run to a mosque to show respect for Allah. A little excessive, I thought at the time, but I might have been rash. Sitting on their knees facing Mecca, backs straight with hands on knees, bending forward they chanted, "Glory be to God the great, and praise to Him." Today, I tell my skeptical friend, Anna, "By expressing our respect for Einar, we may gain reentry into Mecca."

Our persistent knocking couldn't be ignored. I notice that the class was unusually quiet, probably taking greater interest in our adventure than microspore and mitosis. Einar, his gray eyebrows pulled together over the bridge of his nose, opens the door. On our knees, with sincerity that any Muslim would envy, we chant, "Glory be to Einar the Great, we pray for access to the Mecca of Botany." That's the thing about life, you can never predict how people are going to react. Instead of returning to his earlier command of going to the principal's office, he laughs and tells us to get into our seats. But there is another teacher who finds me less humorous.

Kristín, our gym teacher, likes my brother Villi. She quizzes me on his whereabouts. First of all, my own interest in my brother on a scale of 5 is 2. I go with 2, because he was a lot of fun. I use *was,* a state-of-being-verb. Present tense *is*—is no longer. Except for holidays, he isn't much a part of my life. Gunna is a part of my life. She'd get a score of 4 and I'd rather talk about her. Kristín doesn't want to talk about Gunna.

"What's your brother up to these days?" she smiles.

Snickering, my classmates tease me about it later. "Have Kristín and Villi gotten together yet?" Their teasing is good natured, but just letting her ask about my brother makes me feel disloyal to Gunna. I decide to stop her questions.

Kristín takes attendance. "Ingibjörg? OK. Lisa?" Lisa raises her hand. "Magga?"

Our dressing room has forty spaces, divided by a long piece of polished wood. Within each space are two hooks and a sturdy coat hanger with a mesh for our socks and underwear. Polished wood bench, a rectangle missing one side, opens to the short hallway that leads to the gymnasium. Tall windows are set above eye level to guard our privacy. To the left of the dressing room is a communal shower large enough for forty teenagers, a requirement after every gym class.

Aunt Rose is visiting, so the night—gym classes were in the evenings—I carry out my plan, I don't put on my white gym leotard. Aunt Rose is a code for that time of the month. Kristín announces that we'll be jumping over the horse and practicing hand-stands. This Viking need of ours to jump over things when walking around is so much more civil baffles me. Also, what possible explanation or rationalization is there for people to stand on their hands? It took millions of years for *homo sapiens* to learn to stand on our two feet. Isn't that good enough?

"Alda, is Alda here?" she looks around then back at the roster. "Edith." I raise my arm. "Aunt Rose is visiting," She notes it in her book.

"How is that brother of yours?" she smiles waiting.

"My brother Villi?" I act like the question took me off guard. Then, surprising even myself with the tone of my voice, "My brother Villi is happily married. I asked him if he remembered you; he doesn't." Like a stone dropped into a pond, the confrontation sends a ripple through the room. It is hard to look her in the face. She should quit asking. I justify my behavior and hold thoughts of reason at bay. Chanting inside my head while I wait for her next move, "Quit asking stupid question, stop asking stupid questions." She remains calm, a crazy person calm. I feel a knot of fear inside my stomach. She beckons me to follow to her office. There is no escape, or at least not one I can identify.

Sitting down in her chair, she no longer hides her anger. "Sit," she barks. She looks waiting for me to say something, probably to apologize. Head chanting has worked its magic and I'm seized by righteous indignation; her endless questions have to stop. We sit looking at each other, like a matador and a bull. Which am I? We refuse to look away; the pause is heavy with emotions. Finally, she breaks the silence. "Do you know what we talked about at last week's teacher's meeting?" I say nothing. This unexpected turn in the conversation is intriguing and I relax back in the chair. "We talked about you," she spits out the words like Uncle Pétur spits out his Copenhagen snuff chewing tobacco.

Although she's asked a question, her demeanor suggests that she would not be a good listener. Besides, I've probably said enough for one gym period.

"We talked about *you*." She leans towards me and gives me a "got you" look. Not a sound from the thirty-some girls in the locker room. They are eavesdropping. "What do you think of that?" Her barking brings a picture of a seal to my mind's eye. So I'm to understand that Kristín is interested in my opinion? I ponder—what do I think the teachers said about me?

"Must have been a boring meeting," I offer. Her expression tells me that she doesn't like what I have to offer. She doesn't like it even a little bit. I sense she's forgotten all about my brother.

She sits up straighter. No more touchy-feely for this high school student. She's decided that it is time for the straight-talk express. An icy smirk—she's going in for the kill. "We talked about what a waste it was that God gave you a good mind and you choose never to use it. We all agreed that you would never amount to anything." She pauses. She waits. So, God is a personal friend of the teaching staff at my high school? I accept that the teachers at Réttarholts School feel this way, but not God.

"God is in on this?" I raise my eyebrows as I look at her. "God attends your teachers' meetings?" Kristín has heard enough. She motions for me to return to the locker room.

As far as the teachers' comments about me, that surprises me. Not what they said, although I wish I had heard exactly who had said what. Kristinn and Einar, had they agreed with this? In spite of my shenanigans, I'd sensed that Einar liked me. Some days when his lectures intrigued me, I joined Pétur peppering him with questions pleading for more stories. Kristinn, no way did he say anything bad about me. Once he'd told me that he'd heard that I'd been sent out of class. He didn't believe it, so he asked me if it were true. He said he could not imagine that the girl he knew would be dismissed from class for poor behavior. For weeks after his comment, I towed the line in all my classes. His disappointment stirred up buried emotions telling me to grow up. Walking home from gym class, I chose to believe that the two of them had not concurred with the majority. Kristín said that the consensus was that I was capable but lazy. The latter part hurt because a little voice inside wouldn't let me dismiss it as nonsense.

Kristín stopped inquiring about my brother's health. Villi remembered her, actually smiled when I mentioned her name. I forgave him. Not her.

By Christmas of 1964, Mamma was complaining more about her stomach acting up. "Wine doesn't sit well with me."

She takes naps during weekdays and quits smoking. By now all my siblings and friends smoke. I chose not to smoke. Breathing was important to me and my lungs had been invaded enough for one lifetime.

Christmas preparations mean washing and ironing all the curtains, cleaning windows inside and out—washing down walls and ceilings was done in the spring. There isn't a nook or cranny in the apartment that does not meet a washrag sometime during the year. Stella and I clean our rooms to spare our parents' nagging us. Jórunn cleans her clean room.

Christmas Eve, the Mávastell dishes come out of the hutch. It's almost a religious affair. Women whispered when they asked, "*Tók hún fram Mávastellið?*" (Did she take out the Mávastell.)

Pabbi inherited them from his parents. It is a Danish Royal light blue dinnerware with a white seagull and gold edges around every piece. Mamma warns us, "Careful now. Use both hands when you carry the plates. Don't let the kids near it." When we wash them afterwards, the kitchen is a surgical room. Clean towels are laid out, clumsy people told to leave, and voices lowered. Only the most trusted daughters wash the Mávastell. "Mamma is letting her wash the Mávastell." This information was met with awe from the rest of the Andersen females.

New Years Eve, 1964, after listening to six o'clock mass from Reykjavik's cathedral, dinner is lamb, sugared potatoes, red cabbage, and gravy. For dessert Mamma made ice cream and serves it with canned fruit poured on top. Afterwards, Áslaug, Anna, Birna, and I go to a bonfire in a field by our high school. It's what we do every New Year's Eve. Since pagan days, bonfires have been lit on New Year's Eve to chase away evil forces. Icelanders continue this practice even if some of us have quit believing in the evil part.

At the second of midnight on New Year's Eve the sky lights up, a pyrotechnic display of celebration. Rockets and fountain tubes thrust through the air like spaceships escaping Earth's gravitation. Thousand of bright stars explode in colors of red, blue, green, yellow, sending a shower of sparks cascading to the ground or into the sea. Snake-like fireworks hiss and slither on the ground while kids jump up and down screaming. Roman candles, fire flowers, make a loud pop then shoot out bright red flames. Sparklers fulfill my pyro need.

Ships at harbor and fire trucks on land blow their horns and whistle to welcome 1965. It's one of the few times we kiss each other on the cheek, saying thank you for the passing year. Tradition holds that at midnight people should enter their house through the front door and exit from the back door for good luck. We have no back door.

At this time many people head home, but others turn to *Brennivín,* Iceland's national party drink. Drinking, our national addiction, takes off and ends like the rockets, shines brightly for a brief moment then fizzles and dies. Watching my countrymen tip the bottle, I can see the weight of responsibilities and other burdens lift off their shoulders. They become boisterous and uninhibited. Eventually, good natured taunts turn ugly and spatters of fights break out. At Áslaug's house the four of us get a hold a of bottle with a few ounces of Brennivín remaining. One taste of Brennivín and I conclude that future demons will not include alcohol.

On the Twelfth Night of Christmas, January sixth—Gunna's twenty-eighth birthday—elves and trolls come out to celebrate, dancing and singing. It's their way of wishing humans, who sometimes get in their way, best of luck in the coming year. Any remaining fireworks from New Year's Eve are lit on this night. We pack up Christmas decorations and go from a paradise of color to the darkest days of the year. This year, as the days lengthen, a mere month away, Stella leaves for good.

Stella's work gave her a going away party at the National Theater cellar. Now that she is getting pregnant big, she stays home and knits for her baby. For Stella's honeymoon trip, Mamma made her a turquoise suit out of a wool blend with a chiffon lining that matched her blouse. Stella told me that when they landed in New York, it was 32°C (90°F). Inside a wool suit, a tad warmer. This time Mamma was making a green dress with a collar, and Gunna helped sew a dark-brown corduroy coat.

February arrived and left. Stella's room is dead space. Her desk lamp and the metal window frame didn't kill her after all. Standing on her chair, I stick my head out her skylight. It's not really hers anymore. This is the kind of thought that makes me want to sweep a floor or dust. Instead I concentrate on the cold air on my face. It's almost five and already dark outside. From Stella's window you can see Nautholtsvík, Kópavogs Church and new houses built south of Bústaðahverfi. Stella has taken everything from her bedroom with her except the lamp and her doll, Nóma. She will miss the view. I will miss her.

With her departure, the household continues at a softer pace. Adda and kids come on Sundays. Gunna drops over for a quick cup of coffee. When Villi visit, he always makes Mamma laugh. I like that about him. Pabbi makes Saturday visits to Ásta. Mamma listens for the sound of our mail slot and plop-flop, a letter from Stella.

Pabbi's business is struggling and the work physically hard. His migraines are more frequent and Mamma reminds us to keep our voices low while he tries to sleep it off. He plays the piano more often and works at his desk, inherited from his father. He seldom talks to Mamma about his readings, especially books on life after death. Mamma is steadfast in her believe that when this life ends, it's over. Our bodies decompose, worm food. Yet she is intrigued by dreams. In my mind, those two views contradicted each other. If life is a one time thing, where do dreams come from?

In her early twenties, Mamma had a dream. She was walking down a long corridor flanked with heavy wood doors. Faint sound of birds chirping aroused her curiosity. She opened door after door to see fields of flowers, blue skies, and birds. Behind the last door next to an elaborately carved mahogany desk at the far end of the room stood a young man. He was about six feet tall with thick hair, a muscular neck, and broad shoulders. He smiled. Soft wrinkles gathered around his eyes and mouth, the kind you see on people who smile a lot. Closing the door, she noticed a plaque on the door with the inscription "JNKA."

Mamma always remembered the dream, but it wasn't until they were married and she happened to be watching him write his full name that she understood its significance. She said she felt as if a bucket of icy water had been poured down her spine as she pulled out the first letter of each name for Jens Nikolaj Kai Andersen.

My parents' spiritual difference is just one of many. For Mamma, life is work with endless deadlines with occasional breaks. Pabbi sees life as something to be enjoyed. His enchanted childhood remained in his blood. Hardship flowed through her veins.

Less than a week after my sixteenth birthday, Mamma asks me if I've given thoughts about my future. I tell her that I have another year of school left. She says that instead of continuing in school, it be better that I learn English. With this, I know she has made other plans. What to do with Edith? I am about to find out.

She lights a cigarette. I wait. She pours another cup of coffee and offers me one. I'm not thirsty. She butters a slice of bread and asks if I'm hungry. I'm not hungry.

"Few weeks ago," she starts, "I read an interview in Morgunblaðið with Ragnheiður Reichenfeld (Ragga), an Icelandic woman living in England." Mamma looks at me waiting for me to comment. I don't. "I wrote to her and she wrote back." She takes a sip of coffee and another puff. Something tells me that she's not sold on what she is selling. "Anyway," she continues— I'm about to learn what to do with Edith— "you are going to England to live with them."

# Chapter 15

## England

*This chapter is about Arabs, a mouse on fire,
and a guitar playing boy—1965 to 1966.*

A m I a male or a female?" I asked the passenger seated next
to me, a big burly man in a suit that probably fit him better twenty pounds ago. Filling out the customs forms before
landing at Heathrow Airport in London, I'd encountered my
first language difficulty. He looked at me for a few seconds and
smiled, and lines around his eyes and mouth fell into place.
My English was good enough to know that he was a Brit, no
more than that. Mamma had concluded that I was wasting my
time in school, so instead of finishing the fourth year, I'd go to
England to learn English.

"Learning English is the most important thing you can do,"
she'd told me. Now thousands of feet in the air, it dawned on
me that I should have asked why.

Straining the seams of his sleeve jacket my seat mate
pointed to the box next to the word *female.* "Check this one."

I wanted to converse with my seat mate, but that wasn't
going to happen. Draped over my lap, still warm from the needle of the sewing machine, was my new orange coat, a mixture

of polyester and wool. It had a matching skirt lined with satin that blocked the scratchiness of the wool. In the back, it had a pleat from the collar to the hem that created a flair. Mamma had let me pick the pattern. I thought I looked older than sixteen. The V-neckline on the coat ended with a large black button, one of five. Except for the pleat, Mamma had finished the edges with an overstitch. She warned me not to keep money in my pockets. "Pickpockets look out for girls like you."

Last night it had taken a long time to fall asleep. Staring at my wallpaper ballerinas in faded tutus doing the do a rond de jambe—thoughts came and went. Every sound in the house was a part of me. Rain on the roof, wind blowing through the mail slot in the downstairs hall, water whooshing through the radiators, last coughs, and doors closing. In my mind I heard Stella's and Jórunn's laughing, Mamma reminding us to walk slowly down the stairs, Pabbi yelling to us to set the table, grandkids chattering away, and Mamma telling us to get Adda on the phone. Through the years new sounds were added and others left. After me only Jórunn remained at home. Next year my parents turn sixty. It was time for me to move on. My mind knew it. Further down in the deep of my gut—fear fluttered. Little by little the barrage of memories slowed. At long last the whirring of Mamma's sewing machine, a sound as familiar as the beating of my heart, lulled me to sleep.

Ragga is the woman I'd be living with. Claim to fame—she was interviewed in *The Morning News* because her sister was a well-known actress in Iceland. The interviewer asked about her being an Icelandic woman living abroad. I recognized her at the airport from her newspaper picture. She was a middle-aged woman with deep set eyes and a few extra pounds around the middle. She looked too old to have two children in elementary school. Halla, her oldest, was married and living in Ireland, and Kristín, my age, went to a boarding school in Vienna.

At the airport I learned that Ragga was picking up another girl from the plane, Þórunn. She was hired as an au pair for a family that had two little girls. Their house was a twenty-minute walk from Ragga's house so, we could see each other during our free time.

From London to Birmingham, the three of us chatted amicably. Þórunn lived with her father in Reykjavik. Ragga was raised in Seyðisfjörður, in Vestmannaeyjum (Westman Island), Borgarfjörður, and Reykjavík. She was warm and friendly, and her Icelandic was untouched by years abroad. She came home, that's how she phrased it, at every opportunity. Her mother, seventy-two, was still living, but her father had died while in his thirties. She spoke of Iceland with affection and longing.

Birmingham is located in the center of England, in what's called the West Midland region. It sits on a plateau with the Trent River running through it. It's an industrial town with towering chimney stacks spewing dark smoke to the heavens above returning it in the shape of a flimsy blanket soaked in soot. The warm June air smelled like the morning after a family party.

Ragga's two–story red brick home, on the corner of Brecon Road and Heathfield, was in an up-scale neighborhood with a yard with thirteen apple trees. It was a five-bedroom, three-bathroom home with a garage that housed Dr. Reichenfeld's Jaguar. Their kitchen and eating were next to a sitting room with a television where Robert and Stephen planted themselves after school and tea and scones. I learned quickly that afternoon tea, Earl Grey and some tasty treats, was a religiously adhered to custom.

Robert was a tall gangly nine-year old who loved to watch *Captain Scarlet*, a science fiction action show. Stephen was a couple of years younger. He had white-blond hair, light complexion, and a less serious demeanor than Robert had. His physical features were from his Icelandic mother, none from his father, an Austrian Jew. With their daughter, Kristin, a couple of years older than I, it was reversed. She had black wavy hair, big brown eyes, and a nose too large for her face. Ragga had

Halla, a blond Nordic-looking woman, before she and Hans (Dr. Reichenfeld) met.

Hans was tall and lean, with short black thinning hair, long on top, making it necessary for him to sweep it to the side every few minutes. Unlike Ragga's slow pace and responses, he was decisive in movement, logical in thinking, and frank with his opinions. Hans, a general practitioner to Birmingham's Catholic poor, expressed frustration with the Catholic's Church for its stand on birth control. "She has four children she can't feed; a fifth is not going to make them less hungry. She should ask the church to feed them," he'd grump.

Responsibilities in my new home were the boys' rooms, making their beds, picking up toys, dusting, and vacuuming, along with shopping for groceries. In the afternoon Ragga wrote a grocery list and helped me practice to pronounce the words: potatoes, lettuce, bread, jam, carrots, coffee. Broccoli was a though one. Our neighborhood produce man dreaded the sight of me. He wanted to understand me, but it wasn't easy. Whenever I said a word he couldn't understand, he'd smile and hold up a potato.

My Brecon Road bedroom was on the second floor, left of the stairs. All the other bedrooms were to the right. It was smaller than my attic room at home, but without the beams it didn't feel that way. It was drab with white walls and worn linoleum floor with copper-colored stain by the door. My bed had a bright yellow bedspread with a radiator for a headboard and a wardrobe for a footboard. Lying on my back, I could reach the white porcelain sink that sat at the opposite wall. I used my suitcase for a table to stack my books and picture frames, next to a chair. The size of the room necessitated that I keep it tidy. Mamma would have been a skeptic if she'd been told that her youngest took time each morning to make her bed and hang up her clothes. My wash basin was where I washed underwear and socks then dried them on the radiator.

Speaking of laundry, one Saturday Hans came to my room to fix my radiator—the top didn't heat up—I had white cotton panties lined across it like flags of surrender. Outside on Hólm-garður Mamma hung our underwear on the inside lines with the sheets and towels on the outside. I used to think it was silly, now I don't. With Hans already in my room, it was too late to remove my underwear. I didn't want to touch them with him there, although I think it's unlikely that he thought they belonged to someone else. He seemed unfazed by my embarrassment. "There's probably air trapped in the system," he explained. With one knee on the floor, pushing my underwear to one side, he proceeded to unscrew the handle. It gave me a chance to grab them off and stick them under my arm. They were still wet, so for the rest of the time he was there, I had to turn my soaking-wet right side to the wall, out of his sight and hope the puddle on the floor would escape his attention.

School started. Ragga cautioned me to use good judgment traveling to and from school. Although she never identified groups of people—as in, "Watch out for the Arabs" I knew that's what she meant. Birmingham's population included a significant number of people from the Middle East, India, and Pakistan. Arabs thought nothing of yelling rude things, pinching you, and whistling at you. They scared me into alertness.

Kristin, finished with school in Vienna, worked for an optician. We had little in common. Her bedroom, larger than our living room at home, had high bay windows facing Brecon Road. She had more clothes, all store bought, than my sisters put together. Perhaps in an effort to help us find common ground, Ragga suggested activities for us to share. One afternoon we took the bus downtown to see *The Sound of Music*. It was early fall, warm, with the normal pungent smells of vinegar from the fish-and-chips shops. Any homesickness I felt was less for my family and more for the fresh outdoor air, the ocean, and Esja.

At the theater it was rotten luck that I was seated next to an Arab. He was by himself. Twenty minutes into the movie, Mother Abbess tells Maria, who's leaving the convent, "These walls were not meant to shut out problems. You have to face them. You have to live the life you were born to live." It gave me goose bumps—this was good stuff. White-capped Austrian mountains, where the von Trapps lived reminded me Iceland's mountains.

First, I though it was just an accident that the Arab kept touching or bumping into my arm. Keeping my arms close to my body, I surrendered the armrest to him. When his hand crossed into my space, I knew it wasn't an accident. I gave him the meanest look I could muster. He smiled. I hissed at him, "Stop it!" His smile got wider. Dismissing the idea that he didn't understand "stop it," I turned to Kristín for help. "That man keeps touching me. Can we move?" Kristín did not want to be interrupted. I crossed my arms and leaned away from him.

My reprieve lasted long enough for me to once again get interested in Maria's trials and tribulations and enough time for the Arab to lose his interest in Maria. I asked Kristín to change seats with me. After all, she could speak English. I'd hissed so many stops that a synonym was in order. His dark arrogant face was infuriating. My frustration with the Arab and Kristín made a knot in my stomach that kept getting tighter and tighter. I remembered Mamma on the bus when her hand was caught between a metal bar and the door refusing to let me call out to the bus driver for him to close the door to free her hand. Now it was me worrying about being a nuisance. Worrying that Kristín might tell her mother and she would think less of me.

Sensing new movements, I looked over at the Arab. He was smiling and nodding towards his hand. Looking down, I saw that he was holding a wad of money. Lost for words, aghast at the implication, my mouth dropped open in disbelieve. Mr. Nutcake was not fazed. His smile suggested that we were making some kind of deal. Tears of rage braided with feelings of shame and anger poured out like hot lava. I got up and faced him. "Leave me alone!" Helen Keller would have heard my outburst. I fought an urge to kick him, grab his hair, and smack his head against the seat in front. I wanted to stick my fingers into his eye sockets and pop them out. Making my way out of the cinema, Kristín caught up with me and asked if was OK. Rage of this magnitude was new. I was afraid of myself. I was afraid of what I'd wanted to do.

Ragga registered me for a city community school. It was a short bus ride from the house. It was an old building with linoleum floors and high ceilings. Students moved from room to room; the halls were loud and full of life. All my classes were with English–speaking students except one, English for the Foreign Born. My history class of the Middle Ages was the most challenging. In the beginning I was looking up every other word and writing it in the margins of my book. Listening to the teacher, I found that to my disappointment, the vocabulary used on Bonanza episodes, didn't help one iota. Not once did I come across outlaw, round-up, rustler, or chaps. Instead I struggled with words like feudalism, crusades, dungeons, and drawbridge. Granted, my effort in high school was poor, but I should have remembered some of it. At the end of the term, I had a C grade in History of the Middle Ages—I was ecstatic.

At home I turned to Stephen to practice my English. Stephen half listened and half watched the telly while I told him about the Middle Ages. I fictionalized events and restructured them so they'd be appropriate for a seven-year-old. Occasionally, Robert felt compelled to correct my English. This was intimidating. Ragga continued to work with me on the names of various fruits and vegetables, so by the end of my first semester, I had the vocabulary to shop from a farmer's cart under Henry VIII's rule in the sixteenth century.

Þórunn's family lived a few blocks north of Brecon Road close to Holy Trinity Church. Our area was up-scale; hers was up-upscale. Handsworth, our community, served as a buffer to these wealthy residents from the factory row houses and immigrant shacks. Visiting Þórunn was an adventure in beauty. Large ivy–covered Victorian and English Tudor homes were on one side of the street; on the other, a wooded park. Outside the houses circular drives framed islands filled with hundreds of different colored orchids where bees swarmed favoring the brightest among them. Her street was thick with the fragrance of lavender, rose-peach, and a tinge of apricot. Nearing her house, wanting to enjoy every minute, I set my pace slower than a geisha's in a tight kimono.

Entrance to Þórunn's house was a six-paneled oak door surrounded by a cream–colored casing, with a semicircular fanlight window on top. Between the two middle panels was a black iron knocker in the shape of a lion's head; and below that, a brass letter box. The property was groomed to perfection inside and out by a gardener, a maid, and a cook. Þórunn's job was to occupy the Kerrs' two little girls.

Left of the foyer was what Þórunn called the formal room, where children were not allowed. Adjacent was a smaller room where the master of the house spent much time. Mr. Kerr, a banker, was a short, balding man with a stern countenance who wore suits seven days a week. They were members of the Anglican Church (Church of England), and according to Þórunn, Sunday was the only time the girls saw their father.

Right of the foyer were the kitchen and an eating area with a sitting room. It was Mrs. Kerr's, twenty years her husband's junior, favorite place in the house. Before her husband came home, she changed clothes, put on make-up, and waited at the door ready to greet him. Mrs. Kerr was two people, a gregarious full–of–life mother during the day and a bland, beautifully gowned woman at night.

One afternoon, a few months into my stay in England, Þórunn and I were playing cards with the little ones, and I announced that I would read everyone's fortunes. I told the little ones that they would get a pony sometime in the future, disappointing them since they already had two. Then I read Þórunn's making it cautiously rosy. I threw in an aspiring writer, but the relationship wouldn't last. She'd told me about a cute guy at the park who was always reading. It was a nice fit. I told her that her father would soon get a better job and that upon returning to Iceland, good things would happen. Mrs. Kerr listened with greater interest then my spiel deserved.

"Edith, would you read for me?"

I didn't know much about Mrs. Kerr, so I told her that I wasn't good at it, a shameful understatement. Unlike the mediums in Iceland who had contacts with the other world, my contact was my imagination. Þórunn was instructed to take the children. "Please, luv, take the girls outside." I shuffled and shuffled and then shuffled some more. For heaven's sake, I don't even know her first name. I knew from pictures that she had a wedding akin to a royal wedding with twelve brides-maids. I knew what she looked like, a sculpted face and eye-brows, peachy complexion, and a nose that Kristín would give her eyeteeth for. She was small boned and slightly shorter than I, maybe five feet four. If she hadn't been blessed enough, she then had a body you see on front covers of fashion magazines, not on a mother of two.

"Would ya loike sum tea and apricot scones, Mum?" Her cook was probably making sure her mistress was OK. She gave me an evil glance that told me she was on to me. Maybe I shouldn't eat anything she's cooked.

Mrs. Kerr waved the back of her hand in a dismissive ges-ture I would use to shoo off a gnat. God was watching and punishing me with the fresh, sweet aroma from the kitchen, making it hard to concentrate. Apricot scones are nothing short of deee-licious. Mrs. Kerr was quiet and watched me shuffle. If she was concerned about disrupting an aura, some higher being guiding her psychic, she shouldn't be. I wished we could just eat apricot scones and play crazy eight. Her eyes were full of hope that this Icelandic au-pair possessed the gift of foretelling. My card reading would reveal to her moments yet to be lived, moments that would fill her deepest desires, wishes, and dreams. It made me feel shorter than your average Iceland elf until another whiff of scones visited my nostrils and guilt gave way to taste bud wants.

As the shuffling hour came to an unwanted end, I laid out three cards for each category. "These three cards will tell about you, these are your family, then your hopes," saying *desire* didn't seem appropriate, "and this last set of three cards are your future."

It was beyond me how anybody can believe this. The likelihood of any of this materializing was equal to my swimming the Strait of Dover in the English Channel, all twenty miles of it.

"Skuze me mum, yaw husband wull be um late, mum. The bonk is haven ah suppah meeting."

As I picked up each group, I explained to her that the fifty-two cards represented the weeks of the year. Thirteen cards in each suit corresponded to the thirteen lunar months. Where did I come up with this?

Reading the first three cards—queen of club, five of hearts and eight of hearts—I began my predictions in a low, even voice. "There is a woman with dark hair who wants to give you good advice. But you are not ready to hear it." If she had any doubt about my psychic gift, this dispelled it. Maybe I'm good at this. Mrs. Kerr leaned over the table listening as if her life depended on it. By then my vocabulary had evolved beyond *castles*, *knights*, and *potato*. "This eight of heart means an invitation to a party where you will meet someone that takes an important role in your life." I shouldn't have said that. She looked as though she were going to pass out from excitement. I had a chronic ability to surprise myself with the stupid things I got myself into.

It was somewhere between the family and your hope pile that I decided to throw caution to the wind. The old chap was at the bank. His Cinderella wife full of romantic ideas—we had that in common—so why not give her hope that life can be more than running upstairs to change clothes before baldy comes back and sitting over him every night while he reads and smokes cigars?

"King of clubs is a dark-haired, kind-hearted man. He is a generous, compassionate man who despises self-importance and arrogance." I'd just described her husband. She didn't blink. "He loves gardening, children, and travel." All the things she loved. I'd just made her entire year. "There will be a long-distance phone call." Every time I read cards, I throw in a long-distance phone call or a telegraph.

Taking in a deep breath, "You are really good," Mrs. Kerr praises—*if only she knew how good*.

Next time I visited Þórunn she met me at the door. "Edith, the long-distance call—it came." It took me a minute to remember what the heck she was talking about. She restrained herself from hugging me.

Áslaug visited me, and we spent a hot day in London. It was her first time abroad. We saw the changing of the foot guards at Buckingham Palace and Madame Tussaud's Wax Museum with the Chamber of Horrors. She came with me to a favorite dance place, and we visited Þórunn. Even after all that, we both felt it—we had grown apart. She'd finished the fourth year in school and worked at a bank. I'd learned some English and to hate Arabs who continued to pester and follow me around.

Soon after she left, I learned two important pieces of news. First, Tryggvi, MD, Iceland's only plastic surgeon according to Hans, was coming for additional training at Birmingham Accident Hospital. Of greater interest, the Reichenfelds were immigrating to Canada. Hans was seeking change. While waiting for the immigration papers, they'd sell the house and move to Shenley Village, a forty minute drive north where he would work at an insane asylum.

What to do with Edith?—again. Return home to what? I wondered. I'd turned seventeen, the age my sisters met their spouses. I had no desire to be something besides seventeen, and getting married wasn't even on the list of maybes. Second semester ended, my English and grades much improved. For the first time, school was enjoyable. Finally, I was taking responsibility for my learning. Back home, I'd have to find a job, but what

Ragga, in her characteristic quiet way, ended my quandary by inviting me to come with them to Canada. "From Canada," she explained, "you could go to your sister in Ann Arbor." Another door opened, another opportunity to find something to do with my life. I cleaned the boys' rooms, spending extra time organizing their plastic toy men and matchbox cars. They didn't notice; Ragga did.

Before our move to Shenley, Tryggvi arrived. I'd not socialized with physicians, and my experiences with them as gods in white were mixed. There were some good ones, such as Garðar at Vífilsstaðir, my favorite medicine man. Others? Let me think—, let me think, let me think. Can't come up with more names. I could hear Mamma say, "He's a doctor," her voice full of reverence daughter.

Complaining to Þórunn, "He gives me the creeps," was all I could come up with when explaining his behavior, how he stared through me, but it sounded harmless. Þórunn watched me and waited to hear something to justify my creepy feeling. One such time was when Ragga told me to take him shopping at a downtown department store. She and I were not on "share your feelings" terms, so I acquiesced. But hadn't she noticed how he always asked me to see him to the door? At times I'd be rude and actually say "no" to this request. Yet he would stand there and wait and wait until I felt worse not doing it than doing it. Ragga couldn't have missed that.

At the department store, he tells me he'd like to look at infant clothing. "Your kids are seven and nine," I protest. Even so we go to the third floor of Bhs, Ltd. on Fort Parkway. At the top of the escalator, I point him in the direction of the baby stuff.

"No, I want you to come with me." The man is killing me.

"What size aaare you loohking for?" She looks and sounds like Queen Elizabeth without the matching hat.

"What do you think?" He waits to hear my opinion. Turning to the salesclerk he says, "She's two." My eyebrows go north; my jaw goes south. So many thoughts are going through my head and paralyzing me from selecting one to share. I stared at him long enough for the saleslady, Maaary, to look worried. Is her customer having a seizure? He looks back at me with an expression of commonality that didn't exist. Finally, the cause of my unease around Tryggvi has a name, loose screw.

"Well," she says, looking at me. Is she of average size or perhaps ah little plump?" Maaary wants to please.

"I really don't know who he is talking about," I tell her. Maaary looks confused. Tryggvi proceeds to look at bibs, sweater sets, cradle sheets, and baby bottles, of which he buys none. He thanks her and she seems relieved that the curtain has come down on this act.

Next stop, the men's department. By know, I knew like I knew that poor Catholics procreated to their own detriment that I am playing some perverted game. I don't know how to end it. Thoughts to leave him stranded kept my sanity in check and shrugging my shoulders to his questions becomes my only response. Only one of us would play this game.

That evening Hans invited me to join him and Tryggvi at a local pub. After my day of looking at baby clothes and Tryggvi modeling suits, pants, shirt—, everything short of socks, my inclination was to make up an excuse. However, Hans had never invited me to go with him anywhere. We went to their summer home in Wales, but that didn't count. So, I said "yes."

Tryggvi acted normal, and it was a lovely night. Hans joked, teased Tryggvi about some of the nurses he knew at the hospital. When Tryggvi absent mindedly peeled the sticker off his beer bottle, Hans asked him if he knew what that meant. Then they both laughed. With everything so normal again, maybe I was overreacting. Back home, when Tryggvi insisted I walk him to the door, I knew I hadn't.

Hans knew Aarunya. He told me she was looking for a night babysitter. She was a widow to a colleague of his, and if I was interested, he had her address. He had been reserved in his information sharing. There was much more to be learned.

Aarunya is a Hindu name and means full of grace and scent of beautiful white flowers. All those vowels—you can roll them around on your tongue. On the other hand, Edith, EEE-diTH, is articulated by making a donkey sound, eeeee, then by pushing your tongue into the back of your upper teeth, sliding your teeth over it while at the same time sticking out your tongue. My parents wear false teeth. Was this a good choice for a name?

Edith means to strive for wealth or to be successful in war. It's unlikely that I'll be fighting wars, which leaves strive for wealth. Strive is a struggle or conflict. In other words, my destiny, live a life of a struggling poor.

Aarunya, born and raised in the city of Dharamsala in north India, was born to more thoughtful parents than I. Aarunya said that her beautiful home with its landscape of mountains and rivers was known as the "Scotland of India." I'd been to Glasgow and had failed to see any beauty. Of course, there were probably many beautiful places in Scotland, the ones I didn't travel to.

Be that as it may, she was less than ten years older than I and our lives were turning out quite differently. True, nobody can prove that our names affect our lives or decisions, but I think parents should give serious thought to the meaning of names before bestowing them on their babies. My parents gave middle names to their first two kids. After that one name was all the effort they could muster. Adeline Dagmar, my oldest sister, has a handsome name, a aristocratic Scandinavian name. Vilhelm Ingvar, my brother's name, makes you think of a learned man, a gentleman of wisdom. Then it's Ásta, just Ásta. That's four letters and no middle name. It's a name you give to a cleaning lady. Jórunn was named after my grandmother and my aunt Inga. Icelanders are into renaming. This way you spend no time at all finding the perfect name for your baby. Stella comes from Estella, a variant of Ásta.

For my middle name, they could have chosen Hamsini, a Hindu name. Let's face it, my parents were marginal Lutherans, so this shouldn't have bruised their religious sensibilities. Hamsini means one who rides swans. Beautiful Dancer of Lord Indra would have been better. But Hamsini is an improvement over Struggle and Conflict.

On a trip to India, Dr. Moore, Hans's colleague, in his sixties, met then-sixteen-year-old Aarunya, a local beauty from an educated Indian family. Whether Dr. Moore's and Aarunya's first encounter was a moment of perfection—I have no idea. When I met her, she'd been in England for eight years and had two children, two and four. Her husband was in his early seventies when he died a little over a year ago. Imagine, a rich old man marries you and then dies. How cool is that!

Aarunya was small boned, and her skin reminded me of a crayon color, burnished brown. Michelangelo would have been challenged to create her likeness. She had obsidian eyes, thick black eyelashes, and cheekbones that a Mongolian would have envied. Her long black hair looked like silk. It took self-control not to reach out and touch it. She moved unlike other mortals, floating with an occasional tossing of her head, creating black flutter as if a raven flew by.

She and I could have been a study in contrasts. Aarunya came from India and drove a Jaguar; her chauffeur drove her in a Bentley. I came from Iceland and walked. She was twenty-four, educated, and sophisticated. I was seventeen, uneducated, and naive. Men wooed her, sent her flowers, waited on her hand and foot. I went to dances and prayed that someone would ask me to dance and on a good night buy me a drink. Her culinary moments were directing her cook on some exotic preparation. Mine were tea and scones. Yet the starkest difference were in our home, hers on Ward Grove Avenue and mine on Hólmgarður.

Her home at 63 Ward Grove Avenue was a three-story mansion covered with English ivy. The heavy wood doors were flanked by brass lanterns and a cast iron bell with a rope to pull to get the attention of workers in the service quarters. Through the entrance door, as far as delivery people and garden workers would go, another church-size door greets you. Inside, you entered a hall with a cathedral ceiling. Staircase up to the second floor on the left is wide enough for people to sleep on. But it's an orchestra balcony, a foot below the second floor rails, that surpasses my imagination—for party entertainment.

Servants' quarters on the third floor had a separate stair-case from the kitchen area. When Aanurya's husband died, she chose not to have live-in servants. Only a cook, whose senior-ity earned her free room and board, as long as she could work, lived in the house with her. Other servants came in the morn-ing and left after dinner.

First time I babysat, the second time I baby sat, always when I babysat, I'd sleep over. Aanurya's dates included break-fast on the following day. As far as I could tell, her brown chest-nut babies, with eyes like copper pennies, spent their waking hours in the kitchen-family area. When the cook went to her room, and servants left, two-year-old Aidan, four-year-old Esha, and seventeen-year-old babysitter were all that remained in the that space. In spite of the luxury and all the toys, it was a cold, lonely place, the kind old Mrs. Dýrset would enjoy hang-ing around in.

Aarunya had me sleep in her bedroom so as not to be too far from the children. It didn't matter; it was far enough where they could scream for me and I wouldn't hear. They could have been abducted like the Lindbergh baby, and I would have been clueless, or they could have been fixing themselves a scotch, and I would have been equally oblivious. I spent babysitting nights in short fitful naps between tip-toeing to their rooms to make sure they were still in bed and breathing. After a few babysitting opportunities, my routine resembled that of an inmate in a loony bin.

Staff leaves, we play in the kitchen. Bedtime means heading out of safe zone to go upstairs. Aidan crawls up the stairs keep-ing an eye on his bottle in my possession. Esha shares none of my apprehension and runs ahead to select a book. Diaper changed, pajamas on, a hug and a kiss, and Aidan gets his bottle. Tugging the blankets under his little cherub face, I tell him night-night and walk out of his room that's the size of Leifsgata 7 that housed my parents and six kids. Esha is a negotiator. If she picks a short book, then she insists I read two. Babysitting Esha, I decide that if ever I have children, I want them to look like her, petite with straight black hair, permanent tan, and eyes full of trust and curiosity. I was never in a hurry to leave her. As the Brits would say, "She was ah deaaaar deaaaar child."

It could be argued effectively that I lack a thing or ten. Stick-too-itiveness, ability to swim, thinking ahead, and a small waist starts the scroll. On the other hand, imagination would be on my list of plethora traits.

Preparing for bed in their mother's bedroom, pushing the aqua–green silk bedspread to the side, I change into a nightgown wishing I'd brought pajamas instead. Besides, a nightgown conjured up images of an Alfred Hitchcock film of Ingrid Bergman wearing a long swirling satin nightgown over a 19-inch waist chased by an invisible apparition. It is easier to run in pajamas.

Borrowing a bed jacket, I stand at the window and watch the clouds thin out and the moon, a waning crescent, casts an eerie glow. A lone raven sits on a tree. I name him Edgar Allen Poe. The Brits say that if the ravens at the Tower of London leave, the crown of England will be lost. In Norse mythology, Óðinn was the raven-god. They pearched on his shoulder, Huginn and Muninn, and he gave them the ability to speak.

Mansion across the street, the one with a turret, is shutting down for the night. Room after room, lights are extinguished. Where is Rapunzel? Outside noises fade. Inside noises of unknown origin get louder. This is a lonely place—how Mamma described Margrét's state of mind after Ástþór died of cancer.

Trying to sleep, sensing presence in the hall or worse overwhelms me. It takes all my mettle to get out of bed and check the hall. Nothing. If I live through the night, I will be stronger for this experience. Who am I kidding? I will never be one of those people who puffs up her chest and faces the enemy.

Checking on the children means walking down the dark halls, holding on to the wood railing knowing that on the other side is a thirty foot drop to the foyer. It wouldn't be hard to push me, I don't weight that much. If I just jumped, I could get rid of the thoughts. Eeeekkk, snaps, and crackles, it feels as though someone is breathing on me, a cold draft—where is it coming from?

Aidan hasn't budged but his bottle has rolled to the side, and I wipe a milk drool from his face. I cover Esha hoping she'll wake and I can take her to my bed. She doesn't. A few hours and trips to the nurseries later, I fall asleep exhausted from my imagination.

March 1966, letter from home. Mamma writes that Jórunn and Ævar have moved to their new home on Holts Road in Kópavogur. She adds that the grandkids—Kata, Jens and Bragi—visit frequently. I can see them sitting on the white bench eating crepes and talking Pabbi's ear off.

Early summer of 1966, we moved to Shenley psychiatric estate in south-west Hertfordshire between St. Albans and Barnet in Middlesex County. The 22-acre property included several hospital buildings, activity center, mansion for some of the doctors' families to live, orchards, farm on Black Lion Hill, and a chapel. Large green bushes surrounded the land segregating it from Shenley village.

Shenley village was used as the setting for *The Avengers*, a TV series with the characters Emma Peel and John Steed. One of the episodes was actually filmed at the mansion we now shared with other faculty. It was a good suspense series that started with Steed showing up at Emma's apartment, "Mrs. Peel. We're needed."

Without þórunn, school, or my brown babies, I was free to explore at will. My only responsibilities were shopping in the village for Ragga and making the boys' beds. I'd never fully assimilated into the Reichenfeld family and was now eager to create my own life at Shenley for as long as we'd stay here—until the immigration papers came.

Down Ratlett Lane, the main road outside the compounds, were two cottages, Frank and Winnifred. Learning that these were the names of Mr. Raphael's children intrigued me. Mr. Raphael sold the property in 1924, then called Porters

Park, to Middlesex County for building a mental hospital. I wondered if his children were mentally ill. Why were the cottages outside the grounds? Querying the librarian, I found out it opened in 1934 after it was christened by King George V and Queen Mary. At first, patients were locked up and drugged to keep them manageable. Treatment theories changed, and instead of thinking of the hospital as a colony for mental defectives, doors were unlocked and patients given opportunities to work and learn new skills.

Initially, the whole concept of living with loonies was a tad too much for my courage pool. Growing up with Stella and Jórunn prepared me for much, but maybe not this much. Once while I was walking past the chapel, the route to town, one of the patients paced back and forth across the lane. This dude, hunched over in his long gray coat with hair unacquainted with a comb, was barmy. He'd got it in his head that people had to answer a question about some history fact and if the sun was hot on his head—geography.

With arms extended, "Rome is built on seven hills, name them." You could tell three things: first, he knew the answers; second, he believed that walkers had to earn their walking papers; and third; he was the man to issue them. Listen, loony, I'm just going shopping for the Missus via Porters Park Drive not the seven hills of Rome. I'd do a quick soccer like move and evade his hand reaching to grab a hold of me.

Walking around Walled Garden, which provided most of the fruit and vegetables for the kitchen, I found it impossible to tell if the men and women working were patients or paid workers. Hans said that most of the workers in the orchards around the estate and the farm on Black Lion Hill were patients. Learning clerical work, carpentry, and cookery helped them reenter the outside world. Some of the hospital facilities such as the mansion where we lived, the cricket grounds, squash courts, and social club—were for staff only. However, others were mixed—patients, faculty, and workers and their families such as the art center, the game room, and a tea-room.

In the beginning, I kept to myself. Soon I was giving a helping hand and talking to the patients. Many wanted to be left alone inside their head where only God knew what thoughts tortured them. But I quickly loved being at Shenley, and the loony on Porters Park Drive no longer scared me. There was Samantha, a twenty-something retarded patient, wearing hospital garb, meandering the gardens and talking to herself. She reminded me of Gummi the Idiot without the meanness. We sat and talked—as in her repeating what I said and stroking my arm. It seemed unfair that God would let some of us suffer so much. I was beginning to question if there was a God. Then simple things such as pink skies at night, a rainbow, green meadows, and trees in bloom would make a believer out of me.

It was at the art center that I met Eva and William. Soon, we set up our easels next to one another's, talked about nothing, and listened to mostly British groups, including the Beatles whose song, "Eleanor Rigby," had reached the top of the charts. Eva, William, and I sang along with it, replaying the 45 rpm until someone pleaded for mercy.

It was a song about people like the patients at Shenley. I wanted to ask if they agreed. If Paul and John had "their kind" in mind when they wrote it. But then I'd have to reveal that I was not a patient but an outsider. Saying "their kind" felt wrong. Like them, I had voices in my head. The patients were here only because they'd acted on their voices.

Inside Eva's saucer-sized brown eyes there was sadness. It was the sadness I'd seen in Ásta's eyes. Eva never talked about her road to the asylum. She was pretty in a Twiggy sort of way. Her tall, painfully thin body had collar bones that stuck out of her chest like ridges. Her daily attire was a yellow button-down shirt with loose jeans. I wondered if she'd lost weight since she had come to Shenley. I wondered how long she had been here. Eva was indifferent to her clothes and appearance with the exception of her one piece of jewelry, a silver ring with a blue stone—from a friend, she explained.

William was committed after trying to kill his stepfather, twice. He was taller than Eva and had a massive amount of brown curly hair. He looked a little like Bob Dylan, who, like me, had dropped out of high school. William and Eva could have been siblings—oval face, large nose, and long fingers–but their commonality was being mental patients, nothing else. William was out-going, Eva shy. He got angry and lashed out; she pulled inside.

William entertained us with stories of his successes, or lack of, in picking up girls. As doctors reduced his medication—weekend passes started, and his humor blossomed like wild flowers in Cow Banks Woods. "Coffee, tea, or me?" he smirked waiting for us to laugh. We told him that girls would find that lame. "Hey, I'm Batman. Wanna see my bat-mobile?" He'd never really say those things. He was just trying to make us laugh. "Blimey, ya daan't loike any of me ideas. What's a bloke ter do?"

Even by English standards, this one August day was a warm one. After kicking a soccer ball with some patients and staff, Eva and I set up our easels and went to a table by the sink to pick colors. Perhaps it was the heat of the day that made me choose all red paints: brick red, red orange, maroon, and red violet. Humming to herself, Eva painted a field with an orange sun on the horizon and a dark figure of a person in a field of wild flowers. Yikes. Neither of us were artists, but we were creating. One of the doctors came over by us and asked me to tell him about my painting. There wasn't anything to tell. I'd started thinking I could paint red rose petals in different shades of red—this thought grew out of picking too many reds and lack of better ideas—but gave up and drew a mouse. The mouse was so deformed that, at the last minute to conceal my ineptitude, I took a large brush dipped in red orange and with sweeping strokes surrounded the rodent with flames.

"It's a mouse," I said, "surrounded by hell's fire," I liked the name. That was pretty good. I looked at him to see if he agreed.

He gave me a side hug and in his most encouraging voice, "Jolly good. Get your feeling out ohn that canvass."

What? "Wait, I am not one of them." Did he think I was a patient? I was not crazy; I was just waiting to leave for North America. Did I look like one of them? When he patted me on the shoulder, it dawned on me what I'd said. In that second, I realized that I harbored thoughts unbecoming of a friend. My eyes looked to Eva. She was by the sink rinsing brushes. She'd not heard our exchange. A sigh of relieve flooded through me. At least, for this moment, I didn't have to deal with my deception—not yet, I told myself for the umpteenth time. But the longer I waited to tell them, the harder it would be.

Variants, a rock band from Northampton was coming to play at Shenley. It would be a welcome change from listening to records. Some of them were so scratched that we could anticipate when the needle was about to jump over and adjust our sing-along accordingly. Eva and I never talked about clothes, but in my excitement of the coming dance, I asked her what she was going to wear. She looked back at me, surprised. Immediately, I regretted bringing up the subject, but there was no way to take it back. "Dis iz all I brought wiv me," I had no idea how to make this go away. "Yous don't brin party threads to da animal shak, do yah?" Her smile forgave my blunder.

I continued, "Well, I brought this outfit," I opened my arms for a full look, "and some pants and tops."

"You wore a brown skirt whun I met you." Dang, I'd forgotten that. It's easy to get trapped when you lie. Had she seen my summer dress? Another thing about lying is not to compound it by adding to it, which of course is what I did.

"You're sure right about that. A loony bin is not exactly a seashore resort." Eva's eyes have clouded over with doubt about me. Her eyes held a question, but she kept it to herself. Confessing had seemed like a hill to climb, now it was a mountain. Just as Pabbi said, "Dishonest people don't look you in the eyes." I looked away from Eva.

Saturday night we helped decorate the cafeteria along with patients and workers. Before I came to Shenley, I'd imagined the mentally ill like the quiz guy on Radlett Lane. Never like William and Eva.

"Samantha is pregnant agyen," Eva told me in a way of conversation.

"Samantha has children?" It was unimaginable to me that Samantha would have a boyfriend and children. She understands the simplest of directions; otherwise she just repeats what you say. Come to think of it, I'd not seen her for a while.

"She doesn't hev a boyfriend. She gets raped an' then the doctors abort the bairn." Eva continued tying balloons to chairs acting like this was no big deal.

"They can't just take her baby! Who raped her?" My heart rushed blood around my body and my face got hot. "Eva, that can't be." I understood then that in many ways Eva and I were different. This news outraged me. For Eva, it was ho-hum, business as usual. I wished there was something I could do for Samantha. I wish I had a job teaching people to stick up for themselves.

That night, William announced, "This is a class band." He smiled like all the happiness in the world had just rained on his shoulders. By now, the Variants had played a few songs. Eva and I, leaving earlier conversations alone, danced, laughed, and sang with the band. William, unwilling to join us, instead listened to every guitar chord with the intensity of St. Francis when God told him to build up his house.

All the weeks I'd hung out with Eva, she'd never looked as happy as she did this evening. We danced every dance except the slow ones. That'ood been just a bit too daft.

I'd given little attention to the band members. I was caught up in the merriment of the moment when someone tapped me on the shoulder. "Wud yee leek a glass ov lemonyed?" One of the three guitarist from the band, had come up behind me.

He said his name was Brian. He was too tall with green eyes that had a mix of openness and apprehension. He stood waiting, using his fingers to comb his hair. Eva waved her hand to let me know that it was okay that I leave her, so the two of us walked towards the refreshment tray.

Brian came from a large family in Northampton. He'd lived there all his life, and the Variants were his ticket out. He wrote some of the songs they played, and they were getting more and more bookings. I told Brian that I was not a patient, that I came from Iceland and that soon I'd be leaving for Canada. Again, I'd found it necessary to say that. I was ashamed for people to think of me as a patient. What did that say about me as Eva and William's friend? We exchanged phone numbers. The night reminded me of the country western dance, the best night of my life. Since then, I'd given up on Ómar—it takes two to tango.

Brian wanted to walk me home, but his band mates didn't fancy waiting. William, who'd taken an immediate liking to Brian, promised to my ward. "Daan't worry. I'd git the Pope in Rome home safe." I felt physically sick. Indeed, dishonesty was a roller coaster that in a single heartbeat, takes you from the apex of joy to the abyss of remorse. I'd put myself into this trap of deceit thinking I could just keep kicking the can down the road. No more. Why oh why? Edith, you steeewwpid daft filly. There were times when I made a moron look like the sharpest pencil in a desk drawer. I should have told them right from the start. Then they wouldn't have cared. I suspected that now they, or at least Eva, would.

William cared. Eva cared. I lost two good friends. Yet I refused to believe that it would end this way. At the art center, I set up close to William; he moved his easel. Days of playful shoves between us—a sign of familiarity and affection—were gone. Eva acted as though we were so-so acquaintances, a far cry from the two girls who sat in the orchard blowing leaves between our thumbs, braiding each other's hair, and pilfering fruit from the trees. Pain and disappointment had wormed its way into our carefree existence, and none of us could sweep it away—I doubted they wanted to.

My last few weeks in England, I stopped going to the art center. Brian and I saw each other two or three times a week. A bus took me from Shenley Village to Northampton in less than an hour where he paced and waited.

What you noticed most about Brian wasn't his curly hair, like William's, or his clothes which Mamma wouldn't have let us wear outside; you noticed his eyes. Before he could see me get off the bus, his eyes looked worried, preparing for disappointment. The instant he saw me, blink, they changed to relief.

In those few weeks, I learned more about Northampton and England than I had in the year I'd been here. Brian was a twenty-three-year-old history buff and was far more animated talking about British history than about himself. He was also the most considerate, easy to be with boyfriend I'd ever had. We could argue that he was also my first boyfriend. But, why argue?

Northampton was the size of Reykjavik, not quite a city but bigger than a village. Market Square, known as Grosvenor Centre, was a mosaic offering of retail delight with one exception, the Victorian Theater Royal. At moments, I wished Eva were there instead of Brian. Eva was not allowed to leave the grounds yet. Again, I wondered why she'd been committed. Brian's enthusiasm for window-shopping lacked energy. Instead, he was eager to tell me about British's history.

We visited All Saints Church, near Grosvenor Centre. "This is Charles II," Brian pointed to a statue in front of the church of a king-like guy wearing a toga and a wig. "Eee ruled in the seventeenth century ...." He knew a lot about Charley. Any attempt to look back to the shops—deplorable manners. I listened. Surrendering desires to window-shop, I followed Brian down history lane.

After learning that in the seventeenth century Charles had a reputation for being a ladies' man—that happens when you have fifteen mistresses in twenty years and 14 illegitimate children—I was hooked. I was asking questions. Seventeenth century wasn't that long ago. Iceland's *Sagas*, full of blood and revenge, happened a millennium ago. Brian laughed at my interest in this aspect of the royalty and humored me.

"In those days, munarch and mistresses wuz an expected combination," he explained. But he relented that even by permissive standards, King Charles was an active monarch. Charles moved from one mistress to the next like he changed his fur-trimmed, silk-lined cloaks. In 1669, with Moll and Nell as his mistresses, the latter decided that two was one too many. Hearing that Moll was to sleep with the King, Nell prepared sweetmeats with a generous serving of laxative jalap. Charles, whose amorous plans didn't go as he'd hoped, sent Moll packing. I told Brian that Charley wouldn't be remembered in the history books as a role model for chastity. He laughed and agreed, "That's fo' sure."

On another day, we spent two more hours at All Saints Church. Brian said there was more to see. I tried to remember some of my own history. In high school, it was just rote memorization. He was the son of blah who was the son of blah blah. Why spend time on exact years instead of the story with its plots and twists? That was the stuff of history. Then there were reams of poems, pages and pages. Once in a while, there was a description of nature that caught my fancy, but mostly not. For example, a poem about pagan mythology from Edda's Prose by Snorri Sturlson. In this poem, the chief pagan god, Odin, shares how the art of writing (runes) came to him.

I know I hung
on the windswept Tree
through nine days and nights

I was struck with a spear
and given to Odin,
myself given to myself

They helped me neither
by meat nor drink
I peered downward,

I took up the runes,
screaming, I took them -
then I fell back.

Not once did I hear my classmates say, "Hey, this is good stuff." It wasn't. It was enough to convert a perfectly healthy pagan to a withered Christian. Brian ignited a spark within me. Interrupting my thoughts, Brian suggested we take a breather before I went back to Shenley. Next time we'd visit the Madonna and Child in front of St. Matthew's Church on Kettering Road and Ashby Manor.

Sipping tea, indulging on little sandwiches with blackberry preserves, signaled the end of another date with Brian. We were comfortable with each other, now sitting quietly. Around me a sea of people came in waves and "Yellow Submarine" played on a speaker." Breathing in the aroma of cakes, teas, the heat from the sun, and fragrance of flowers agreed with me. Bzzzzz, I tired to refrain from whacking the bees remembering what Pabbi said when I tried to squash them in our backyard. "Don't swat them, they are working, pollinating to ensure the plants' survival." Across the table, Brian, wearing his velvet hip huggers and paisley button-down looked content, and like me, enjoying this yellow sunshiny day.

At the end of a day together, in front of the bus to Shenley Village, passengers and the deep blue sky, he kissed me. In romance novels the heroine sees a flash of light, feels butter-flies in her stomach, and hears music of the angels. I didn't see, feel, or hear that. What I heard was the bus driver, "If yaouw wanna get on this buzz, noo is the toyme. Let's goo, luv."

I waved to the tall beanpole of a boy with hunched shoul-ders from hours of playing his guitar. All Saints Church steeple shrunk from view, and my British boyfriend, a distant shape, faded. Was I in love with him? How do you know? Short of cupid with a Cockney accent informing me, "Listun, luv, this is fo real," I wouldn't know.

Falling in love was supposed to be like coming down with a terrible bout of insanity. Your inside became a raging inferno. I should be consumed with thoughts about Brian. Truthfully, I thought more about Ómar during Ómar Era—what he ate, what he wore, who he hung out with, what he was doing every minute—than I thought about Brian. I enjoyed Brian's company but as I would a brother's or a good friend's. When we weren't together, I didn't think about him. However, if you asked me who'd I most like to go to a museum with, I'd say Brian. Of course, nobody is ever going to ask me that.

Brian and I continued to date until October of 1966 when I left on the *Alexandr Pushkin*, a Soviet cruise ship, headed west. When I resisted his affection, he assigned it to a nonexistent moral fortitude. Our last evening together, walking the grounds of Shenley, he acted nervous and giddy. "Did you get a new gig?" I asked. This could explain his out of character behavior.

"Nay, ee didn't."

We walked Porters Park Drive, the orchard on our left, the chapel ahead. Leaves of orange, yellow, and red covered the paved road making crisp crackling sounds when we stepped on them. Shenley's orchards were in their last stages of preparation for winter. Everything was changing again. Even the geography–history guy was nowhere in sight. Too bad. I bet Brian could answer any question he'd throw at us.

"I'd leek tuh hav' met the history bloke," Brian said, "Bein sick in the heed leek that, bad luck."

At the chapel, he asked if we could step inside. It was a splendid little church that remained open day and night. Ever since coming to England, I'd started visiting churches just to walk around or sit in them. Also, it didn't cost anything. St. Martin Church by Bullring Shopping Centre in Birmingham was one of my favorites. It was built hundreds of years ago, then rebuilt and improved when the powers to be took interest. Its tower with its spiral point and cement statues of screaming angel heads were mesmerizing, but it was the inside of the church that brought me back to it. Sometimes I sat in the pews for an hour, not thinking, just feeling. The feeling was akin to a balloon expanding, filling my ears and entire being. After a while I'd feel light headed. Was this what it was like inside a mother's womb?

Thoughts returned to present situation and Brian seated in a pew digging into his pocket like a starving man remembering a morsel of food. He motioned for me to sit next to him. A part of me wanted him back on the bus to Northampton. I needed to iron and finish my packing. Kristín and I would be cabin mates on the *Alexandr Pushkin* on an eight-day trip that ended in Quebec, Canada. After tomorrow, I'd never see my friends again. If life was a card game, I'd played the wrong card when I didn't tell Eva and William. If wild cards allowed you to replay a card, what I wouldn't give to have one now. I'd play one where we were parting as friends, each better because of our friendship. My behavior had trumped that wish.

When I turned my attention back to Brian, he was pulling a small jewelry box out of his pocket; I felt as if I'd been kicked. My hands gripped the pew in front. A statue of Jesus was looking at me wondering how his mortal sister keeps getting herself into these situations. Brian's hand, reaching out to me like an offering, an open box with a gold ring adorned with one tiny diamond, "Edith, I love ya' well much. Will yee be me missis?" I didn't see this coming. I really truly didn't see this coming. This never made it on the radar screen. For a moment, I couldn't remember a single English word. Maybe that was good. Perhaps it wouldn't have made any difference if I had known what he was going to do. But I couldn't faze that. It would have. Yes, if only he ….

"When yaouw retn, I'll come and meet yer family in Iceland." His eyes were full of hope, enough to wish good things for all mankind. We'd live in Northampton. His voice seemed far away.

He'd told his parents, whom I'd never met, and they looked forward to meeting me even though I was five years younger. "Wha't yaouw say, luv?"

I wish he'd keep talking. As long as he talked, I didn't have to say anything. Come on, Edith, think. Desperation teaches a naked woman to spin. A man is only as good as his word. A Viking quote cautions talking too much. Often it's best for the unwise man to sit in silence …. It's the ill fortune of unwise men that they cannot keep silent. These were good thoughts, but I still had to answer Brian. Hope in his eyes shone bright, the North Star in a pitch black sky. There was no escape.

I sat up straighter, rested my hands in my lap, took a deep breath, and said, "Yeah, I will marry you, Brian."

For the remainder of our time together he talked nonstop. We could live with his family until his band started making good money. I'd like his mother; she'd love me. I doubted that. I declined the ring, asking him to bring it when he met my family. Tossing and turning in bed that night, a last thought— what goes around comes around. If the ship went down, there would be one passenger who deserved to drown. Perhaps this was the reason I'd never learned to swim.

# Chapter 16

## United States of America.

*This chapter is about turbulent waters, life in America, and education—1966 to 1967.*

October 1966, the *Alexandr Pushkin*, a mother of all ships, left the shores of London, England. It had come from Leningrad with a stop in Copenhagen. Standing at the bow looking toward the horizon where miles of green and aqua blue sea seemed to end or drop off, I found it easy to believe that beyond there were dragons. It was a calm day. Without the wind, it felt warmer than the thermometer suggested. Below me, waves, mere ripples licked at the keel and dissipated without a sound. The surface of the waves moved up and down like a mother rocking her baby to sleep. It was unlike the sea I knew, thundering and crashing against the shores spreading thick white-wave spume over the shore. That was an angry sea that took lives of our fishermen without regret. With that thought, dark clouds moved inside my head and a squall of emotions washed over me. I crossed my arms and squeezed my shoulders together in an effort to keep feelings at bay.

At home, sticking my head through my attic window settled any angst, known or unknown. Locating the North Star reassured me that all was as it should be. Under the starry night sky, any problem I could have seemed inconsequential. Holding the rails, I leaned back letting the wild blue yonder mesmerize me. Being seventeen years old was a good place to be, I reminded myself. Farther out in the distance I saw where the cottony-blue sky divided itself to a deeper blue heaven, sharp as a razor's edge. Demarcation of the two colors symbolized my life. I was moving toward a new color.

Suddenly, a deafening burst of sound, the ship's horn, blasted loud enough to knock filings out of teeth bringing my attention to the here and now mighty fast. The port side of the ship sat against the dock, now crowded with people waving good-by. I remained at starboard covering my ears hoping for no repeat. Who would challenge this massive ship for sea lanes? *Alexandr Pushkin*, like a giant ogre stumping down Pool Street, earned its right away for no other reason than size.

Kristín and I had a cabin with two bunk beds and one porthole. Russian workers cleaned our room and knew English words for sheets, towels, pillows, coat hangers, but that's it. If you were in the cabin when they were cleaning, they acted like stray cats cornered. I was convinced that their English was better than they let on. "Are you from Leningrad," I asked Alona— she wore a name tag—the younger of the two. No response and no eye contact.

Alona was shorter than I and had gray eyes, round cheekbones, and a small straight nose. She never smiled, and when an accidental eye-contact occurred, she ended it before I could blink. "What is it like in Russia?' What came to my mind about Russia was their leaders' desire to annihilate the rest of the world, oppression of their citizens, Dr. Zhivago and vodka. There was something exciting in the notion of befriending a Russian. If Alona got to know me, she'd see that the rest of the world, which I represented, was good and caring and that we liked Russian people—just not their leaders. Shenley memories mocked my good and caring thought.

Valli told Pabbi that in his travels to Moscow for our government, he was watched by the KGB. While he read *Time* magazine, a cab driver kept eying him in the rear view mirror. As they pulled up to the hotel, Valli asked him if he'd like to keep the magazine. He looked frightened but took it, almost ripped it out of Valli's hand, and stuck it under a seat cushion.

Early days of calm sea on the *Alexandr* came to a screeching halt in the middle of the night. To prepare us for the daily assaults, an agenda that included the weather report was delivered under our cabin door. So this was not unsuspected. For the remainder of the trip until we reached the St. Lawrence Seaway, it was either bad, very bad, or outright terrible. As the wind from the north increased, our nautical knots slowed. The size of the waves from crest to trough reached up to 20 feet flooding the lowest level—crew's cabins. Couple of floors up, passengers swung from port to starboard like drunken sailors swaggering. I remembered reading a poem about a sea captain caught in a storm realizing that his ship is going down.

I have a wife in London town tonight she'll be a widow. Then he spies a lovely mermaid holding a mirror and combing her hair. Just like that, the captain's gloom is replaced with a desire to join the lovely nymphet, forgoing his ship and sailors. Looking at my own lovely face of green, I prayed I'd spy the captain on a rock polishing buttons on his coat beckoning me to join him.

Two people of the Reichenfeld family unfazed by the turbulence were Hans and Robert. Hans said that we should force ourselves out of bed, get our sea legs, under us and breathe fresh air. He calls himself a doctor? Father and son roamed the slippery decks, enjoying Russian cuisine and making friends with the equally inhumanly unaffected.

Late one evening, we reached the southern part of Newfoundland, the worst was over. Night clouds had thinned, and a new moon peaked through. My face lost its green hue, my appetite returned, and thoughts besides envy of mermaids returned.

St. Lawrence River, the last stretch, is the longest water-way in the Western Hemisphere and one of the most beauti-ful places I'd visited. Feeling like myself again, I spent hours watching the banks as we sailed by. Leaves of yellow, orange, bright red, and purple hung on the trees and covered the ground. Heavens filled up with birds. It was impossible to see what kind they were. Up high, they all looked like terns. Looking down the river, I could see in my mind's eye Indians in canoes rowing down the river,. It must have been a magnifi-cent place before the white man came, populating the river banks to own the views.

After spending a day in French Quebec, we went to Montreal for a train to Hamilton, the final destination. Dr. Pierce, from Hans's new hospital, picked us up and took us to the family's new home. I'd be moving on, visiting Stella and her new daughter, Dísa, in Ann Arbor, Michigan. Plans from there on—murky.

In 1966, much of what I knew about the United States was what was covered in the news. Lyndon B. Johnson signed a new law, The Voting Rights Act, that banned colored people from voting if they couldn't pass a literacy test. Ever since the Russians, under the leadership of Khrushchev had taken the lead in what they called a space race, then—President Kennedy announced that Americans would be the first to put a man on the moon. Anti-war rallies, protesting America's involvement in Vietnam, were popping up around the country like small fires. Martin Luther King had led a march on Washington in 1963.

From the Americans I'd met in Iceland, I'd concluded that they were loud, spirited—as in not following rules—wore white socks and had great teeth. Natalie Wood, Elizabeth Taylor, and Paul Newman were popular Hollywood stars, and the Beat-les visited the United States, once performing at a place called Olympia Stadium in Detroit. Of interest to me was a group of young people in America that called themselves hippies.

Sitting on the bus headed for Detroit, I practiced saying Ann Arbor. In England, I conversed easily and people understood me. Now, listening to the white, brown, and banana-colored people on the bus, I understood very little. They spoke fast, running the words together. They sing-songed, the sound coming from the throat through the nasal passage. It sounded awful. Some of the black people—a news reporter had said that colored want to be called *black*—frankly, it couldn't be English. Straining to hear, I understood nothing, zippo.

To let some air in, I tried to pull down the window, but it didn't budge. With my purse between my legs, I gave it another attempt, pulling down with all my might. This was a heck of a well-built window casing. Defeated, I sat down, hugged my purse, and remembered my mother's warnings, "People look for girls like you." Some of the people looked at me, but nobody stared.

A middle-aged Indian woman with a pink dot between her eyes sat next to me. Her hair was long, wavy with gray around the temple. She wore a greenish-blue dress with a fabric shawl draped over her right shoulder. If our eyes met she smiled, but neither of us said anything. Considering that the Mafia owned politicians and judges and there were daily killings on every street corner, people were admiringly calm.

At the Greyhound terminal ticket booth in Detroit, I said, "Ann Arbor, please." Thick oppressive air, people running from somewhere going somewhere else, reminded me of Glasgow.

"Whaaat?" It was not an unkind voice, just one who couldn't understand my British accent.

"Ann Arbor."

"Whaaaat?" We were not making progress. Had Stella given me the wrong town? She must know where she lives. I tried again. Then a fourth time. A man behind me said something, and Ticket Man nodded his head. It was nice that they understood each other, but I needed a ticket. He held up a brochure pointing to the word Chicago. Come on, Ann Arbor sounds nothing like Chicago.

Ticket Man, in his white shirt with a tie, wanted to help. His eyes under a haystack of gray eyebrows and ears large enough to hear paint dry were at full attention. He kept talking, holding up brochures, looking for help from the man behind, who was still without a ticket. I didn't even pretend to understand.

Waiting for Ticket Man and Man Behind to figure out where I was going, I looked around me. An old tattered man with a tin cup walked around begging. Floors were littered with trash, gum, and sticky popsicles. I tightened the grip around my purse and held my suitcase between my legs.

Man Behind was talking louder looking from me to Ticket Man. I listened hard like an old woman losing her hearing. "Givehersomethingtowritewith." Who is supposed to understand this?

Ticket Man handed me a paper and pencil. Of course, why didn't I think of that? On the paper I wrote, "Ann Arbor.".

"AnnArborwhydidn'tyousaythat?"

Whatever! They both smiled, pleased with themselves. I paid for the ticket, and they pointed past a sign that read "Grand River" then "Lansing" to one with "Ann Arbor." A bus seat, even one with a big tear in the seat, felt mighty good. Looking out the window, driving through Detroit, I thought Michigan was dirty.

Stella, Norman and eighteen-month-old Dísa waited at the bus stop. Stella looked older, but when she smiled I saw that familiar twinkle she shared with Villi and Pabbi. Norm drove a beautiful American car, a 1957 Ford. When I said, "That sure is ah daaarling motor caar," he laughed loudly. It was embarrassing.

Dísa was the first American I had no trouble understanding."No. Mine. No, no." Next to her father, they were a striking contrast his darkness to her pale skin, blue eyes and blond hair. She bounced around in the car, grabbed my arm she sunk her teeth into my hand. Stella was so proud of her that I didn't have the heart to tell her that her kid was a bitty biting monster in angel disguise.

Michigan, it turned out, was not all full of trash and noise. We drove through neighborhoods of single homes, yards filled with flowers reaching up for a last feel of warmth before frost arrived, and trees in bright red and orange. I asked my sister why there were so many young people in the center of town. Stella said that the University of Michigan housed thousands of students during the winter. Indeed, my wish to see hippies was already granted. Strolling the streets, kids my age wore oversized peasant shirts, patched jeans with frayed hem seams, sandals with no socks, along with dangling beads. Mamma might not care about the beads, but it would be the only thing she'd not shake her head at. I was in awe of the idea of living with your peers, attending classes that you chose.

Staying with Norm's family, I caught on to American accent. Now I worked on getting rid of my British accent and adopting Yankee talk. The Briggs family had a three–floor colonial house on a friendly–looking street of similar homes. Stella and Norm occupied the lower level, which had a bedroom and a sitting area, but they shared a kitchen. Stella's mother-in-law, Bertha, was a first–generation Greek in her second marriage, a family secret Stella and Norm discovered while rummaging through the attic.

Bertha worked at a cleaners' until she got a job at a post office. Like Mamma, she stayed busy. She worked, took care of the house, cooked, and made crafts she donated to her church. Their house was cluttered with her hobbies and unfinished projects. It lacked a homey feeling that had existed in my child-hood home. Everyone had his own space and preferred it over mixing with the rest of the family. Terry, Norm's fifteen-year-old attractive blond sister, was expecting a baby. She was a quiet girl who stayed in her room a lot, or maybe she just resented all these people invading her home. Steven, the younger brother, was more social.

Bertha's husband, Norman, was a postal carrier for a living and, like Pabbi, a gardener for pleasure. His British parents, one English and the other Irish, had passed away before Stella joined the family. Home from work, Norman fixed himself a vodka and tonic. Then with a transistor under his arm, he worked outside or sat at the kitchen table drinking and listening to a broadcast of a baseball team, the Detroit Tigers.

He was a peaceful man who said little. One exception was when he told me about a doctor who lived on his route. It was around Christmas time ten or so years earlier. "Many people," he told me, "leave a gift for their mailman, a token of appreciation." So when Norman took out of the mailbox an envelope with his name on it, it was not a surprise. He continued, "Inside the card there was a signed check, made out to Norman Briggs, but the amount was blank. 'Norman,' the doctor had written, 'you fill in the amount.'" He looked at me and shook his head still in disbelief.

I adjusted quickly to America's ways and liked it. There was a feeling of freedom I'd never felt before. Rules were questioned and challenged. Like my American peers, up close to what was happening in the world through the eyes of the American press, I began to formulate my views but lacked opportunities to discuss them.

Stella and I took Dísa for walks to monitor the progress on their soon-to-be home in a new subdivision. Builders in America are a friendly bunch and let us walk through, although not much changed when you came as often as we did. We'd start in the kitchen, then the dining area leading to a hall with a bathroom and three bedrooms. Stella showed me my bedroom, and we daydreamed about moving away from Lillian Road and having our own space.

In the meantime, via letters, I told mother that I knew what I wanted to learn. It wasn't true. I just knew that I wanted to stay in America. Watching how teenagers lived—wearing hippy clothes, demanding to be heard—I wanted to be a part of it. I wanted to speak up, stand for something. Learning what you wanted to learn instead of meaningless sagas of poverty, starvation, and death intrigued me. I wanted control over my destiny. But I was a realist and doubted that I'd be one of those university kids driving around in her own car. Going to school in America was expensive. Going to school in Iceland didn't cost anything.

I wrote to Mamma: "I know what I want to do. I want to go to beauty school. There is one close to Stella's house. It cost $360. You learn not only to do hair, but how to do make-up, eyebrows, and manicure." Writing it was hard because it rang false. I didn't even wear make-up, kept my hair long and straigh,t and found doing my own nails less interesting than changing Dísa's diaper. But I saw no other way to stay here. Two weeks passed before I heard back.

"Who is Brian? He called the house and said you were engaged." Ouch. That wasn't supposed to happen. Her English was better than I'd expected. Mamma believed with passion that you conduct yourself in honorable fashion, and she suspected that her youngest had strayed. She wrote and waited for me to explain myself, hoping her suspicion was unfounded. But she also said that she was getting overtime at the fish factory and would have enough money for me to go to school since this is what I really wanted. This was the kind of news that called for dancing with elves in the sun. But the elves were in Iceland and the sun in America. Logistically impossible. Gnawing at me, impairing this best of all news was thinking of Brian's hurt.

What if I finished beauty school and then went to England to live? It wouldn't be so bad. I sat at the kitchen table on Fernwood—we'd move in two weeks earlier, just in time for Christmas—tapping my fingers in a pattern of index to little fingers, then all four fingers, tap, tap. I wanted people to think well of me. I could make it all right. Brian was crazy about me. I imagined how happy he'd be if I wrote him this news. I also knew I wouldn't.

In my next letter, I told Mamma that Brian was just a friend. He must have misunderstood. I wrote those words. I was disgusted with myself. I should just tell her that I'd said yes to a marriage proposal that I never intended to keep. But she might tell me to forget beauty school and move back home. We never spoke of Brian again.

January 1967, beauty school started, and I had a basin full of new friends. Sandy, blond with the help of hair dye, looked like Sandra Dee and had a small convertible. Her parents wanted her to go to college, but since she couldn't get into University of Michigan where her boyfriend went, this was her way to stay close to him. It was mind-boggling to think that she'd give up going to school for a boy. For lunch, we'd go to a restaurant where she'd order whatever she wanted with no thought to cost. Most days I ordered Coke and ate saltine crackers; they were free. Sandy accepted my explanation that I was dieting, making me wonder if I needed to lose weight. After a few weeks of working on dummy heads, we progressed to the floor where we earned tips and my diet ended.

Stella got a job at JC Penny's, and Terry, who had a baby boy, babysat Dísa. Norm worked for a tree service. At night, he and his friend Bud Royal rented a large garage where they started an auto shop. Two of their clients were Tom and James Monaghan, who started a business called Domino's Pizza. They wanted Norm and Bud to join their adventure, but they declined. Just as well. Pizza smelled bad and tasted worse.

Participants at weekend parties in the unfinished basement on Fernwood were their twenty-something friends with a huge appetite for fun and forgetting. A keg of beer did the trick. Unlike Iceland, in America, you can buy alcohol of any kind at your local grocery story or drug store. In Iceland, the government sold it from one store downtown. On weekends, lines down several city blocks were the norm. Even so, a limit was enforced on how much people could purchase.

Stella and Norm's relationship was turbulent. When he was home, his restlessness created tension. Norm found sitting still torturous. He was quick tempered, loud, and opinionated. Stella was stubborn, and, like Pabbi, moved slowly and desired peace and quiet around her. She was fiercely protective of Dísa.

Dísa's vocabulary increased daily, and she'd developed a sense of independence. She was also learning that she couldn't always get what she wanted. This would bring on the fireworks. That girl could throw temper tantrums with the best of them.

Once when we were having lunch at a restaurant, Stella let Dísa walk, actually bounce, ahead of us. A black man was paying his check at the register. Seeing him, Dísa took off like a jack popping out of a box, arms extended yelling, "Dad, dad, dad." After seconds of confusion, observing Goldilocks reach out to this black man, some of the patrons laughed.

It had been close to ten years since I had asked Mamma if drinking chocolate milk made your skin brown. My new world was a mixing bowl of color, race, and ethnicity. I'd become a news junky. A militant group that called itself the Black Panthers promoted black power. Martin Luther King, who'd received the Nobel Peace Prize, worked in Chicago helping poor blacks. This subject aroused people at parties and resulted in heated debates. Shirley, a black girl, had a work station next to mine. Her husband was in dental school. She was full of funny stories, and after a while I forgot that she was dark brown. What made her different escaped me. Stella's group of friends was divided. Some said that the black man's violent nature was forcing whites out of their homes. Eventually, the city of Detroit would be all black. In the summer of 1967, riots broke out in the city, and people in the suburbs armed themselves. So much fear, yet nothing happened around us.

Any disagreements between Stella and me faded after days of stewing and never saying. It was how we were raised. Confrontations quelled, complaints dismissed. That aside, we always managed to happen upon moments to our liking.

Norm was giving a bachelor party for a buddy. Stella explained to me that this is for guys only—a celebration of a man's last moments as a free man. In their basement, we came upon round flat metal containers for the big night. Norm had said, "Stay out of them." We got into them.

With Dísa propped in her highchair with Cheerios and toys, we went to work. Light, there had to be light—light, film, our eyes. Standing on the kitchen table with the shades of the French doors pulled shut, unwinding reel after reel of film, we were aghast. It was disgusting. It took many arm lengths to get to that part, the disgusting part, but my goodness, who would do this? Worse yet, I told Stella, "Who would want to watch this?" Dísa's interest perked, and she started throwing Cheerios around, squirming to be released. Careful not to say no, no, I told her, "This is not for babies." Actually, it really wasn't for a seventeen and a twenty-year-old either. Stella added M&M's to Dísa's highchair tray.

Answering my question of who would want to watch this filth and eager for her turn, Stella pointed out, "You do. You are looking at it." It was hard to stop looking. Although unrelated, her Formica kitchen table was one sturdy beast. This could be an ad for the company; no probably not. The ceiling light bulb should have been 100 watts though. "OK, come down," Stella was tired of waiting.

Not willing to quit quite yet, I pleaded, "Let me finish this scene. Ohhh, oh noooo." Stella's usual patience cresting, she climbed upon a chair ready to push me off. One scene took hundreds of pictures to evolve. This was the most horrible thing I'd ever seen. Comparing my health book, page 82, and these films was like comparing Attila the Hun to Mahatma Gandhi. Knowing my turn was coming to an end, I asked, "Did Norm bring the projector?"

"It's in the basement. He'll kill me."

I had three more sisters—I mean, if something happened to Stella. But I also knew the ugliness of Norm's temper, and an hour later, with aching arms, we packed them away. We lamented over the fact that men found this entertaining. Then we looked at each other and started laughing so hard that Dísa joined in shrieking twisting her little body back and forth, which made us laugh even more.

By late winter of 1967 Stella and I, without drivers' licenses, were driving any car that friends would trust us with.

Americans expected to have a good life. There were opportunities to make a good living even without a college degree. You could work in a factory and make good money. Beauty school—with it various coiffures, perms, hair colors—was enough to keep me in the country, but I could not imagine doing it for a living. Haircuts I was good at; everything else mediocre. Soon, I'd have my 1200 hours and be done with beauty school. Then what? I wanted to go to college. This thought consumed my waking hours.

One night Norm and his friend Ron taught us to play euchre. While Stella cleaned up the kitchen, I took care of Toddler Girl. She liked baths, and on this night, she got to wear her yellow sleeper with brown bears. After a glass of juice, she gave a slobber kiss to her mom and dad and waved good-night. In the last few months, her language development and vocabulary had exploded. She was putting words together such as "Out mommy!" Or when Stella had fed her oatmeal that morning, "No, hot!" Dísa now understood when you talked to her. I tell her to get a book, and she'd bring one. Sometimes when I heard her during the night, I'd go and fetch her. She fell right back asleep. It was better than having a pet. Stella hearing her laughter when I should have been getting her to bed yelled, "Nú er upp á ykkur tippið," then I heard her laugh.

Ron loved to tell stories. I wondered if card night would also be a story night. I like stories. I just don't like Ron's stories. His stories go on and on, and listeners have to exercise great self-discipline not to fall asleep. His stories lasts so long that every one of us, listening, had made trips to the bathroom, some two. Usually, his stories have good beginnings but are followed by a middle the size of an encyclopedia. It takes so long to get to the end, if there is one, that I'd often meander off before I find out.

One night he tells a story he insists is true, about a young Algonquian Indian woman who had been kidnapped, a retaliatory measure, by another tribe—you've got to admit, it is a catchy beginning. Nobody goes to the bathroom. We listen with rapt attention. I want to know the fate of this enslaved, demeaned creature. Ron's voice drops, we are silent.

"She was tied to a tree. Twigs and branches piled around the base of the trunk. Her high cheek-bones and almond-shaped eyes were partly hidden by her hair. Her clenched teeth and fist showed defiance, a trait common of the Crow tribe. Her crime was running away and taking her daughter, Little Butterfly, with her." Ron's voice lowers another octave. Listeners lean towards him. "They had brought her back, and there was no escape. She knew it. Looking at the people who had gathered, people she'd lived with for three years," Ron's voice is so low you can barely hear him. In a whisper he asks us, "Guess what she said?"

I meant to think it, but it just comes out of me. I jump up and scream, "FIRE!" Ron grabs his coat and leaves. Sandy Royal admonishes me for ruining his ending. Norm is disgusted with me. Stella, instead of helping me field the hostility of Norm's friends, moves around in the kitchen. I hear her laughing. Bud says that actually Indians didn't burn people, so there must have been another explanation. Because of me, we would never learn of Little Butterfly's mother's fate. Two Icelanders are OK with that.

April 30, 1967, Dísa turned two years old, and Mamma wrote to say she and Pabbi were coming to visit. I'd been negligent in my correspondence to Mamma after she gave her consent for me to stay in America to attend beauty school. She had sent me checks for school and to live. I was ashamed of not having written more, but now that they were coming, I'd catch her up on what was going on at home.

In the record shop next to the beauty school, a clerk, Frank, a stutterer, had taken a fancy to me. He was awkward in mind and body. He got off work at three and waited for me to get off at five. Each day he offered to drive me home. "Can n n n I d d d drive you home?" I told him no and asked him to leave. Frank reminded me of the patients at Shenley. His eyes revealed him as a reluctant owner of inner insecurity. At other times, a glance, something in his eyes brought up my antennas—safety alert, safety alert. I remembered Mamma's putting her hand on me when I left for England, "you'll be careful won't you?"

Being emotionally disturbed was a rough road to travel. Unlike cancer or tuberculosis, this problem made a suffer-ers an outcast—a person to be feared. At Shenley, Samantha was raped by other patients or workers. Eva said that they'd drag her into some bushes. She'd had her second abortion. In my mind, unwanted abortion was another form of rape. Yet I had no answers for what should be done. Whenever I'd expressed outrage about some injustice, Pabbi would ask, "How would you handle it?" Also, if I said "they"—as in "they say"—he'd look at me and ask, "Who are they?"

Eventually, Frank accepted that I'd never ride in the car with him and quit following me home. On cold winter days, facing an hour walk to Fernwood, it was tempting. But I made sure that I held out no hope that a potential of a relationship existed. Then he brought me gifts, mostly popular records from the Beatles, Rolling Stones, and Bob Dylan. I declined.

July 1967, Mary Fleszar, an Eastern Michigan University stu-dent, a few miles from Stella's house, was found murdered with her fingers and feet cut off. It was a reminder for me to listen to my inner voice. America had a lot to offer, including crime.

Sandy and I, now two of the senior students, ate lunch at Big Boy on Washtenaw Avenue in Ann Arbor. To me, Slim Jims and Big Boys were the best food America had to offer. When not busy, Pat, one of the waitresses, came and sat with us. She attended Washtenaw Community College. She was taking her basic classes and then transferring to Eastern Michigan Univer-sity to get a teaching degree to work with mentally retarded people. I peppered her with questions. "Yes, there was a pro-gram for teaching the emotionally impaired." She said that anybody could attend and that you could even work at the school. Every waking second, I thought of nothing but going to school. An old proverb states: "The wind can't favor your sails until you pick a direction." Within me, a storm great enough to sail ships was brewing.

But, of course, Mamma would never go along with this. How on earth would I come up with the money? Would I pass the test of English proficiency? I didn't have a car or a driver's license, so I'd have to move closer to the school.

Beauty school exit exams came and went. I passed. Beauty school was over, and my parents would be here in two weeks. Stella and I cleaned and prepared, telling Dísa that her *amma* and *afi* were coming to visit her. I made an appointment at Washtenaw Community College to take the English Proficiency Test. It was free.

At WCC I was led to a room and had the test explained. If I passed, I'd receive a letter that I would take to the Immigration and Naturalization Office in Detroit to extend my student visa. The test covered math—my best subject—and English reading and writing. I worked slowly, checked and rechecked my answers. It was warm in the room, and a bumble bee buzzed around seeking an escape route. Another student finished and left the room. Maybe I was taking too long. For my essay, last part of the test, the topic was describe your most rewarding experience. Ron's stories did not come to mind. Misleading Brian or pretending to be a seer, not rewarding. Time was ticking. Nothing came to me. Could I write about the Christmas when I got my watch? How could I live seventeen years and not have a single rewarding experience worth writing about? *Bzzz*, Mr. Bumble Bee hovers around the window. Go left, I think. Move left to the opening. You are almost there. Bzzzzz. Mesmerized with his persistence, I remembered the bees at Grosvenor Centre in Northampton. It came to me; my most gratifying experience was in England, talking and helping patients at Shenley. When I finished, I looked up, Mr. Bumble Bee had found freedom.

It'd been a while since I'd seen my parents. Mamma looked older to me. I could tell from what she didn't say, how my thoughtlessness of not writing to her had caused her grief and worry. Having them here was like having a root of a plant visit a leaf. But this plant was seeking to blossom away from the root. Whether I passed, occupied waking hours. I might have failed. I would be taking my state test for a hairdresser in September. After that I go back home.

For the two weeks they were here, temperatures were above 30°C (90°F), with high humidity—mist on your skin. There was no air conditioning in the house. My parents were very uncomfortable and sleeping was difficult. Norman went out and bought an air conditioner and placed it in their bedroom. Mamma was bit by some bug and her ankle swelled up making walking hard, but it didn't stop her. Pabbi was like fish out of water without his garden, piano, and books. His clothes looked crumbled in the heat, like a handkerchief left out in the rain. He shaved in silence. He tapped his fingernails on Stella's kitchen table. Father, an intelligent man in an unintelligent world, had moved inside for answers. He conversed less and saw more. An unsettling feeling came over me as I sensed that he would never have answers to life's big questions, to make sense of his life. Would this also be my fate?

Unlike Pabbi, Mamma found things in America that amazed her. Frozen TV dinners in the freezer section of the grocery store. "Why does anybody bother to cook? This is so inexpensive." She was like a kid in a candy store. Stella's washing machine took dry clothes, washed them, rinsed them, and delivered them clean. It was almost too much for her. Clothes dryer? Mamma was dumbfounded. "You don't have clothes'-lines?" At restaurants she'd ask us to order for her. When the food came she'd blurt out, "This can't be for one person." Mamma was not one to bring attention to herself or complain. America was pushing out the perimeter of her world of reality. We'd laugh and she'd continue, "No person can eat this much."

Later she concluded that Americans had large mouths. Her reasoning, extrapolated from ten days in America, rested with hamburgers. Generations of Americans eating hamburgers had resulted in a large-mouth-breed of Americans who now could get their gills around a Big Mac. This evolved to how overweight Americans were. It surprised her enough to make frequent comments. "It would be difficult to make slacks for a person of this size"; followed with, "It would take a lot of material"; ending with, "The seams would have to be reinforced." My mother had applied Darwin's theory of evolution to Americans and their love of hamburgers. Impressive. Looking at Stella's modest-sized-mouth, her children's chances of surviving in Hamburger land were not so good.

Norm, a driver who liked to pretend he was falling asleep at the wheel, drove the speed limit plus ten. Of course my parents didn't complain. I knew as I knew where Dísa hid her pacifier that they were afraid. They clung to the front-seat and door handles. Stella was furious and snapped at him as much as she could without creating more tension. Compounding the problem was Mamma's borderline neurosis with crime in America. Norm, taking a different route back from a restaurant, she'd want to know why he was doing that. It uneased her.

When Sandy came in her white convertible to meet my parents, they were taken back. It was the first time they'd met a teenager who owned a car. Sandy's outgoing personality didn't charm them. Mamma didn't care for her. I couldn't understand why. Perhaps she could see how much I admired and desired Sandy's lifestyle.

After my parents left sadness visited, sadness I couldn't sweep away. A part of me wanted to go home. I remembered glorious red and yellow sunsets, pink skies, and green cloud tongues you could see right after the sun drops below the horizon. I could hear waves crash against the shoreline, gulls squealing attempting to snatch fish from each other. I remembered mild summer winds that blew my hair around like a taffeta petticoat, the smell of sulfur, and how my body felt as I submerged into a hot tub. Never to see my Esja, my rock of Gibraltar. Denying that the frigid island was in every liter of blood pumping through my body was like the sea denying it had salt. My melancholy deepened. No word came for Washtenaw Community College.

Even Stella, uncharacteristically subdued, struggled. She found solace in sleep. I became an insomniac. I had a sense that I'd turned a page and that the winds were blowing full force moving me along, but where? For a seventeen-year-old, I was acting like a baby. Maybe Mamma was right; I didn't have enough to do. I started babysitting more for Stella's friends and memorized the classes I needed at WCC before going to Eastern Michigan University—just in case.

August 17, a letter in the mailbox was addressed to me. Return address was Washtenaw Community College. Dust on the unpaved street kicked up and sailed in my direction. I held the letter against my chest. Sometimes you want something so bad that you can feel it as an entity banging around inside your body. My future was in a white nine by four envelope. How crazy is that? I told myself that a rejection was not the end of the world. In a couple of weeks, I'd take my state exams for a hairdresser, a job I didn't want. This line of thinking didn't make the envelope's content any less important. I should go inside the house and fix myself a drink, a drink in a tall glass, a strong drink in a tall glass. That was a good idea only if I wanted to feel sick.

I stood at the kitchen table with the letter unopened on the table in front of me. Dísa was with Terry; Stella and Norm were at work. "What is inside you?" I asked the letter. "Did I pass? Did I fail?" I'm talking to myself. What happened to looking fear in the face? I was like a ship in harbor, safe but going nowhere. I knew that if I didn't move forward, I'd be moving backwards. Sliding a knife under the flap I pull out a folded sheet of paper.

"Dear Edith Andersen, we congratulate you on your acceptance …"

# Timeline

Timarit.is an online newspaper archive

1888 (*Þjóðviljinn*, Feb. 27) Faein orð um Keppinauta Vora um Saltfisk Verzlunina. Controversy for how to process fish.

1900 (*Fjallkonan*, Jan. 2): Giftingar. 2. jan. Ingimundur Pétursson, namsm. á stýrimanna-skólanum og ungfrú Jórunn Magnúsd. My maternal grandparents marry.

*1900 (Þjóðviljinn,* April 27*)* Stýrimannapróf. Maternal grandfather graduates from maritime school.

1914 (*Ýsafold,* June 6*)* Jarðarför okkar elskaða sonar, Karls Björgvin, er ákveðin Þriðjudag 9. juní kl. 1 og hefts með húsakveðju frá heimili okkar, Sellandsstíg 32. Jórunn Magnúsóttir. My maternal grandparents announcing the funeral of their son.

1947 (*Morgunblaðið*, April 20) "Adeline (Adda) D.Andersen fermd í Dómkirkjunni kl. 2" (Sjera Bjarni Jónsson). Adda confirmed.

1947 (*Morgunblaðið*, Sept. 9) "Farþegar með Heklu frá Kaupmannahöfn til Rvíkur 6. sept. Adda Andersen, Wilhelm (Villi) Andersen." My two oldest sibling, then 11 and 14, return from a visit to paternal family in Denmark.

1947 (*Morgunblaðið*, Sept. 19) "Í-DAG kveðjum við einn af okkar efnilegustu æskumönnum, Karl Björgvin Sigurðsson, járnsmíðanema, Hverfisgötu 117, hjer í bæ." Obituary for Aunt Inga's son who died at 17.

1950 (*Morgunblaðið*, April 23) "Hallgrímskirkja kl. 2 Sjera Jakob Jónsson. Vilhelm Andersen..." *Villi confirmed.*

1951 (*Morgunblaðið*, January 9) "Elsku dóttir okkar HELGA HJÖRLEIFSDÓTTIR verður jarðsungin frá Fossvogskapellunni. Þriðjudaginn þann 9. jan. kl, 2 e. h. Margrét Ingimundardóttir, Hjörleifur Jónsson og börn. Skipasundi 39." Six year old cousin's funeral. Burn.

1951 (*Morgunblaðið*, Agust 15) "Tilboð óskast í lagningu hitaeining í 22 hús Reykjavíkurbæjar, C flokk, í Bústaðavegshverfi. Bjóða má efni eða vinnu hvort í sínu lagi eða saman. Eins ma bjóða í eitt eða fleiri hús, en ekki koma til greina tilboð frá öðrum en þeim, sem eiga allt aðalefni, eða eiga von á því mjög bráðlega. Teikningar og útboðs-lýsingu má fá í skrifstofu Hitaveitunnar, Pósthússtræti 7, gegn 100 kr. skilatryggingu. Reykjavík, 13. ágúst 1951 Helgi Sigurðsson." Beginning of Bústaðahverfi, low income housing construction—city seeking independent contractors.

1953 (*Þjóðviljinn*, April 26) "Ferming í Fossvogskirkju kl. 2 e.h. Stúlkur, Ásta Andersen." Ásta confirmed.

1953 (*Tíminn*, June 24) "72 Nemendur voru í Núpsskóla. Hæstu einkunnir í Miðskólaprófi hlutu Valdimar Gislason, Mörum, Dýrafirði og Guðrún (Gunna) Alda Kristinsdóttir, Garði, Gullbrs." Gunna, one of two students earning the highest test score on an exam that was taken around the age of 16. This exam practice ended in the mid-seventies.

1953 (*Morgunblaðið*, Dec. 5) "Nýlega hafa opinberað trúlofun sína ungfrú Adda Andersen, Hólmgarði 26 og Valgeir Ársælsson, Lokastíg 11." Adda and Valgeir's (Valli) engagement.

1954 (*Morgunblaðið*, April 22) "Ég þakka innilega börnum mínum, tengdabörnum og barnabörnum, sem glöddu mig með blómum, gjöfum og heimsóknum á áttræðisafmæli mínu 20. apríl s. 1. — Guð blessi ykkur öll, og gefi ykkur gæfuríka framtíð. Ingimundur Pétursson, Framnesveg 57." Maternal grandfather thanking his children and in-laws for visiting and bringing him gifts on his 80th birthday.

1954 (*Morgunblaðið*, July 25) "Húsmæður í Bústaða- og smáíbúðahverfi Heimabakaðar smákökur og margs konar tertur seldar að Hólmgarði 26, uppi." Adda selling homemade cookies and cakes.

1954 (*Alþýðublaðið*, Nov.13) "...umsóknum um kaup á 16 íbúðum Bústaðahverfi með líkum skilmálum og verið hafa fyir sölta fyrri húsa í Bústaðavegshverfi. Þó hefur lánstími verið styttur í 25 ár og vextir hækkaðir." Second building phase in Bústaðahverfi. Application will begin soon.

1955 (*Morgunblaðið*, Oct. 4) "Bókasafn Hólmgarður 32, Mondays, Wednesdays and Fridays from 5 to 7." Neighborhood library opens three days a week from 5 p.m. to 7 p.m.

1955 (*Morgunblaðið*, Oct. 23) "Nýlega hafa opinberað trúlofun sína ungfrú Guðrún Alda Kristinsdóttir og Vilhelm I.Andersen." Gunna and Villi's engagement.

1955 (*Morgunblaðið*, Nov. 5) "KLÆDASKÁPUR úr Ijósu bnki (4ra dyra). Hæð 16.3. Breidd 232 cm, til sölu Verð kr. 3.000,00. Stig in saumavél á sama stað. — Verð kr. 750,00. Hólmgarði 26, uppi." Armoire and sewing machine for sale.

1956 (*Morgunblaðið*, June 17) "Valgeir (Valli) Ársælsson, Jórunn Haraldsdóttir MEISTARA-PRÓF." Valli earns a Master's Degree.

1957 (*Vísir*, September 23) "VEL með farið barna-rimlarúm óskast. Sími 33615." Looking for a crib in good condition for Jens Ágúst Andersen.

1957 (*Vísir*, November 13) "TELPUKJOLAR; öllum stærðum til sölu. Sanngjarnt verð. Hólmgarði 26, uppi. Bústaðahverfi." Girls' dresses for sale, all sizes, reasonably priced.

1958 (*Morgunblaðið*, April 24) "Hjartkær sonur okkar og bróðir ÁSTÞÓR HJÖRLEIFSSON verður jarðsunginn frá Fossvogskirkju föstudaginn 25. kl. 3. þeim, sem vildu minnast hins látna, er bent á minningarsjóð fatlaðra og lamaðra. Margrét Ingimundardóttir, Hjörleifur Jónsson og systkini." Fourteen-year-old-cousin's funeral. Cancer.

1958 (*Morgunblaðið*, Sept. 20) "Bifreiðueigendur and Bifreiðastjórar: Hef opnað aftur, hjólbarðaviðgerðaverkstæði í Rauðarárhúsinu. (Beint á móti gatnamótum Rauðarásstígs og Skúlagötu. Framkvæmum alls konar viðgerðir hjólaböðrðum og slöngum. Fljót og góð afgreiðsla. Kai Andersen." Pabbi advertising his tire shop.

1958 (*Tíminn*, October 19) "Ferm. í dag í Fríkirkjunni, Séra Gunnar Árnason. Stúlkur: ... Jórunn Andersen, Hólmgarði 26." Jórunn confirmed.

1959 (*Morgunblaðið*, August 9) (Pabbi) "Loftdælur hentugt fyrir gúmmíviðgerðar verkstæði, óskast. Sími 33615." Pappi looking for an air pump to be used in his tire shop.

1959 (*Vísir*, May 22) "UNGLINGSTELPA óskar eftir að komast í sveit í sumar. Uppl. í síma 33615." A young girl (Jórunn 15) seeks to work on a farm.

1958 (*Alþýðublaðið*, April 24) "Ferm. í dag í Fríkirkjunni, Séra Gunnar Árnason. Stúlkur: ... Stella Andersen, Hólmgarði 26." Stella confirmed.

1960 (*Tíminn*, June 2) "14 ára telpa óskar að komast á gott sveitaheimili í sumar. Uppl. í síma 33615." A 14-year-old girl (Stella) seeks to work on a good farm home.

1961 (*Tíminn*, April 25, 1961) "12 ára telpa óskar að komast á gott sveitaheimili í sumar. Upplýsingar í síma 33615." A

12-year-old (Edith) wants to spend a summer on a good farm.

1962 (*Morgunblaðið*, April 27) "2ja tíl 3ja herbergja íbúð óskast til leigu nú þegar. Uppl. í síma 33615." Ásta advertising for an apartment.

1962 (*Morgunblaðið*, Dec. 13) "Þjónustu í framtíðinni. Hárgreiðsludama er: Jórunn Andersen. Guðfinna Breiðfjörð. (Minna). Hárgreiðslustofan LORELEI. Laugavegi 56. — Sími 19922." Jórunn's place of employment changes hands.

1963 (*Alþýðublaðið*, April 21) "FERMING í Kópavogskirkju 21. apríl kl. 10. 30 f. h. Séra Gunnar Árnason. Stúlkur : Edith Andersen, Hólmgarði 26." I'm confirmed.

1963 (*Vísir*, Oct. 31) "ATVINNA ÓSKAST Tvær stúlkur óska eftir vinnu á kvöldin. Margs konar störf koma til greina. Uppl. í síma 35379 og 33615 milli kl. 6 og 8 eftir hádegi." Áslaug and I looking for evening work.

1964 (*Morgunblaðið*, Jan. 21) "Vel með farinn barnavagn óskast." Simi 33615 Jórunn advertising for a baby buggy for Arnþór.

1964 (*Vísir*, March 27) "Ferðaritvél óskasts til kaups uppl. í síma 33615." Someone in the household looking to buy a typewriter.

1964 (Morgunblaðið, June 18) "... opinberuðu trúlofun sína Stella Andersen Hólmgarði 26 of Norman Briggs, Lillian Road, Michigan, USA" Stella and Norman engaged.

1964 (*Vísir*, Aug. 16) "óska að komast í samband við mann, sem hefur lóð og bygingarleyfi (í Reykjavik eða Kópavogi). Stærð íbúðar 80—100 ferm. Fokheld ílbúð kemur einig til greina. Uppl. í síma 33615." Jórunn and Ævar looking for a lot to build on.

1965 (*Vísir*, Sept. 7) "Mótatimbur til sölu. Uppl. i sima 33615." Selling left over timber from Jórunn's new apartment in Kópavogur.

1966 (*Vísir*, Nov. 1) "Gott herb. til leigu fyrir stúlku eða konu, í Vesturbæ. Kópavogs. Barnagæzla æskileg. Uppl. í síma 33615 frá kl. 5—7." Jórunn renting a room to someone willing to babysit.

1966 (*Morgunblaðið*, Sept. 3) Loftdælur hentugt fyrir múrara eða verkstæði. Einnig slöngu-suðuvél til sölu. Sími 33615." Pabbi selling equipment from his tire shop.

# Bibliography

*Listed in order as they appear in the book.*

*Íslendingabók.is*; Source for names of ancestors and dates throughout the book.

*HI.is Háskóli Íslands. SKARÐSBÓK POSTULASAGNA, SÁM 1 fol. Retrieved January 1, 2010, from http://www.3.hi .is/HI/Ranns/SAM/nokkur.html#skard.*

*Wikipedia.org. List of Historical Plagues. Retrieved January 1, 2010, from* http://wn.wikipedia.org/wiki/ List_of_historical_plagues.

Thomasson, R. F. (1980). *Iceland: The First New Society* (1st ed.). Minnesota, U.S.A. Univ of Minnesota Pr;. Retrieved January 1, 2010, http://www.amazon.com/ dp/0816609136/ ref= rdr_ext_sb_ti_hist_1.

*The Axe and the Earth* by Ólaf Gunnarsson, historical fiction of Iceland's last Catholic Bishop (1548-1634).

Gunnarsson, G. (1949). *Svartfugl* In (M. Ásgeirsson, Trans.). Reykjavík, Iceland: Útgáfugélagið Landnáma Reykjavík.

Magnusson, S. E. Celebration of Women Writers. *http://digital .library.upenn.edu/*. Retrieved January 1, 2010.

Thorsson & Scudder, B. (Eds.). (2001). Egil's Saga. *The Sagas of Icelanders* Vol. 1. (First pp. 3-183). New York New York 10014, U.S.A. Penguin Books.

*http://en.wikipedia.org*. Church of Iceland. Retrieved January 1, 2010.

*http://www.hi.is/*. The Árni Magnússon Institute in Iceland. Retrieved January 1, 2010.

*http://www.aq-verlag.de/*. The Laws of Later Iceland: Jónsbók. Retrieved January 1, 2010.

Made in the USA
Lexington, KY
15 September 2010